Augustus Ely Silliman

A Gallop among American Scenery

Or, Sketches of American Scenes and Military Adventure

Augustus Ely Silliman

A Gallop among American Scenery
Or, Sketches of American Scenes and Military Adventure

ISBN/EAN: 9783337180447

Printed in Europe, USA, Canada, Australia, Japan

Cover: Foto ©ninafisch / pixelio.de

More available books at **www.hansebooks.com**

A GALLOP

AMONG

AMERICAN SCENERY:

OR,

SKETCHES

OF

American Scenes and Military Adventure

BY

AUGUSTUS E. SILLIMAN.

NEW YORK:
A. S. BARNES & CO., 111 & 113 WILLIAM STREET.
1881.

TO

BENJAMIN D. SILLIMAN,

THIS

LITTLE VOLUME

IS

AFFECTIONATELY INSCRIBED,

BY

HIS BROTHER

CONTENTS.

	PAGE.
BANKS OF THE POTOMAC,	1
THE COUNTRY PASTOR,	7
MOUNT VERNON,	12
THE MEDICAL STUDENT,	22
THE RESURRECTIONISTS,	34
OLD KENNEDY, THE QUARTERMASTER, I,	44
OLD KENNEDY, THE QUARTERMASTER, II,	51
OLD KENNEDY, THE QUARTERMASTER, III,	56
OLD KENNEDY, THE QUARTERMASTER, IV,	64
THE PARTISAN LEGION,	73
HUDSON RIVER,	99
NIGHT ATTACK ON FORT ERIE,	104
BATTLE OF LUNDY'S LANE,	112
LAKE GEORGE AND TICONDEROGA,	122
MONTREAL,	130
THE NUN,	134
CATARACTS OF NIAGARA,	137
MOUNT HOLYOKE,	143
WHITE MOUNTAINS,	147
BASS FISHING OFF NEWPORT,	155
BRENTON'S REEF,	161
OLD TRINITY STEEPLE,	168

	PAGE
OLD SCIPIO,	181
THE PEQUOT,	187
CAPTAIN KIDD,	191
SPIRITIANA:	
No. I.—Hydrachos	198
No. II.—Winter,	216
A PEEP OVER THE BLUE RIDGE,	220
THE DEAD MAN'S SERMON,	231
A TRIP THROUGH LONG ISLAND SOUND:	
No. I.—Hell Gate,	249
No. II.—Burning of Fairfield and Danbury,	255
No. III.—Night Alarm,	261
No. IV.—"The Boys,"	265
No. V.—The Unfortunate Lover,	271
No. VI.—Adventure on the Mississippi,	273
No. VII.—New London and Stonington,	279
THE BLIND OFFICER,	283
GREENWOOD CEMETERY,	293
APPENDIX,	305

PREFACE.

THE *larger part of this volume (now long out of print) was published many years since. The various sketches of which it is composed were written for recreation, amid the cares of business; reviving, as they did, recollections of attractive scenery and passages of military and naval history, the latter made specially interesting to the writer by oral narratives of persons themselves engaged in them.*

When the book was written, we had little of military history except that of the Revolution, and the events of "the War of 1812" were cherished with deep regard by the public; but since then, the smoke and carnage of the Mexican War, and the gigantic horrors of the conflict with the South, have thrown them almost entirely in the shade.

It is hardly necessary to say that most of the dramatis personæ which figure in these sketches are ideals, improvised for the purpose of telling their various stories, nor that in a work so tinged by the imagination a degree of poetic license is taken to give continuity to the narration.

To occupy some idle hours, the writer has prepared this edition; adding to it a number of chapters not contained in the first.

JUNE, 1881.

BANKS OF THE POTOMAC.

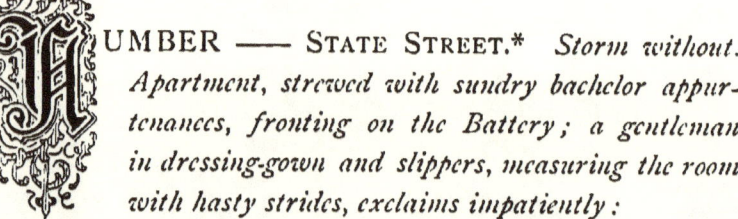UMBER —— STATE STREET.* *Storm without. Apartment, strewed with sundry bachelor appurtenances, fronting on the Battery; a gentleman in dressing-gown and slippers, measuring the room with hasty strides, exclaims impatiently:*

Northeast, by the flags of the shipping in the bay! Northeast, by the chill rain dashing on the window panes! Northeast, by the weather-cocks on all the steeples, from St. Paul's to the dog-vane on the stable end! NORTHEAST, by the ache of every bone in my body! Eheu! What's to be done? No going abroad in this torrent. I've read all the landlady's little library. How shall I kill the enemy? I'll whistle; vulgar. Sing; I can't. There are the foils and the gloves. Pshaw! I have no friend to pommel or pink; besides, the old lady in the room below has nerves. Whew! how it pours! I'll—I'll—stand and look out into the street. Jupiter! how near the bread-cart came to going over the chimney-sweep. Poor Sooty—how he grins! He owes the worm no silk, whatever obligations his rags may be under to the sheep. Poor fellow! Halloa! ho! blackey; catch this quarter, and get you a hot breakfast. There goes that confounded battery gate again! bang! bang! night and day.

Alas! me miserable. What shall I do? The spirit of ennui rides me as thoroughly as did the " old man of the sea," Sinbad the

*On this street, at that time, were the residences of the *élite* of the city.

sailor. *Eh! there are the dumb-bells: diminish nervous excitability by muscular exertion. Good!—humph; and there are the old lady's nerves below.* How the wind roars and rumbles round the chimney-tops. RAIN, RAIN, RAIN! *The tin spout is choked, and the gutter is pouring over, a young cataract. Oh! that I were a whale, or the sea-serpent, chasing the down-east fishermen—in short, anything, so that I need not mind the wet. Hum—hum—what shall I do? I have it. Eureka! I have it. I'll sit down and give my friend ———————— an account of my last ramble.*

(*Rolleth his chair up to the table at the fire, crosseth his legs on the fender, and proceeds to nib his pen.*) Now for it (*Writes*).

You well recollect, my dear ——————, the arguments I used, to induce you to make a short journey to the South with me last summer; and your answer: "I can't leave my business." You well recollect that I urged that we were not born to work, alone; that life was short; that, sixteen or sixty, its term was but a flash: that we were rushing on with increased velocity to that bourne, whose sands are marked by no returning foot-print: that bourne, where the sceptre and diadem of the monarch lie contemptuously hurled, with the goad and chain of the slave; where, their service ended, the broken wain of the yeoman, and the grim cannon of the soldier, interlock their shattered wheels; the bayonet and pruning-hook, the sword and the ploughshare, rest without a name. You well recollect that I reproached you, the rather, with too great love for the green fields and giant elms around your rustic cottage; that I swore by my faith—an' I believed in the doctrine of Pythagoras—that I should look to see thy immortal part transferred, on its exit from its present habitation, to one of those huge trees towering into the blue ether; that there, in the sunny mornings of summer, for sonnets which do enliven thy library, I should hear the joyous call of the robin, the shrill whistle of the scarlet oriole; for sparkling wit, the dew of night glittering on thy leaves in the early sunbeams; for wise old saws and dreamy legends, venerable moss gathering upon thy trunk and branches; while, alike in the evening wind or howling blast, thou shouldest stand firm against casuistry or dictation. "Wilt go?" "Wilt join me?"—with soft persuasion murmured I. "*My business,*" quoth thou. "Presto," quoth I; and without more ado started in my usual heels-over-head fashion alone on my journey.

I swept over the broad breast of the Delaware; dashed down the enemy-insulted Chesapeake; bounded through the city of riots and beauty, and came down on my feet at the cottage of my whole-souled friend, Tom B———, on the banks of the Potomac. The afternoon of my arrival was warm and still, and everything in nature, even the birds, seemed wrapped in indolent repose. Slowly sauntering through the long vistas of sycamores and elms which adorned the grounds in picturesque avenues, the airy East Indian cottage of my friend suddenly broke upon my sight, peering from a whole load of flowering vines and sweet-briers, tall white lilies and moss roses, from thick beds of myrtle at their feet, climbing into the half-open lattices, while two towering pines almost crossed their extended branches above its lowly roof. I stole quietly through the open door, examining the choice Italian landscapes hanging upon the walls of the airy grass-matted hall; slid through the drawing-rooms, stopping for a moment to scan the crouching Venus and dying Gladiator on their pedestals, to admire the exquisite Magdalen of Carlo Dolce, the lovely Claude, the Cenci, and Flora, beneath their silken tassels; and, coming out upon the verandah overlooking the river, suspended in his grass hammock, found master Tom enjoying his luxurious siesta. His double-barrelled gun, and game-bag, shooting-jacket, huge sombrero and hunting-boots, were tumbled into one corner of the piazza, while a dozen fine plover, turning up their plump breasts, a partridge, and a score of yellow-legged snipe, with the powder-flask and shot-belt, were thrown across the back of the rustic settee, trophies of his morning's sport, beneath which, with their noses extended between their legs in like luxurious repose, lay the huge old Newfoundlander, "Bernard," and his favorite pointer, "Soho."

The mild breeze bore in the sweet perfume of the honeysuckle from a neighboring arbor, and the broad Potomac, stretched tranquilly onwards, undisturbed save by the occasional jibe of the boom or lazy creak of the rudder of some craft, reflected with her white sails upon its surface. The garden, with its white-gravelled walks, bordered with box, descended in parterres to the river's edge—an embroidered carpet of flowers; and lemon and orange trees, released from their winter's confinement, displayed their golden fruit, hanging amid the green leaves in tempting profusion. I bent over and looked into the hammock, and could not but admire the serenity of the manly features, the measured heave of the broad chest, and the masses of raven locks playing around the white forehead of the sleeper, as they were slowly lifted by the play of the passing wind. I thought it were a sin to disturb him, so, drawing out my cigar case, I stretched myself on the settee at his side, complacently reclining my head upon its arm. Whiles watching the blue smoke of my "cigar," as it slowly wreathed and floated above my head, whiles watching the still dreamy flow of the river, and whiles—if I must confess it—cogitating which had been the wisest, myself the bachelor or Tom the married man, Tom, myself, the dogs, forming a tolerably correct picture of *still* life, a still life that remained unbroken for some half hour, when through the glass doors of the drawing-room a beautiful boy of three or four years came galloping into the piazza, and bounding towards the dogs threw himself full length upon the shaggy Newfoundlander, manfully striving to pull open his huge jaws with his little hands. The Newfoundlander, opening his eyes, saw me, and raising himself on his legs gave a low growl, while the child, relinquishing his hold upon the ears to which he had clung as the dog arose to his feet, came slowly up to me, and placing his plump little hands upon my knee, looked curiously and inquiringly into my face, his golden locks falling in a profusion of ringlets down his superb sunburnt shoulders. I was charmed with the confidence, and innocence, and sweetness beaming from his gaze, and took him upon my knee, his hand playing with my watch-guard, while his beautiful blue eyes remained fixed in the same look of curious inquiry on mine. I said it was a picture of *still* life. Tom, aroused by the dog, slowly lifted his head over the edge of the hammock, rubbed his eyes as if uncertain whether he were in a dream, as I calmly and silently returned his astonished gaze, and then, with a single swing, was at my side, both of my hands clasped in his. The next moment, I fancy, the picture was other than *still* life.

Why should I tell you of the tea-table, loaded with delicacies in the matted hall, as the soft evening sunset poured its last rays through it; of the symmetrical figure clad in snowy whiteness; the Grecian features; the dark, Andalusian eyes, beaming with kindness from behind the glittering silver at its head? Why, that the youngster, tied by the handkerchief in the high chair at his mother's side, pertinaciously kicked his tiny red shoes about him in frolic glee, while my little knight of the golden locks did the duty of the trencher at his father's elbow? Why, that as the shades of evening faded into twilight, the young gentry were snugly ensconced in their little bed, the mother's soft cheek pressed against the forehead of the eldest as he lisped his evening prayer? And why, as soon—"like twin roses on one stalk"—as they were wrapped in innocent slumber, we sat in the fading twilight, talking over old scenes and boyish recollections, retracing our steps back to those days which, softened by the lapse of time, appear divested of everything save brightness and sunshine? Why, but to tell you that we were aroused from those retrospections by the sound of the church-going bell, musically chiming in the distance.

THE COUNTRY PASTOR.

THE slow tolling—now almost dying away, and now striking more strongly upon the ear—arose from the church in the neighboring village, where my friends were in the habit of worshipping, and where they were to have the opportunity on that evening of hearing the voice of their time-honored pastor—an opportunity which his great age and increasing infirmities had made equally rare and valuable. I gladly accepted the invitation to join them, as, aside from a desire to see the aged man, of whom I had so often heard, if there is a time for devotion more consonant to my feelings than another, it is when the quietness and serenity of a summer's evening dispel all external impressions, and everything appears in unison with harmony and benevolence.

As we walked the short half mile between the cottage and the church, the stars shone in beauty amid the still rosy tints of the west; the night-hawk stooped towards us, as he wheeled in his airy circles; the whip-poor-will in the adjoining meadows sounded his mournful note, and the crickets, with the chirping frogs in the neighboring ponds, sustained a ceaseless chorus. Arrived at the churchyard, we picked our way among the old brown tombstones, their quaint devices contrasted here and there with others of more modern pretensions in white marble, and entering the church took our seats in silence. We were early; but, as the church gradually filled, it was interesting to watch group after group, as it noiselessly measured the aisles, and sunk quietly upon the cushioned seats. Now and then a pair of bright eyes would glance curiously around from beneath a gay bonnet, and a stray tress be thrown hastily aside; but, alas! those clad in the habiliments of woe, too, too often

moved, phantom-like, to their places; the lights, as they threw a momentary glare on their pale and care-worn faces, making more dark the badges which affection has assumed as a tame index of inward grief. The slow toll of the bell ceased; the silence became more deep; an occasional cough, the rustling of a dress, the turn of a leaf, alone breaking the perfect stillness.

The low tones of the organ rose gently and sweetly, and

the voluntary floated softly and mist-like over the assembly, rising, falling and undulating, with like dreamy harmony, as if the Æolian harp were answering, with the passing airs playing among its strings, the ocean laving his pebbly shores, till, gradually rising and increasing in depth, it grandly and solemnly ascended upwards, thrown back, reverberated from the walls of the circular dome above us, in deep and distant thunders. All became again silent. The venerable form of a man of four-score years, his hair bleached with the sorrows of eighty winters, rose slowly in the pulpit; and as, with eyes closed, yet lifted to Heaven, he feebly supported himself with outstretched arms upon its cushion, we heard, almost in a whisper: "Let us pray, my brethren," fall tremulously from his lips. Nought but the perfect stillness enabled us at first to hear the sentences, pronounced with evident and painful effort; but, as he advanced in prayer, that almost whisper became firm and distinct, and his pallid cheek lighted up with a hectic flush, as he waxed eloquent in the presence of his Maker.

His venerable features appeared to glow almost with inspiration, and the hearts of the mourners beat more calmly, as they felt themselves carried into the Divine presence. More thoughtless than the swallow that skims the summer skies must he have been, who could have heard that prayer, and not have joined with reverence in its solemnity. His closing words still ring upon my ear, and long will remain stamped upon my memory.

"My children: your fathers, and your fathers' fathers, have listened to my voice. Generations have passed by me to their long account, and still I have been left, and still my voice hath arisen from this holy place. Woe! woe is me, if my Master hath looked upon me as a slack and unworthy servant to his people. But a few short days, and this trembling voice, that still strives to teach his blessed will, shall be hushed, this tottering form be laid beneath the mould from whence it came; but, with the last tones of this quivering voice, the last grasp of these trembling hands, I extend to you this sacred volume, as your guide to happiness in this, your surest light into the world to come.

"The sneers of human reason and vain philosophy will desert you assuredly, my children, as you stand upon the edge of that awful precipice, where each of you *alone* must take the fated plunge into the deep darkness of the future; but this shall make clear your passage as brightest noon-day. My children:—I look back upon you as I speak; my hand is on the door-latch; my foot upon the threshold—oh! when your short days, like mine, are numbered, may you, with the same reliance in his mercy, say Amen!"

As the service ended, it was good to see the kind-hearted feeling with which the congregation gathered around the venerable man, for he was pure, and sincere, and true; and of a verity, as he said, his voice had arisen among them above the infant's wail, at the baptismal font; had joined them with cheerfulness at the marriage feast; and still been heard in solemn sympathy at the side of the dark and silent grave. It was the last time that he addressed them. Not many days, and another voice pronounced the burial service of the dead in that green churchyard, and the form of the good old man was covered from their sight beneath its sod.

As we returned to our cottage home, the crescent moon

was streaming in silvery brightness, the constellations and galaxy resplendent with "living fires," and the far, far worlds, rolling in immeasurable distance, as twinkling stars, trembled upon our human vision. The dews of night were moist upon the grass, as we remeasured the lawn that led to the cottage, where, after planning our visit for the following morning to Mount Vernon, we soon were wrapped in contented and grateful repose.

MOUNT VERNON.

THE sun raised himself in a huge globe of fire above the eastern horizon, as my friend's spirited bays stood saddled at the door of the cottage, pawing, champing the bit, and playfully endeavoring to bite the black boy who held them. Finishing an early breakfast, we were soon in our saddles and full gallop on our journey; the dogs in an ecstacy of delight, bounding along at our sides, overhauling and putting in bodily terror every unfortunate cur that came in their way, as they sportively tumbled him over, old Bernard, with glistening eyes and wagging tail, bestriding in grim fun the prostrate form of the enemy. We passed rapidly through the rough-paved streets of Alexandria, watching eagerly for its famed beauties at their casements, and clearing the town were soon on the rustic road that leads to the sacred place of America.

The meadows were glistening in the morning dew; the sweet perfume of the clover filled the air; the white daisy and delicate cowslip danced over their luxuriant grassy beds, as the fresh morning breeze fanned them in its passage; and amid the sea of melody, high above the merry gossip of the bob-link, the chattering volubility of the mocking-bird, his yellow-spotted breast swelling with delight, his keen eye gazing into the distance, the saucy "*you-can't-see-me*" of the meadow lark sounded in merry challenge; while the clear "whistle" of the quail from the golden wheat-field was echoed by his eager companion far down in the green vales, as they stretched softly and gently into the distance, in the long shadows of the early morning. Oh! let him that would scan the benevolence of the Creator, leave his restless bed in the sweltering city, and walk forth with the day in its youth; for verily, like man, it hath its youth, its manhood

MOUNT VERNON.

and its old age, and the sweetness of morning is the youth of the day.

The hedges on the road-side were covered with a tangled mass of verdure, from which wild vines and green ivy crept to the surrounding trees, wreathing gracefully their trunks and branches; the undergrowth loaded with wild roses and honey-suckles. The graceful fleur-de-lis, curving its blue flowers, trembled upon the green banks, and the pond-lily, floating on its watery bed, threw forth its grateful fragrance, as we occasionally passed through the swampy bottoms. Fat cattle grazed indolently in the meadows, while now and then, as we cantered by their pastures, the horses, with tails and manes erect, accompanied us on our journey, till, arriving at their confines, with eager neighing they would look after us, throw their heels high in the air, and gallop down into the broad fields in the very jollity of freedom. Everything seemed contented and joyous. The hearty, happy-looking negroes, trudging along to their agricultural labors, doffed their hats to us with a cheerful "good morning," as we passed, or laughingly displayed their white teeth and big eyes, as they led the dew-wet horse to the bars, to mount, and drive to the milking, the smooth, fat kine. A ride of an hour brought us to the woods that adjoin Mount Vernon, which are cleared of undergrowth, but in other respects as wild and untamed as if naught but the savage had ever placed foot in them. Silence reigned through the deep glades, unbroken, save by the hoofs of our horses as they resounded with hollow echo, the sharp chirp of the squirrel, jumping among the dry leaves, or the quick rap-rap of the wood-pecker, as his scarlet head and blue back glanced momentarily from some dead trunk upon our eyesight. We met with nothing to intercept our progress. Now and then, to be sure, a drove of hogs, feeding upon the mast in the forest, would marshal themselves in our path, stupidly staring at us with a sort of ludicrous, half-drunken gravity, snuffing the air as if determined to intercept our progress; but as we came nearer they would whirl short about, and with a simultaneous grunt, their tails twisted in the air, gallop off with desperate precipitation into the depths of the forest. Journeying a mile or two farther, we came upon the porter's lodges at the entrance of the domain proper, which were old and ruinous. Proceeding still farther, over a very bad and rough carriage-road, we came suddenly in view of the Potomac; and Mount Vernon, with its mansion-house and smooth, green lawn, lay extended before us, Fort Washington's battlements and cannon-filled embrasures in stern silence guarding it from the opposite side of the river.

Fastening our horses, under the guidance of a grey-headed old negro, born in the family of General Washington, we entered the lawn and came upon the rear-front, if the term may be allowed, of an old-fashioned mansion, surmounted by a cupola and weather-cock, semi-circular piazzas extending around from each end, connecting it with the kitchen and servants' apartments. Various buildings, all bearing the impress of time, were scattered about, evidently in architectural order and plan, and the two large gardens, rendered interesting by the flowers and plants still blooming in the beds where they had been placed by the hands of the General, extended back to the forest from which we had just emerged. As we stood for a moment looking at the old building, we almost expected to see the yellow travelling carriage of his "Excellency," with its four beautiful bays and liveried out-riders, draw up at the great hall door in its centre. Having sent in our address, we received permission to enter and survey the interior. We were struck with its extreme simplicity, the lowness of the walls and ceilings, and the bare floors, which were waxed—not, as with us, carpeted. The sides of the rooms were composed exclusively of wooden panels, upon which hung some old oil paintings, engravings of naval actions between the English, the Dutch, and the French; and a small enamel miniature,* which is considered the best likeness extant of Washington. Curiosities of various kinds covered the shelves and the mantels, and the painted porcelains and china jars stood in stately display behind the glass doors of the old-fashioned beaufets in the corners.

Our attention was arrested for a moment, as we passed through one of the rooms, by a large rusty key of iron enclosed in a glass case. It was the key of the Bastile, that monument of centuries of grinding cruelty and oppression, where men vanished and were seen no more of their day and generation; where, by the intrigues of the courtier, the subtle blandishments of the minion of the palace, letters de cachet plunged equally the innocent, the imprudent and the generous, into the jaws of living death; that congerie of dungeons where, from mid-fellowship of rats and spiders, such scrap of soiled paper, written in the blood of the poor prisoner, fluttering from a loop-hole in its lofty towers, arrested the footstep of the casual passenger upon the causeway:

"Masses de Latude, *thirty-two* years prisoner in the Bastile, implores good Christians to intercede for him, that he may once more embrace his poor old father and mother, if they yet live, and die in the open world."

One side of the great drawing-room was ornamented with a sculptured mantel in Italian marble, presented by Lafayette; the other was covered with cases containing books, while from the third, its green silk curtain drawn aside, was suspended a portrait of the then family, by Chap-

* Cut out from a common China pitcher.

man. The figures of the portrait, as large as life, presented a lady of middle age, clad in mourning, surrounded by a group of children advancing into youth. It was well executed, and in the dignified and saddened serenity, in the simple and natural grouping, and the pure and unaffected expression of the countenances, an American in any part of the world would have at once recognized a family group of the more intellectual and refined of his own country. As we walked through the various rooms, from which the family had withdrawn, we were so overcome with the illusion—the work-basket with its scissors and thread, the half-opened book lying upon the table, the large Bible prominently, not ostentatiously, in its place, the portraits on the walls, the busts on their pedestals, all causing such a vivid impression of present life and being—that we almost expected to see the towering form of the General entering the doorway, or passing over the green lawn spread between us and that Potomac which he had so often viewed from the same windows. We were at first disappointed at not seeing in some conspicuous place his sword, but our disappointment vanished as we were referred to and read this clause in his last testament:

"To each of my four nephews I bequeath one of the swords of which I may die possessed. These swords are accompanied with the injunction not to unsheath them for the purpose of shedding blood, except it be for self-defence, or in defence of their country and its rights; and, in the latter case, to keep them unsheathed, and prefer falling with them in their hands to the relinquishment thereof."

Passing through the great hall, ornamented with pictures of English hunting scenes, we ascended the oaken stair-case, with its carved and antique balustrade; we stood at the door—we pressed the handle—the room and the bed where he died were before us. Nothing in the lofty drama of his existence surpassed the grandeur of that final scene. The cold which he had taken from exposure, in overseeing some part of his grounds, and which resisted the earlier domestic remedies that were applied, advanced in the course of two short days into that frightful form of the disease of the throat, laryngitis. It became necessary for him to take to his bed. His valued friend, Dr. Craik, was instantly summoned, and, assisted by the best medical skill of the surrounding country, exhausted all the means of his art, but without affording him relief. He patiently submitted, though in great distress, to the various remedies proposed; but it became evident, from the deep gloom settling upon the countenances of the medical gentlemen, that the case was hopeless; advancing insidiously, the disease had fastened itself with deadly certainty. Looking with perfect calmness upon the sobbing group around him, he said: "Grieve not, my friends. It is as I anticipated from the first; the debt which we all owe is now about to be paid. I am resigned to the event." Requesting Mrs. Washington to bring him two wills from his escritoire, he directed one to be burnt, and placed the other in her hands, as his last testament, and then gave some final instructions to Mr. Lear, his secretary and relative, as to the adjustment of his business affairs. He soon after became greatly distressed, and as, in the paroxysms which became more frequent and violent, Mr. Lear, who was by his side, assisted him to turn, he, with kindness, but difficulty, articulated, "I fear I give you great trouble, sir;—but perhaps it is a duty that we all owe, one to another. I trust—that you may receive the same attention—when you shall require it."

As the night waned, the fatal symptoms became more imminent, his breath more labored and suffocating, and his voice soon after failed him. Perceiving his end approaching, he straightened himself to his full length, folded his own hands in the necessary attitude upon his chest, placing his finger upon the pulse of the left wrist, and thus calmly prepared, and watching his own dissolution, awaited the summons of his Maker. The last faint hopes of his friends had disappeared. Mrs. Washington, stupefied with grief, sat at the foot of the bed, her eyes fixed steadfastly upon him; Dr. Craik, in deep gloom, stood with his face buried in his hands at the fire; his faithful black servant, Christopher, the tears, uncontrolled, trickling down his face, on one side, took the last look of his dying master; while Mr. Lear, in speechless grief, with folded hands, bent over his pillow on the other.

Nought broke the stillness of his last moments but the suppressed sobs of the affectionate servants collected on the stair-case, the tick of the large clock in the hall, as it measured off, with painful distinctness, the last fleeting moments of his existence, and the low moan of the winter wind, as it swept through the leafless, snow-covered trees. The laboring and wearied spirit drew nearer and nearer to its goal; the blood languidly coursed slower and more slowly through its channels—the noble heart stopped—struggled—stopped—fluttered—the right hand slowly slid from the wrist upon which its finger had been placed—it fell at the side—and the manly effigy of Washington was all that remained, extended upon the death-couch.

We left that room as those who leave a sick room; a suppressed whisper alone escaped us, as, with a sort of instinctive silence and awe, we drew the door slowly and firmly to its place behind us. We again descended the antique staircase and emerged upon the lawn in front of the mansion. Passing through several coppices of trees, we approached the sepulchre where rest his remains. In the open arch of a vault composed of brick, secured and firmly protected by gates of open iron-work, were two large sarcophagi of white marble, in one of which, carved in high relief with the arms of the republic, were deposited the remains of him "who was first in war, first in peace, and first in the hearts of his countrymen." A marble slab, set into the brick wall of the exterior, bearing in black letters simply this inscription:

"The remains of
Gen'l George Washington."

There rested all that was mortal of the man whose justice, virtue and patriotism meet with few parallels in history. There, within the smoke of his own hearth-stone, mouldered the remains of that towering form, whose spirit, whether in the battle or in the council-hall, in the fierce dissensions of public discord or in the quiet relations of social life, shone with stern and spotless purity.

The Potomac glittered like silver, between the trees, in the noonday sun, at our feet; the soft mild breeze gently moved the leaves upon the tree-tops; the chirp of the wren, the drowsy hum of the locust, the quick note of the thrush, as she hopped from twig to twig, were all that showed signs of life; and those huge sarcophagi lay still, motionless, far, far from voiceless.

We were struck with the truthfulness of the "Sweet Swan of Avon," as we saw above the sarcophagi (free passage to which was open over the large iron gates) the clayey nest of the martin, or common house-swallow, built in the corner of the ceiling, where, in perfect security and confidence, she fed her chirping brood, directly over the head of the departed hero. Pure, indeed, was the air; "nimbly and sweetly" did it play upon our senses. Oh! bard of England, as, standing upon that hallowed spot, the spirit of the unfortunate Banquo whispered again to our memories his words to the murdered Duncan:

> ———— "This guest of summer,
> The temple-haunting martlet, does approve,
> By his lov'd mansionry, that the heavens' breath,
> Smells wooingly here: no jutty, frieze, buttress,
> Nor coigne of vantage, but this bird hath made
> His pendent bed, and procreant cradle: Where they
> Most breed and haunt, I have observed, the air
> Is delicate."

We lingered at the tomb, and with reluctance withdrew, as the advancing day warned us of our homeward-returning ride.

The setting sun, streaming in radiance through the trees, measured in long shadows the persons of the two men dismounting at the cottage door, from whence they had departed so buoyant and joyous in its morning brightness. That setting sun, sinking beneath its gorgeous bed of crimson, gold and purple, left those men more chastened, true, more elevated, from their pilgrimage to the shrine of him whose name is the watchword of human Liberty.

THE MEDICAL STUDENT.

I REMAINED several weeks on my friend Tom's plantation, enjoying the course of life that he pursued, which was entirely consonant to my tastes. His plantation consisted of about three hundred acres, principally laid down in wheat, Indian corn and tobacco, though some of it still remained in meadow and woodland. This, with a handsome productive property in the neighboring towns of Alexandria and Washington, afforded him an abundant income to indulge his liberal, though not extravagant, tastes. He usually arose at five in the morning, mounted his horse, and rode over the plantation, overseeing and giving instructions to the laborers; and returning, was met by his smiling wife and beautiful children at the breakfast-table; after which, he again applied himself to business until eleven, when he threw all care aside and devoted himself to pleasure or study for the remainder of the day. He thus avoided the two extremes to which country gentlemen are liable, over-work on the one hand, or ennui on the other. His library, the windows commanding a view of twenty miles down the Potomac, was crowded with a varied store of general literature, among which I observed, shining conspicuously, the emblazoned backs of Shakspeare and the worthy old Knight of La Mancha. History, Travels, the Classics, English, French, Spanish and Italian, and works on Natural History and general science, were marshaled on their respective shelves. There was also a small but very select medical library, for my friend had taken his degree in that profession, and, although relieved from the necessity of practising for support, he was in the habit of attending gratuitously on the poor in the neighboring country. Marble busts of Shakspeare, Milton and Columbus, stood on pedestals in the corners of the room, and fine old portraits of Cervantes, Lope de Vega, Dante and Ben Jonson, besides an exquisite gem of Ruysdaels, hanging over the fire-place, adorned the walls. On one side of the room, fronting the entrance, an effigy in complete polished armor of the fifteenth century stood erect and grim, the mailed gauntlet grasping the upright spear, while on a withered branch above it was perched, with extended wings, a superb American eagle in full preservation, his keen eye appearing to flash upon the intruders at the entrance. In the centre, on the soft thick carpet, which returned no sound of footsteps, was a circular table surmounted with an Argand lamp and writing apparatus, on one side of which was one of those exquisitely comfortable lounging chairs that admit of almost every position of ease, and on the other a crimson fauteuil stuffed with down, which Tom laughingly said was for the peculiar benefit of his wife when she saw fit to honor his sanctum sanctorum with her presence. He tasked his invention to the utmost to make my time agreeable. Horses, dogs, guns, books, everything, were at my disposal. Among other excursions, he proposed, a few days after my arrival, that we should take a run down the Potomac in his boat. Now this boat was none other than a beautiful clipper-built schooner-rigged yacht, of about seven tons burden, with a very ample cabin in her centre, and from the gilt eagle on her stern, and the gaudy pennant streaming at her masthead, to the taught stay running out to the end of her mimic jib-boom, the most complete thing of the kind that I ever laid eyes on. In so expressing myself when I first saw her, I received an approbatory and very gracious nod from "Old Kennedy," a regular old salt, with one arm, for whom Tom had built a cottage on his estate, and to whom she was beauty personified, a beauty which he could the more readily appreciate from the fact that the far greater part of his time was devoted to her decoration. "Many a time," says Tom, "have I found him lying by himself on the banks, looking at her in admiration with half-open eyes; and I much doubt whether my Mary looks more beautiful to me than does her namesake, as she floats yonder, to old Kennedy."

But to come to our story. We appointed the following day for our excursion, and having first ascertained that Walter Smith, an old friend, whose plantation was a couple of miles below, would join us, we early the next morning got up our anchor, and under the influence of a smacking breeze were soon cutting our way down the river, the white canvas stretching clean and taught out to the stays, our long pennant streaming proudly behind us, and our little jack shaking most saucily from its slender staff at the bowsprit, as we merrily curveted and jumped over the waves. Running down to a point on Smith's plantation, we got him on board, and were soon under way again, the water bubbling and gurgling into our scuppers as we lay down to it in the stiff breeze. Occasionally she would sweep gunwale under when a flaw would strike her, but old Kennedy, wide awake, would bring her up with a long curving sweep as gracefully as a young lady sliding out of the waltz in a crowded ball-room, till, stretching out again, she would course along, dancing over the mimic waves with a coquetry equal to those same fair damsels when they find an unfortunate wight secure in their chains. We were all in fine spirits, Tom's negro boy, seated at the heel of the foremast, showing his white teeth in a delighted grin as old Kennedy, with his grave face, played off nautical wit at his peculiar expense. We saw a number of ducks, but they were so shy that we could with difficulty get a shot at them, but we now and then succeeded in picking half a dozen snipe out of a flock as it rose from the shore and flew across our bows. We continued running down the river in this way for three or four hours, passing now and then a fisherman or other craft slowly beating up, but towards noon the breeze slackened; we gradually lost our way, merely undulating, as the wind fanned by us in light airs, till finally it entirely subsided, our long pennant hanging supinely on the shrouds, and the water slopping pettishly against our bows, as we rested tranquilly upon its surface. The after part of the yacht was covered with an awning which, although sufficiently high to prevent its obstructing the view of the helmsman, afforded us a cover from the rays of the sun, so that we lay contentedly reclining upon the cushions smoking our cigars, enjoying our refreshments and reviving old recollections and associations; for it must be confessed that we three, in our student days, had "rung the chimes at midnight." I had not seen Smith for several years. He was a descendant of the celebrated partisan officer who commanded a dashing corps in the Revolution, and inherited, in a marked degree, all the lofty courtesy and real chivalry that characterized that officer. He was exceedingly well read in the military history of the country; and, indeed, so thoroughly imbued with military spirit, that, should the signal of war ring through the country, I know of no man whose hand would so soon be on the sword-hilt and foot in the stirrup. My introduction to his acquaintance was marked by an incident, so peculiarly painful and exciting in its character, that I cannot refrain from relating it. Having been let loose from the care of my guardians at a very early age, I made the first use of my liberty in traveling in a good-for-nothing sort of way over Europe, determined to see for myself the grandeur of Old England; to climb the Alps; to hear the romantic legends of Germany in her own dark forests; to study the painters and sculptors of Italy on her classic soil; to say nothing of visions of dark-eyed girls of Seville, of sylphs and fairies floating through the ballets and operas of Paris, and midnight adventures in the gondolas of Venice. Arriving at London, I fell in with and gladly availed myself of the opportunity to take apartments in the same house with my friend Tom and his fellow-student Smith, both Americans, and both completing a course of medical education by attending the lectures of the celebrated John Hunter.

It so happened that on the very first evening that we came together, in conversation upon the peculiar features of their profession, I expressed a desire to visit a dissecting-ing-room, never having been in one in my own country. Smith immediately invited me to accompany them to the lecture on that evening, which was to be delivered in the rotunda of the college, and where, by going at an early hour, my curiosity could be satisfied, besides the opportunity that

I should have of hearing that eminent surgeon. So, putting on our hats and taking our umbrellas in our hands, we plunged into the dense fog and groped our way over the greasy pavements to the college. It was a large building in a dark and retired court, with something in its very exterior sepulchral and gloomy. Entering the hall door, we ascended one pair of stairs, stopping for a moment as we passed the second story to look into the large rotunda of the lecture-room. The vacant chair of the professor was standing near the wall, in the rear of a circular table of such peculiar construction as to admit of elevation and depression in every part. This table was the one upon which the subjects were laid when under the hands of the demonstrator. Two skeletons, suspended by wires from the ceiling, hung directly over it. The room was as yet unoccupied and silent. Ascending another flight of stairs, we came to a third, secured at its entrance by a strong oaken door. This appeared to put a stop to our further ascent, but, upon a small bell being pulled, a sort of wicket in the upper part of the door was cautiously drawn aside, discovering the features of a stern, solemn-looking man, who, apparently satisfied of the right of the parties to enter, drew one or two heavy bolts, and dropping a chain, admitted us. A small table was placed at the foot of the stairs, at which, by the light of a lamp, this gloomy porter was perusing a book of devotion. Ascending the stairs, it was not until three several attempts that I was enabled to surmount the effects of the effluvia sufficiently to enter the green baize door that opened into the dissecting-room. As it swung noiselessly to behind me, the first sensation produced by the sight was that of faintness, but it almost immediately subsided. There appeared a sort of profanity in speaking aloud, and I found myself unconsciously asking questions of my friends in a low whisper.

On small narrow tables, in different parts of the large room, which, though lighted by a dome in the centre, required, in the deep darkness of a London fog, the additional aid of lamps, were extended some five-and-twenty human corpses in different stages of dissection. Groups of students were silently engaged with their scalpels in examining these wonderful temples of the still more wonderful human soul. Here a solitary individual, with his book open before him upon the corpse, followed the text upon the human subject, while there two or three together were tracing, with patient distinctness, the course of the disease which had driven the spirit of life from its frail habitation. I observed one of the professors, in his gold spectacles, pointing out to a number of the students, gathered around one of the subjects, the evidences of an ossification of the great aorta, which had, after years of torture, necessarily terminated the life of the sufferer. There was almost as much individuality in those corpses as if they had been living, and it required the most determined effort on my part to divest myself of the idea that they were sentient and aware of all that was passing around them. I recollect, particularly, one which was lying nearest the door as I entered; it was the body of a man of about forty, with light hair and fair complexion, who had been cut down in the midst of health. His face was as full and his skin as white as if he had been merely sleeping: but the knife had passed around his throat, down his body, and then in sections cross-ways, the internal muscles having been evidently exposed, and the skin temporarily replaced during the casual absence of the dissector. There was something peculiarly horrid in the appearance of that corpse, as, aside from a ruffianly and dissolute expression of the features, the gash around his throat conveyed the impression that it was a murdered man lying before me. A middle-aged female was extended just beyond, her long hair hanging down over the end of the table, but not as yet touched by the hand of the surgeon. While just beyond her, the body of an old man, from which the upper part of the skull had been sawn to take out the brain, appeared to be grinning at us with a horrid sort of mirth. In another part of the room, directly over which the blackening body of an infant was thrown across a beam like a piece of an old carpet, was extended the body of a gigantic negro; he lay upon his back, his legs somewhat apart, one of his arms thrown up so as to rest upon the top of his head, his eyes wide open, his nostrils distended and his teeth clenched in a hideous grin. There was such evidence of strength, such giant development of muscle, such appearance of chained energy and ferocity about him, that, upon my soul, it seemed to me every moment as if he was about to spring up with a frantic yell and throw himself upon us; and wherever I went about the room my eyes involuntarily turned, expecting to see that fierce negro drawing up his legs ready to bound, like a malignant demon, over the intervening space. He had been brought home for murder on the high seas, but the jail-fever had anticipated the hand of the executioner, and his body of course was given over to the surgeons. A far different object lay on the floor near him. It was the body of a young girl of about eleven or twelve years old. The poor little creature had evidently died of neglect, and her body, drawn up by the action of the flexor muscles into the form of a bow, stiffened in death, rocked forward and backward when touched by the foot, the sunken blue eyes staring sorrowfully and reproachfully upon us from the emaciated features. Beyond her, in most savage contrast, was thrown the carcass of a Bengal tiger, which had died a day or two before in the royal menagerie, his talons extending an inch beyond his paws, and there was about his huge distended jaws and sickly eyes as perfect a portraiture of disease, and pain, and agony, as it has ever been my lot to witness in suffering humanity. There was no levity about the students, but, on the contrary, a sort of solemnity in their examinations ; and when they spoke, it was in a low tone, as if they were apprehensive of disturbing the dead around them. I thought at the time that it would be well if some of those who sneer at the profession could look in upon one of these even minor ordeals to which its followers are subjected in their efforts to alleviate the sufferings of their fellow-men.

As the hour for the lecture approached, the students, one by one, closed their books, washed their hands, and descended to the lecture-room. We descended with the rest, and as we passed the grim porter, at the bottom of the stair-case, I observed in the corner behind him a number of stout bludgeons, besides several cutlasses and muskets. A popular commotion a short time previous, among some of the well-intentioned but ignorant of the lower classes, had induced the necessity of caution, and this preparation for resistance. Entering the lecture-room, we took our places on the third or fourth row of seats from the demonstrator's table, upon which a subject was lying, covered with a white sheet, and had time, as the room gradually filled, to look about us. Besides the students, Smith pointed out to me several able professional gentlemen, advanced in life, who were attracted by the celebrity of the lecturer. Shortly after we had taken our seats, a slender, melancholy-looking young man, dressed in deep mourning, entered the circle in which we were seated, and took his place on the vacant bench at my side. He bowed reservedly to my companions as he passed them, but immediately on sitting down became absorbed in deep sadness. My friends returned his salute, but did not appear inclined to break into his abstraction. At the precise moment that the lecture was announced to be delivered, the tall form of the eminent surgeon was seen descending the alley of crowded seats to his chair. The lights in the various parts of the room were raised suddenly, throwing a glare on all around; and one of the skeletons, to which an accidental jar had been given, vibrated slowly forward and backward, while the other hung perfectly motionless from its cord. In his short and sententious manner, he opened the subject of the lecture, which was the cause, effect, and treatment of that scourge of *our* country, consumption. His remarks were singularly lucid and clear, even to me, a layman. After having gone rapidly through the pathology of the disease, consuming perhaps some twenty minutes of time, he said: " We will now, gentlemen, proceed to demonstration upon the subject itself." I shall not readily forget the scene that followed. As he slowly turned up the wristbands of his shirt sleeves, and bent over to select an instrument from the case at his side, he motioned to an assistant to withdraw the sheet that covered the corpse. Resuming his erect position, the long knife glittering in his hand, the sheet was slowly drawn off, exhibiting the emaciated features of an aged woman, her white hair parted smoothly in the middle of her forehead, passing around to the back of the head, beneath the plain white muslin cap. The silence, which always arrests even the most frivolous in the presence of the dead, momentarily checked the busy hum of whispers around me, when I heard a gasp—a choking—a rattling in the throat—at my side; and the next instant, the young man sitting next to me rose to his feet, threw his arms wildly upwards, and shrieking in a tone of agony, that caused every man's heart in that assembly momentarily to stop—"*My m-o-t-h-e-r!*"— plunged, prostrate and stiff, head foremost upon those in front of him. All was instant consternation and confusion. There was one present who knew him; but to the majority of the students he was as much a stranger as he was to my friends. He was from one of the adjoining parishes of London, and two weeks before had lost his mother, to whom he was much attached, and by fatal mischance that mother lay extended before him upon the demonstrator's table. He was immediately raised, but entirely stiff and insensible, and carried into an adjoining rooms. Sufficient animation was at length restored to enable him to stand; but he stared vacantly about him, the great beads of sweat trickling down his forehead, without a particle of mind or memory. The lecture was of course closed, and the lifeless corpse again entrusted to hands to replace it in its tomb. The young man, on the following day, was brought sufficiently to himself to have memory present the scene again to his mind, and fell almost immediately into a raging fever, accompanied with fierce and violent delirium; his fever gradually abated, and his delirium at intervals; but when I left London for the continent, three months after, he was rapidly sinking under the disease which carried off his mother—happily in a state of helpless and senseless idiocy; and in a very short time after, death relieved him from his misery. The whole scene was so thrilling and painful, that, connecting it in some measure with my introduction to Smith, his presence always recalled it to my memory.

THE RESURRECTIONISTS.

AS we returned to our lodgings, our conversation naturally turned upon the agitating event that we had just witnessed, and the extreme caution necessary in the procuring of subjects for anatomical examination. Smith related an occurrence that had happened to Doctor Huger, a gentleman of high standing in South Carolina.

Shortly after the American revolution he visited Europe, for the purpose of pursuing his medical studies, and was received into the family of the same distinguished gentleman whom we had just heard lecture, then beginning to rise to eminence and notice, an advantage which was necessarily confined to a very few. In one of the dark and stormy nights of December, Mr. Hunter and his wife having been called to the bedside of a dying relative in the country, as Dr. Huger was quietly sitting at the parlor fire, absorbed in his studies, he was aroused by a hurried ring at the street door, and rising, went to answer it himself. Upon opening the door a hackney coach, with its half-drowned horses, presented itself at the side of the walk, and two men, in slouched hats and heavy sailor coats dripping with water, standing upon the steps, inquired in a low tone if he wanted a subject. Being answered in the affirmative, they opened the carriage door, lifted out the body, which was enveloped in a sack, and having carried it up stairs to the dissecting-room, which was in the garret, received the two guineas which they had demanded, and withdrew. The affair was not unusual, and Dr. Huger, resuming his book, soon forgot the transaction. About eleven o'clock, while still absorbed in his studies, he heard a violent shriek in the entry, and the next instant the servant-maid, dashing open the door, fell senseless upon the carpet at his feet, the candlestick which she had held rolling some distance as it fell.

Perceiving that the cause of alarm, whatever it might be, was without, he caught up the candlestick, and, jumping over her prostrate form, rushed into the hall, where an object met his view which might well have tried the nerves of the strongest man. Standing half-way down the staircase was a fierce, grim-looking man, perfectly naked, his eyes glaring wildly and fearfully from beneath a coarse shock of dark hair which, nearly concealing a narrow forehead, partially impeded a small stream of blood, trickling down the side of the face from a deep scratch in the temple. In one hand he grasped a sharp long belt-knife, such as is used by riggers and sailors, the other holding on by the bannister, as he somewhat bent over to meet the gaze of the doctor rushing into the entry. The truth flashed across the mind of Doctor Huger in an instant, and with admirable presence of mind he made one spring, catching the man by the wrist which held the knife, in a way that effectually prevented his using it. " In the name of God! where am I?" demanded the man in a horror-stricken voice, " am I to be murdered?" "Silence; not a whisper," sternly answered Dr. Huger, looking him steadily in the eyes. " Silence, and your life is safe." Wrenching the knife from his hand, he pulled him by the arm passively along into the yard, and hurrying through the gate, first ran with him through one alley, then into another, and finally rapidly through a third, till, coming to an outlet upon one of the narrow and unfrequented streets, he gave him a violent push; retracing his steps again on the wings of the wind, pulling to and doubly locking the gate behind him, leaving the object of his alarm perfectly bewildered and perplexed, and entirely ignorant of the place from whence he had been so summarily ejected. The precaution and presence of mind of Dr. Huger most probably saved the house of Mr. Hunter from being torn down and sacked by the mob, which would have been instantly collected around it, had the aggrieved party known where to have led them to wreak his vengeance.

After a few days, inquiry was carefully and cautiously made through the police, and it was ascertained that three men, answering the description of the resurrectionists, and their victim, had been drinking deeply through the afternoon in one of the low dens in the neighborhood of Wapping; that one had sunk into a stupid state of intoxication, and had, in that situation, been stripped and placed in a sack by his companions, a knife having been previously placed in his hand that he might relieve himself from his confinement upon his return to sensibility, and that, in addition to the poor wretch's clothes, they had realized the two guineas for his body.

It is certainly painful, that the requirements of suffering humanity should make the occasional violation of the grave indispensably necessary. Whether the Spirit, released from its confinement, lies in the Limbo of the fathers, the Purgatory of the Catholics, awaiting the great day of doom; whether called from a life of virtue, all time and distance annihilated, it sweeps free and unconstrained in heavenly delight through the myriads and myriads of worlds rolling in the vast sublimity of space; whether summoned from a course of evil, it shudders in regions of darkness and desolation, or writhes in agony amid flaming atmospheres; or whether its germ of life remains torpid, as in the wheat taken from the Egyptian pyramids, thousands of years existent, but apparently not sentient, must, of course, be to us but the wild theories of imagination, and so remain in the darkness with which, in inscrutable wisdom, the Almighty has enveloped it.

But that the Spirit can look with other than indifference, if not loathing, on the perishing exuviæ of its chrysalis existence, which, to its retrospective gaze, presents little other than a tasking house of base necessities, a chained prison of cruel disappointments, even to our human reason, clogged as it is with bars and contradictions, appears hardly to admit the opportunity of question and of consequence. To that Spirit its disposition can but be a matter of indifference. Still, to the surviving friends, whose affection cannot separate mind from matter, those forms, lying in the still and silent tomb, retain all their dear associations; and surely, it most gravely becomes the members of that profession, which, next to the altar, stands foremost in benevolence, that the deepest prudence should be exercised in this gloomy rite required by the living from the dead.

But, upon reflection, we should hesitate to speak in terms of disparagement of the human body; for, of all of the physical works of God, which we think we can comprehend, it bears most strongly the impress of design, in its wonderful, complex, and perfect adaptation, of means to ends. In it we recognize machinery of exquisite order, temporarily furnished to the Spirit to place it in communion with the other material works of God, so that, by their study, it may increase in intelligence and elevate itself in love to Him, who, however incomprehensible to our as yet feeble minds, in many of his dispensations, we feel to be the exhaustless fountain of benevolence and love.

We have learned to define the functions of this body into what we call Senses—three: taste, smell and feeling, intended for its preservation and continuous reconstruction; and two, more noble: sight and hearing, through which, by contemplation of his creation, we are to approach the Deity. The inferior, though necessary, senses, each with appropriate stimulus to achieve its appointed end, and confined within its proper limits, furnish a lower order of pleasure to, and are servants of, the soul; but if the Spirit—this ethereal emanation from the Deity, whose errand here is study of his works, and through them appreciation of his goodness, his love and elevation to intelligence of higher order still—if this beautiful Spirit permits itself to be over tempted by the pleasures of the inferior senses, and withdraws from the contemplation of the Supreme, then its purity is dimmed; it sinks degraded into that lower mental stratum which it participates in, in common with the brutes; and there, its snowy vestments soiled, and struggling in the sensual mire, God still continuously calling it back through the voice of conscience, it lies and wails and sobs despairingly in what we call SIN. Is it not this continual conflict which the soul maintains with the lower senses that constitutes its school of probation here?—the dual nature that Paul complains of?

But let us turn from this sad picture for a moment to the nobler senses—to vision and its organ. The Spirit directs its mimic telescope, the eye, on the surrounding world, and instantly, reflected on the retina through the little pupil, it beholds, pictured as if by magic, oceans, mountains, forests, rivers, valleys, tropic vegetation, arctic snows, parents, children, friends—all the machinery of life and being, now stationary, now floating in ever changing panorama—panorama, itself alone, fraught with study for ages, till, with the declining sun, darkness insensibly draws its veil around, and all is lost to view, all hushed in silence.

But in the darkness, the Spirit still seeks its proper stimulus, the light, and elevates its gaze up to the o'erhanging canopy. Again, the little optic mirror, faithful to its purpose, performs its duty ; now reflects the blazing glories of the starry firmament, the constellations moving on in their appointed journeys in silent majesty ; the moon in serene splendor, sailing amid her sister planets through the cold blue ether, now struggling with, now joyously passing through, the flying clouds, temporarily obscuring her, to cast again her soft and benignant light on all the world beneath ; apt portraiture of the soul in her struggles with the murky clouds of sense.

Amazed, the delighted Spirit begins to reason. It reasons out the Lens, places it auxiliary to the little mirror; and straight it finds the distant stars increase in brilliancy ; that some are nearer,[*] and that other stars appear, " which were not there before." In exultation it enlarges its artificial aid, and then present themselves far distant in the dark o'erhanging chasms, other and yet other stars: and far beyond them still, fleecy, fog-like nebulæ. It increases the optic stimulus and the dim light is resolved to glittering " star dust," the

[*] Planets.

star dust to stars. It adds yet other power, and lo! the fleecy[1] nebulæ expand themselves to firmaments, firmaments glorious with Suns and their surrounding worlds; here scintillating in their own proper silver splendor; here in colors of orange, gold, and pale blue sapphire; and here, glowing with ruby and emerald, blazing in all the gorgeousness of regal diadem,[2] firmaments, compared with which its own, that which first met its uneducated gaze, is but as a point, a unit.

But does the Spirit here stop and fold its wings? No, 'tis but in its novitiate. With increasing aid, which its intelligence reasons forth, and which God continuously extends in exact accordance with its patient effort, it speeds still onward, plunges yet deeper into the great awful[3] voids of space, and sweeps in exultation o'er vast congeries, islands, continents of worlds, millions, countless myriads of worlds, which, like huge starry billows,* crowd the limitless aërial ocean; and still unsated, still unsatisfied, rushes on as the blazing glories continuously unfold themselves to its enchanted gaze! This is but the beginning of education in the Deity; but the first lisping of the infant Spirit in its study of the Infinite!

Nor does the Spirit confine itself alone to aërial study, nor to unassisted vision in the examination of other of Nature's great volume open spread before it, but with microscopic aid dives into the equal wonders of the unseen beneath its feet; hovers o'er and studies with eagerness the movements of the insect nation crowded in the bottom of the lily[4]; each member of the busy throng instinct with life, defined in individuality, each with its loves, and hates, and proper stimulus to action; watches with like curiosity

* See Nichols' Stellar Universe, pp. 72, 73.

the infusoria millions, sporting and fighting in the single liquid drop; invisible nothings to its naked eyesight, through magnifying power springing into entity and being; discovers the gaudy unsuspected plumage on the insect's wing; detects the crystal's angles; with its prism, even dissects and delightedly holds suspended, quivering in its constituent colors, light itself, its own natural stimulus; scoops from the ocean of Eternity a drop, and calls it time; and weighs in like exquisite balance the minute grain and distant worlds. Yet this little eye, this retina, this organ so indispensable, the key to open these wondrous mysteries, is a part and but a portion of the much-despised body.

But what were all this to the gentle Spirit whose law is love, love which tends continually back to its great Creator, who Himself is love, if, locked up in loneliness, it could not, through the sense of hearing, receive the tones of tenderness, gentleness, devotion—the interchange of thought with other intelligences—hear the mother's deep accents of affection, the prattle of the child, the gentle voice of Charity, the glorious harmonies which float it away as if by magic, until in ecstacy it is merged and almost lost in the unseen Infinite; or the louder and terrific crash which frightens it, cowering into more immediate apprehension of the Deity? Doubtless the body is the servant of the soul; but the connection of a minister of such necessity, provided by the Infinite, may well startle us when we reflect to what account we shall be held for its abuse and injury; injury inevitable, when in the least degree we o'erstep the bounds of rigid temperance; injury that paralyzes the harmony of action, which is its appointed function.

[1] A *nebula* in the constellation "Aquarius" is estimated to be

three thousand six hundred millions of miles in extent. One in "Lyra," to be distant from the earth forty-seven thousand billions of miles; another, in the constellation "Triangulum," seventeen thousand billions of miles. The nearest (!) star to our system is Alpha, in "Centaurus," which is computed to be twenty billions of miles distant. Our own Solar system, although it is five thousand seven hundred millions of miles in diameter, is a mere *point* in the Universe. (Bouvier's Astronomy.)

² This magnificent scene presents itself near "Kappa," in the constellation "Crux." See Bouv. Ast., pp. 250–284. For others, see Nichols' Stellar Universe, p. 172.

³ While it is hopeless for us to form even a faint idea of these awful distances, yet we may make a feeble effort at approximation towards their reality, by considering that a railroad car, traveling night and day, at the rate of twenty miles an hour, would require three hundred millions of years to reach the star "Sirius;" (Bouvier's Ast.)—that with the electric fluid flashing through space at a velocity of twenty thousand miles a second, it would alike require, were such transmission possible, ninety years to convey a telegraphic message to star 67, "Cygni;" and thirty years to Alpha "Centauri," the nearest fixed star to the earth. (Bouvier's Ast.)

⁴ The flies which I had observed were all distinguished from each other by their colors, their forms and their manners. Some were of the color of gold, others of silver, and others of bronze; these were spotted, those striped; some were blue, some green, some dull, and others shining. In some, the head was rounded like a turban, in others lengthened into a point like a nail; in some it appeared dark like a spot of black velvet, in others it sparkled like a ruby.

We may therefore conclude, by analogy, that there are animals which feed on the leaves of plants like the cattle in our meadows, which recline in the shade of hairs imperceptible to human eyes, and which drink from their glands, formed like suns, liquid gold and silver. Every part of a flower must present them with spectacles of which we have no idea. The yellow antheræ suspended on white threads appear to them like double bars of gold balanced on columns more beautiful than ivory; the corallæ like vaults of rubies and topazes, of immeasurable extent; the nectaria like rivers of sugar;

the other parts of the blossom like cups, urns, pavilions and domes, which the architecture and workmanship of men have never imitated.   *   *   *

The animals which live beneath their rich reflections must have ideas very different from ours concerning light and the other phenomena of nature. A dew-drop, filtering through the capillary and transparent tubes of a plant, appears to them like a thousand fountains; collected into a globule at the extremity of one of its hairs, it is a boundless ocean; and when evaporated in the atmosphere, an aërial sea. (St. Pierre, "*Studies of Nature.*")

OLD KENNEDY, THE QUARTER-MASTER.

(CONSTITUTION AND GUERRIERE.)

(See Frontispiece.)

No. I.

THE sun became more and more powerful as it ascended towards the meridian, and was reflected with effulgent intensity from the mirror-surface of the river. As we bent over the side and looked far down into the deep vault reflected from above, and saw our gallant little yacht, with her white sails and dark hull, suspended with even minute tracery over it, we could almost imagine ourselves with the Ancient Mariner, " in a painted ship upon a painted ocean." The white sand-banks quivered and palpitated in the sultry glare, and the atmosphere of the adjoining swamps hung over them in a light blue vapor, the deadly miasma, their usual covering, dissipated in the fervent heat, while the silence was unbroken, save by the occasional scream of the gull, as it wheeled about in pursuit of its prey, or the quick alarmed cry of the kingfisher, hastily leaving some dead branch upon the shore to wing its way farther from the object of its terror. The black boy, in perfect negro elysium, lay stretched fast asleep, with his arm resting upon one of the dogs, in the blazing sun on the forecastle ; while we ourselves reclined upon the cushions with our refreshments before us, indolently puffing our cigars under the awning ; Old Kennedy, perched upon the taffrail, coxswain fashion, with the tiller between his legs. While thus enjoying ourselves, like true disciples of Epicurus, the guitar was taken from its case in the cabin, and accompanied by the rich tones of Walter Smith, "Here's a health to thee, Mary," in compliment to our kind hostess, swept over the still surface of the river till dissipated in the distance, and anon the " Wild Huntsman," and " Here's a health to all good lassies," shouted at the pitch of three deep bass voices, bounded over the banks, penetrating the deep forest, causing the wild game to spring from their coverts in consternation at such unusual disturbance of its noontide stillness. " We bade dull care begone, and daft the time away." Old Kennedy, seated at the tiller, his grey hair smoothed down on one side, and almost falling into his eyes, his cheek distended with a huge quid of tobacco, which gave an habitual drag to a mouth whose expression indicated surly honesty and resolution, was a perfect portrait of many an old quarter-master, still in the service, while his scrupulously clean shirt, with its blue collar open at the neck, discovering a rugged throat encircled by a ring of grey hairs, and his white canvas trowsers, as tight at the hips as they were egregiously large at the ankles, indicated the rig in which he had turned up for the last thirty years to Sunday muster. The old seaman had seen a great deal of service, having entered the Navy at the opening of the difficulties with the Barbary powers, and had been engaged in several of the signal naval actions which followed in the subsequent war with Great Britain. Previous to that time, he had been in the employ of Tom's father, who was an extensive shipping merchant at Alexandria, and now, in his old age, influenced by an 'attachment for the son, who had built a snug cottage for him on his estate, and, vested with the full control of the yacht, he had been induced to come down to spend the remainder of his days on the banks of the Potomac, enjoying the pension awarded by government for the loss of his arm.

I had previously had the hint given me, that a little adroit management would set him to spinning a yarn which would suit my fancy. So, watching a good opportunity, knowing that the old man had been with Hull in his fight with the Guerriere, I successfully gave a kick to the ball by remarking: "You felt rather uncomfortable, Kennedy, did you not, as you were bearing down on the Guerriere, taking broadside and broadside from her, without returning a shot? You had time to think of your sins, my good fellow, as conscience had you at the gangway?" "Well, sir," replied he, deliberately rolling his tobacco from one side of his mouth to the other, squirting the juice through his front teeth with true nautical grace—"Well, sir, that ere was the first frigate action as ever I was engaged in, and I am free to confess, I overhauled the log of my conscience to see how it stood, so it mought be I was called to muster in the other world in a hurry; but I don't think any of his shipmates will say that Old Bill Kennedy did his duty any the worse that day, because he thought of his God, as he has many a time since at quarters. There's them as says the chaplain is paid for the religion of the ship, and it's none of the sailors' business; but I never seen no harm in an honest seaman's thinking for himself. Howdsomever, I don't know the man what can stand by his gun at such time, tackle cast loose, decks sanded, matches lighted, arm-chests thrown open, yards slung, marines in the gangways, powder-boys passing ammunition buckets, ship as still as death, officers in their iron-bound boarding caps, cutlashes hanging by lanyards at their wrists, standing like statues at divisions, enemy may-be bearing down on the weather-quarter—I say, I doesn't know the man at sich time, as won't take a fresh bite of his quid, and give a hitch to the waistbands of his trowsers, as he takes a squint at the enemy through the port as he bears down. And as you say, at that particular time, the Guerriere (as is French for sojer) was wearing and manœuvering, and throwing her old iron into us, broadside and broadside, like as I have seen them Italians in Naples throw sugar-plums at each other in Carnival time. Afore she was through, tho', she found it was no sugar-plum work, so far as Old Ironsides was consarned. You observe, when we first made her out, we seen she was a large ship close hauled on the starboard tack, so we gin chase, and when within three miles of her took in all our light sails, hauled courses up, beat to quarters and got ready for action. She wore and manœuvered for some time, endeavoring to rake, but not making it out bore up under her jib and topsails, and gallantly waited for us. Well, sir—as we walked down to her, there stands the old man (Hull), his swabs on his shoulders, dressed as fine in his yellow nankin vest and breeches, as if he was going ashore on leave—there he stands, one leg inside the hammock nettings, taking snuff out of his vest pocket, watching her manœuvres, as she blazed away like a house a-fire, just as cool as if he was only receiving complimentary salutes. She burnt her brimstone, and was noisy, but never a gun fires we. Old Ironsides poked her nose steady right down for her, carrying a bank of foam under her bows like a feather-bed cast loose. Well, as we neared her, and she wears first a-starboard, and then a-larboard, giving us a regular broadside at every tack, her shot first falls short, but as we lessened the distance, some of them begins to come aboard, first among the rigging, and cuts away some of the stuff aloft, for them Englishmen didn't larn to fire low till we larnt 'em. First they comes in aloft, but by-and-by, in comes one—lower—crash—through the bulwarks, making the splinters fly like carpenters' chips, then another, taking a gouge out of the main-mast, and pretty soon agin—'*chit*,' I recollects the sound of that ere shot well—'chit,' another dashed past my ear, and glancing on a gun-carriage, trips up the heels of three as good men as ever walked the decks of that ere ship, and all this while never a gun fires we, but continues steadily eating our way right down on to his quarter, the old man standing in the hammock nettings watching her movements as if she was merely playing for his amusement. Well, as we came within carronade distance, them shot was coming on board rather faster than mere fun, and some of the young sailors begins to grumble, and by-and-by, the old men-of-wars-men growled too, and worked rusty—cause why—they sees the enemy's mischief, and nothing done by us to aggravate them in return. Says Bill Vinton, the vent-holder, to me: 'I say, Kennedy,' says he, 'what's the use; if this here's the way they fights frigates, dam'me! but I'd rather be at it with the Turks agin on their own decks as we was at Tripoli. It's like a Dutch bargain, all on one side. I expects the next thing, they'll order pipe down and man the side-ropes for that ere Englishman to come aboard and call the muster-roll.' 'Avast a bit,' says I; 'never you fear the old man. No English press-gang comes on board this ship; old Blow-hard knows what he's about.'

"Well, by-and-by Mr. Morris, our first lieutenant, who all the while had been walking up and down the quarter-deck, his trumpet under his arm, and his eyes glistening like a school-boy's just let out to play; by-and-by *he* begins to look sour, 'ticularly when he sees his favorite coxswain of the first cutter carried by a shot through the opposite port. So he first looks hard at the old man, and then walks up to him and says, by way of a hint, in a low tone: 'The ship is ready for action, sir; and the men are getting impatient.' The old man never turns, but keeps his eye steadily on the enemy, while he replies: 'Are—you—all ready, Mr. Morris?' 'All ready, sir,' says the lieutenant. 'Don't fire a gun till I give the orders, Mr. Morris,' says the old man. Presently up comes a midshipman from the main-deck, touches his hat—'First division all ready, sir. The second lieutenant reports the enemy's shot have hurt his men, and he can with difficulty restrain them from returning their fire.' 'Tell him to wait for orders, Mr. Morris,' says the old man again, never turning his head. Well, just, you see, as the young gentleman turned to go below, and another shot carries off Mr. Bush, lieutenant of marines—just as we begins to run into their smoke, and even the old gun-boat-men, as had been with Decatur and Somers, begins to stare, up jumps the old man in the air, slaps his hand on his thigh with a report like a pistol, and roars out in a voice that reached the gunners in the magazines: 'Now, Mr. Morris, give it to them! Now give it to them, fore and aft, round and grape! Give it to 'em, sir; give it to 'em!' and the words was scarce out of his mouth before our whole broadside belched at half-pistol-shot; the old ship, trembling from her keel to her trucks like an aspen, at the roar of her own batteries, instantly shooting ahead and doubling across his bows, we gave him the other with three cheers, and then at it we went, regular hammer and tongs. You would a thought you were in a thunder storm in the tropics, from the continual roar and flash of the batteries. In ten minutes his mizzen-mast went by the board. 'Hurrah!' shouts the old man; 'hurrah, boys; we've made a brig of her; fire low; never mind their top hamper! Hurrah! we'll make a sloop of her before we've done!' In ten minutes more over went her main-mast, carrying twenty men overboard as it went; and sure enough, sir, in thirty minutes that 'ere Englishman was a sheer hulk, smooth as a canoe, not a spar standing but his bowsprit; and his decks so completely swept by our grape and cannister that there was barely hands enough left to haul down the colors, as they had bravely nailed to the stump of their main-mast. 'I say, Kennedy,' says the vent-holder to me, lying across the gun after she struck, looking out at the wrack through the port, and his nose was as black as a nigger's from the powder flashing under it, 'I say, I wonder how that 'ere Englishman likes the smell of the old man's snuff.'"

OLD KENNEDY, THE QUARTER-MASTER.

(Sailors Ashore.—Hornet and Peacock.)

No. II.

WELL, well; sailors is queer animals, anyhow, and always ready for a fight or frolic, and, so far as I sees, it don't much matter which. Now, there was Captain McL——, he was a lieutenant then; I was up in a draft of men with him to the lakes in the war, and as there was no canals nor steamboats in them days, they marched us up sojer fashion. As we marched along the road there was nothing but skylarking and frolic the whole time. Never a cow lying in the road, but the lads must ride; nor a pig, but they must have a pull at his tail. I recollects, once't, as we was passing a farm-yard, Jim Albro, as was alongside of me —what does Jim do, but jumps over the fence and catches a goose out of the pond, and was clearing with it under his arm; but the farmer, too quick for him, grabs his musket out of his door, and leveling at Jim, roars out to drop the goose. Jim catches the goose's neck tight in his hand, as it spraddles under his arm, and then turning his head over his shoulder, cries out, '*You fire*—I'll wring his neck off.' And so Jim would have got off with the goose, but one of the officers, seeing what was going on, orders Jim to drop the goose and have a care how he aggravates the honest farmers in that 'ere sort of a way; for, 'By the powers!' said he, 'Mr. Jim Albro, this isn't the first time, and if I hear of the like ag'in from you, but your back and the boatswain's mate shall scrape an acquaintance the first moment we come within the smell of a tarred ratlin.'

"It was wrong, to be sure, for Bill to take the man's goose, seeing as how it was none of his; but there was one affair that same day, as the lads turned up to, and, though a steady man, I'm free to confess I had a hand in't. Why, what do you think, sir, but as we what was bound for to fight the battles of our country—what do you think, but as we comes to one of them big gates they has on the roads, but the feller as keeps it—dam'me, sir, what does he do but makes all fast, and swears that we shan't go through without paying! I'm free to confess, sir, that that 'ere gate went off its hinges a little quicker than the chain of our best bower ever run through the hawse hole. A cummudgeonly son of a land lubber—as if, because we didn't wear long-tail coats and high-heel boots, we was to pay like horses and oxen! If the miserable scamp hadn't 've vanished like a streak into the woods, we'd have paid him out of his own tar-bucket, and rolled him over in the feathers of one of his wife's own beds. But, d'ye see, that wasn't the eend of it. Them 'ere lawyers gets hold of it, and it was the first time any of them land-sharks ever came athwart my hawse.

"When we gets to the next town, up comes a constable to the midshipman, supposing as how he was in command of the draft; up comes the constable and says, says he, 'Capting, I arrests you for a salt and battery, in behalf of these here men, as has committed it,' meaning, you understand, the affair of the gate. Well, the midshipman, all ripe for frolic and fun himself, pulls a long face, and says gruffly that his men hadn't been engaged in no salt on no battery; but that they was ready at all times to fight for their country, and asks him whereaway that same English battery lay, as he would answer for the lads salting it quick enough. Then the lawyer, as was standing with his hands behind him, up and tells him that 'it's for a trespass in the case.' 'Oh! a trespass in the gate, you mean,' says the midshipman. But just then the lieutenant comes up to see what's the muss, and bids me put on my jacket, for, d'ye see, I had squared off to measure the constable for a pair of black eyes. Hang me, if the feller didn't turn as white as a sheet. 'Put on your jacket, sir,' says he, 'and leave the man alone.' And then, turning to the midshipman: 'Mr. ——, take the men down to the tavern and splice the main-brace, while I walk up to the justice's with the gentleman, to settle this affair. And, hark'ee, ye rascals,' says he, 'don't disgrace the name of blue jacket in this quiet village, but behave yourselves till I return.' Well, he and the lawyer walks up to the justice's, and there they took a glass of wine together, and that's the last we hearn of that 'ere business.

"There ag'in, when we took the Peacock—you all knows about that 'ere action. It was what I calls short and sweet. Fifteen minutes from the first gun, he was cut almost entirely to pieces, his main-mast gone by the board, six feet of water in the hold, and his flag flying in the fore-rigging, as a signal of distress. The sea was running so heavy as to wash the muzzles of our guns as we run down. We exchanged broadsides at half-pistol-shot, and then, as he wore to, to rake us, we received his other broadside, running him close in upon the starboard quarter, and a drunken sailor never hugged a post closer nor we did that brig till we had hammered daylight out of her. A queer thing is war, though, and I can't say as I was ever satisfied as to its desarts, though I've often turned the thing over in my mind in mid-watch since. There was we, what was stowing our round shot into that 'ere brig, as if she had been short of kentcledge, and doing all we could to sweep with our grape

and cannister everything living from her decks; there was we, fifteen minutes after, working as hard as we could pull, to keep her above water, while we saved her wounded and the prisoners, like as she had been an unfortunate wrack, foundering at sea. But all wouldn't do. Down she went, carrying thirteen of her own wounded, besides some of our own brave lads as was exerting themselves to save them, and mighty near did Bill Kennedy come to being one of the number, and having a big D marked ag'in his name on the purser's book, at that same time. The moment she showed signals of distress, all our boats was put in requisition to transport the prisoners and wounded to the Hornet. I was in the second cutter with Midshipman Cooper. He was a little fellow then, though he's a captain now. Well, we stowed her as full as she could stow, and I was holding on by the boat-hook in the bows, jist ready to push off, when Midshipman Cooper jumps aboard ag'in and runs back to call a couple of the Englishmen as was squared off at each other, at the foot of the main-hatch ladder, settling some old grudge (for, d'ye see, sir, all dis*cy*pline is over the moment a ship strikes). He runs back to tell them to clear themselves, for the ship was sinking; but before he could reach them she rolls heavily, sways for an instant from side to side, gives a heavy lurch, and then down she goes head foremost, carrying them fellers as was squared off ag'in each other, and her own wounded, besides four or five of our own brave lads, right down in the vortex. Our boat spun round and round like a top for a moment, and then swept clear, but the midshipman barely saved himself by springing into an empty chest as was floating by, and there he was, dancing about in the heavy sea like a gull in the surf, and it was nigh on two hours afore we picked him up; but the little fellow was jist as cool and unconsarned as if he was in a canoe on a fish-pond. The next day we opens a subscription and furnishes all the British seamen with two shirts and a blue jacket and trowsers each, 'cause why, d'ye see, they'd lost all their traps in their ship when she went down.

OLD KENNEDY, THE QUARTER-MASTER.

(Perry's Victory on Lake Erie.)

No. III.

"BUT," says I, "Kennedy, I think you said your draft was bound for the lakes. Which did you go to, Ontario or Erie?" "I was on both, sir," says he, "afore the war was over, and we got as much accustomed to poking our flying jib-boom into the trees on them shores as if the sticks was first cousins, which, seeing as how the ships was built in the woods, wouldn't be much of a wonder. Part of that 'ere draft staid down on Ontario, with the old commodore as was watching Sir James, and part was sent up to Erie. I went up to Erie and joined the Lawrence, Commodore Oliver H. Perry; and I hopes that old Bill Kennedy needn't be called a braggart, if he says he did his part in showing off as handsome a fight on that same freshwater pond as has ever been done by an equal force on blue water. Our gallant young commodore made as tight a fight of it as it has ever been my luck to be engaged in; and seeing as how half of his men was down with fever and ager, and not one in a dozen knew the difference between the smell of gun-powder and oil of turpentine, blow me! but I think it was about as well done.

"You see, our squadron was lying in a bay as they calls

Put-in-Bay, and when the enemy first hove in sight it was in the morning, about seven o'clock. I knows that that was the time, because I had just been made quarter-master, by Captain Perry, and was the first as seen them through my glass. They was in the nor'-west, bearing down. As soon as we made them out to be the enemy's fleet, up went the signal to get under way, our ship, the Lawrence, in course taking the lead. Well, as we was working slowly to windward, to clear some small islands—one of 'em was Snake Island—I hearn Captain Perry come up to the master and ask him, in a low voice, whether he thought he should be able to work out to wind'ard in time to get the weather-gage of the enemy; but the master said as how the wind was sou'-west, and light, and he didn't think he could. 'Then,' said the commodore, aloud, 'wear ship, sir, and go to leeward, for I am determined to fight them to-day.' But just then the wind came round to the south'ard and east'ard, and we retained the weather-gage, and slowly bore down upon the enemy. They did all they could to get the wind, but not succeeding, hove into line, heading west'ard, and gallantly waited for us as we came down.

"There lay their squadron, all light sails taken in, just like a boxer, with his sleeves rolled up and handkerchief tied about his loins, ready to make a regular stand-up fight; and there wasn't a braver man, nor better sailor, in the British Navy, nor that same Barclay, whose broad pennant floated in the van of that squadron.

"Pretty soon, up runs our motto-flag, the dying words of our hero Lawrence—'*Don't give up the ship*'—and floats proudly from our main; and then the general order was passed down the line by trumpet: '*Each ship, lay your en-*

emy alongside;' and if you ever seen a flock of wild geese flying south'ard in the fall of the year, you'll have some idea of us as we went down into action. The men was full of spirit and panting for a fight, and even them as was so sick as to be hardly able to stand insisted upon taking their places at the guns. I recollects one in particular, he was a carpenter's mate, a steady man from Newport, he crawls up when we beat to quarters and seats himself upon the head of one of the pumps, with the sounding-rod in his hand, looking as yellow as if he had just been dragged out of a North Carolina cypress swamp; but one of the officers comes up to him as he was sitting there, and says: 'You are too sick to be here, my man; there's no use of your being exposed for nothing; you had better go below.' 'If you please, sir,' says the poor fellow, 'if I can do nothing else, I can save the time of a better man and sit here and sound the pump." Well, sir, as we bore down, the English occasionally tried our distance by a shot, and when we was within about a mile of 'em, one comes ricochetting across the water, bounds over the bulwarks, and takes that man's head as clean off his shoulders as if it had been done with his own broad-axe. I have hearn say, that 'every bullet has its billet,' and that is sartin, that it's no use to dodge a shot, for if you are destined to fall by a shot, you will sartin fall by that same shot; and I bear in mind that an English sailor, one of our prisoners, told me that in a ship of their'n a feller, as skulked in the cable-tier, during an action with the French, was found dead with a spent forty-two resting on his neck. The ball had come in at the starn-port, struck one of the beams for'ard, and tumbled right in upon him, breaking his neck, as he lay snugly coiled away in the cable-tier. No, no; misfortins and cannon shot is very much alike; there's no dodging; every man must stand up to his work and take his chance; if they miss, he is ready when they pipes to grog; if they hit, the purser's book is squared and no more charges is scored ag'in him.

"But, as I was saying, it wasn't long before we begun to make our carronades tell, and then at it we went, hot and heavy, the Lawrence taking the lead, engaging the Detroit; and every vessel, as she came up, obeying orders and laying her enemy alongside in right good arnest, except the Niagara. She hung back—damn her!—with her jib brailed up and her main-topsail to the mast; consequence was, the Charlotte, as was her opponent, avails herself of her distance, runs up close under the starn of the Detroit, and both ships pours their combined fire into our ship, the Lawrence. I hearn the master myself, and afterwards two or three of the other officers, go up to the Commodore during the action and call his attention to the Niagara, and complain of her treacherous or cowardly conduct. Well, them two ships gin it to us hot and heavy, and in three minutes we was so enveloped in smoke, that we only aimed at the flashes of their guns, for we might as well have tried to track a flock of ducks in the thickest fog on the coast of Labrador, as their spars or hulls. I was working at one of the for'ard guns, and as, after she was loaded, the captain of the piece stood waiting with the trigger lanyard in his finger, ready to pull, one of the officers calls out, 'I say, sir; why don't you fire?' 'I want to make her tell, sir,' says the gunner; 'I am waiting for their flash—there it is;' and as he pulled trigger a cannon shot came through the port and dashed him to pieces between us, covering me and the officer all over with his brains. Their fire was awful, the whole of the shot of the two heaviest ships in the squadron pouring into us nigh on two hours without stopping. Our brig became a complete slaughter-house; the guns dismounted, carriages knocked to pieces, some of our ports knocked into one, hammock-netting shot clean away, iron stancheons twisted like wire, and a devilish deal more daylight than canvas in our bolt ropes, the wounded pouring down so fast into the cockpit, that the surgeons didn't pretend to do more than apply tourniquets to stop the bleeding, and many of the men came back to the guns in that condition, while others was killed in the hands of the surgeons. One shot came through the cockpit, jist over the surgeon's head, and killed midshipman Laub, who was coming up on deck with a tourniquet at his shoulder, and another killed a seaman who had already lost both arms. Our guns was nearly all dismounted, and finally there was but one that could be brought to bear, and so completely was the crew disabled, that the commodore had to work at it with his own hands. The men became almost furious with despair, as they found themselves made the target for the whole squadron, and the wounded complained bitterly of the conduct of the Niagara, as they lay dying on the decks and in the cockpit. Two shots passed through the magazine, one knocked the lantern to pieces and sent the lighted wick upon the floor, and if the gunner hadn't have jumped on it with his feet before it caught the loose powder—my eyes! but that 'ere ship and everything on board would have gone into the air like a sheaf of sky-rockets, and them as was on board never would have know'd which side whipped. Out of one hundred men that went into action, eighty-three were either killed or wounded, and every officer was killed or hurt except the Commodore. Our lieutenant of marines, Lieutenant Brooks —him as was called the Boston Apollo—the handsomest man in the sarvice, was cut nearly in two by a cannon shot and died before the close of the action.

"It was nigh on all up with us. The men was real grit though, and even the wounded cried, 'Blow her up,' rather than strike. Well, as things stood, there was an end of the Lawrence, so far as fighting went,—and our Commodore says, says he,—'Lieutenant Yarnall, the American flag must not be pulled down over my head this day, while life remains in my body: I will go on board that ship and bring her myself into action, and I will leave it to you to pull down the Lawrence's flag if there is no help for it.' So we got our barge alongside, by the blessing of Heaven, not so much injured but what she'd float, and off we pushed for the Niagara—the Commodore standing with his motto-flag under his arm; but as soon as the enemy caught sight of us they delivered a whole broadside directly at the boat, and then peppered away so briskly, that the water all around us bubbled like a duck-pond in a thunder-shower. There Perry stood, erect and proud, in the starn sheets, his pistols strapped in his belt and his sword in his hand, his eyes bent upon the Niagara, as if he'd jump the distance, never heeding the shot flying around him like hail. The men begged him to sit down; they entreated him with tears in their eyes, but it was not until I dragged him down by main force, the men declaring that they would lay upon their oars and be taken, that he consented.

"There's them as says the Niagara *wouldn't* come down, and there's them as says she *couldn't*; all I know is, that when our gallant young Commodore took the quarter-deck, she walked down into the thickest of it quick enough—my eyes! how we did give it to 'em, blazing away from both sides at once. We ran in between the Detroit and Charlotte, our guns crammed to the muzzle, and delivered both of our broadsides into them at the same time, grape, cannister and all, raking the others as we passed, and the Niagara lads

showed it wasn't no fault of their'n that they hadn't come earlier to their work. I never know'd guns sarved smarter, than they sarved their'n, till the end of the action, nor with better effect. We soon silenced the enemy, and run up the stars again on the Lawrence as she lay a complete wrack, shattered and cut up among them, for all the world like a dead whale surrounded by shirks. They struck one after another, much like you may have seen the flags of a fleet run down after the evening gun; and as the firing ceased, and the heavy smoke-bank rolled off to leeward, shiver my timbers! but it was a sight for a Yankee tar to see, the striped bunting slapping triumphantly in the breeze over the British jacks at their gaffs.

"If there's any man, tho', as says that their Commodore wasn't a man, every inch of him, aye! and as good a seaman, too, as ever walked a caulked plank, there's one here, and his name is Bill Kennedy, as will tell him that he's a know-nothing, and talks of a better man nor himself. Aye, aye! scrape the crown off his buttons, and he might mess with Decatur and Lawrence, and splice the main-brace with Stewart and Hull, and they be proud of his company. He was badly cut up, tho', and I have hearn tell, that when he got home to England, he wouldn't go for to see the lady what he'd engaged to marry, but sent her word by a friend, —I don't know who that friend was, but suppose it was his first lieutenant, in course—he sends her word that he wouldn't hold her to her engagement, ' 'cause why,' says he, ' I'm all cut to pieces, and ain't the man I was when she engaged for to be my wife.' Well, what d'ye think the noble girl says when she hearn this? 'Tell him,' says she, 'as long as there's enough of him left to hold his soul, I will be his.' I say, Master Tom, that's most up to the Virginny gals. Well, well, there never was but one, as would have said as much for Bill Kennedy, and she, poor Sue, she married curly-headed Bob, captain of the main-top in the Hornet, in a pet, and was sorry when it was too late. She was a good girl, though, and I've lent her and her young-ones a hand once't or twice since in the breakers.

OLD KENNEDY, THE QUARTER-MASTER.

(CHESAPEAKE AND SHANNON—BOAT FIGHT ON LAKE ONTARIO.)

—

No. IV.

"WELL, Mr. Kennedy," says Smith, "you have told us of your victories—have you always been victorious? Have you always had the luck on your side? Where did you lose your arm?" The old man took a long and deliberate survey of the horizon astern of us, apparently not well pleased with a dark cloud just beginning to lift itself above its edge, but whatever inferences he drew from it he kept to himself, and having relieved his mouth from the quid, and replenished the vacuum by a fresh bite of the pig-tail, he leisurely turned to us again and replied with some emphasis: "Them as fights the English, fights men; and though its been my luck to be taken twice by them, once't in the unlucky Chesapeake, and once't on the lakes, and though I owes the loss of my flipper to a musket marked G. R., I hopes I bears them no more grudge than becomes a true Yankee sailor. Now, speaking of that, I've always observed, since the war, when our ships is in the same port, that however much we always fights when we falls in with each other, that the moment the English or Americans gets into a muss with the French, or the Dutch, or the Spaniards, that we makes common cause and tumbles in and helps one another But I'm blest! but that Chesapeake business was a bad affair. They took the ship. Let them have the credit of it, say I, but no great credit neither; for half the men was foreigners in a state of mutiny and none of the men know'd their officers. I hearn Captain Lawrence say himself, after he was carried below, that when

he ordered the bugle-man to sound to repel boarders, the cursed Portuguese was so frightened, or treacherous, that no sound came from the bugle, though his cheeks swelled as if in the act. And I hearn a British officer say to one of our'n, that Captain Lawrence owed his death to his wearing a white cravat into action, and that a sharp-shooter in their tops picked him off, knowing as how no common man would be so dressed. I don't complain of their getting the best of it, for that's the fortune of war, but they behaved badly after the colors was hauled down. They fired down the hatches, and," lifting his hat and exhibiting a seam that measured his head from the crown to the ear, "I received this here slash from the cutlash of a drunken sailor, for my share, as I came up the main-hatch, after she surrendered. My eyes! all the stars in Heaven was dancing before me as I tumbled back senseless on the gun-deck below. And when they brought the ship into Halifax, she smelt more like a slaughter-house nor a Christian man-of-war. Howsomever, they whipt us, and there's an end of the matter, only I wish't our gallant Lawrence might have died before the colors come down, and been spared the pain of seeing his ship in the hands of the enemy. It was what we old sailors expected, though. She was an unlucky ship, and that disgraceful affair between her and the Leopard was enough to take the luck out of any ship. Now, if it had been old "Ironsides,"* or the "Old Wagon,"† I'm blessed! but the guns would have gone off themselves, had the whole crew mutinied and refused to come to quarters, when they heard the roar of the British cannon; aye, aye, Old Ironsides' bull-dogs have barked at John Bull often enough, aye, and always held him by the nose, too, when they growled; but the Chesapeake's colors was hauled down, while the Shannon's was flying. That's enough; we had to knock under; let them have the credit of it, say I. They'd little cause, except in that 'ere fight, to crow over the Yankee blue jackets. They whipt us, and there's an end to the matter, and be damned to 'em. But that ain't answering your question, as how I lost my larboard flipper. It wasn't in that

* Frigate Constitution. † Frigate United States.

'ere unfortunate ship, altho' if it would have saved the honor of the flag, Bill Kennedy would willingly have given his head and his arms, too; but it was under Old Chauncey on Lake Ontario. It was in a boat expedition on that 'ere lake, that I first got a loose sleeve to my jacket, besides being made a pris'ner into the bargain. You see, Sir James was shut up in Kingston, and beyond the harbor there was a long bay or inlet setting up some three or four miles. Now, the Commodore thought it mought be there was more of his ships in that same bay; so he orders Lieutenant Gregory, him as the English called the 'Dare-devil Yankee,' the same as went in with a barge the year before and burned a heavy armed schooner on the stocks, with all their stores, and came away by the light of it at—at—I misremember the place—he orders him to proceed up the bay to reconn'iter, to see whether there was any of the enemy's ships at anchor there, to get all the information he could of his movements, and to bring off a prisoner if he could catch one, that the Commodore mought overhaul him at his leisure. So the lieutenant takes a yawl as we had captured some days before, having Sir James's own flag painted upon her bows, with midshipman Hart, and eight of us men, and pulls leisurely along shore, till we made the entrance of the bay. It was a bright summer afternoon, and the water was as calm as the Captain's hand-basin, not a ripple to be seen. Well, the entrance was narrow, and somewhat obstructed by small islands; but we soon got through them, never seeing two heavy English men-of-war barges, as was snugly stowed in the bushes; but about three miles up we spies a raft of timber, with two men on it. We gave way, and before long got up abreast of it. When we got close aboard the raft, the lieutenant hailing one of the men, calls him to the side nearest the boat, and says: ' My man, what are you lying here for, doing nothing? The wind and tide are both in your favor; don't you know we are waiting down at Kingston for this here timber for his Majesty's sarvice; what are you idling away your time for here?' The feller first looks at Sir James's flag painted upon the bows of the yawl, and then at the lieutenant, and then again at the flag, and then at the lieutenant, and then opens his eyes, and looks mighty scarey, without saying anything, with his mouth wide open. ' I say,' says the lieutenant ag'in, ' I say, you feller with the ragged breeches, do you mean to swallow my boat? Why don't you answer; what the devil are you doing here?' The feller scratches his head, and then stammers, ' I—I—*I* know *you;* you are him as burnt Mr. Peter's schooner last year.' 'Well,' says the lieutenant, ' what are you going to do with this here timber?' ' I'm carrying it down for a raising,' says he. ' What!' says the lieutenant, 'do you use ship's knees and transom beams for house-raising in this part of the country? It won't do, my man. Bear a hand, my lads, and pile all the boards and light stuff in the centre, and we'll make a bonfire in honor of his most sacred Majesty.' So we set fire to it, and took the spokesman on board the yawl, towing the other man in their skiff astarn, intending to release them both when we got all the information we wanted out of them. We returned slowly down the bay again, the blazing raft making a great smoke; but as we neared the outlet, what does we see, but them two heavy barges pulling down to cut us off. We had to run some distance nearly parallel with them, an island intervening, so we every moment came nearer to them, and soon within speaking distance. The men gave way hearty, in fear of an English prison, but as we came nearer each other, some of the officers in the English boats recognizes Lieutenant Gregory, 'cause why, they had been prisoners with us, and hails him. 'Gregory,' says they, ' you must submit, it's no use for you to resist; we are four to your one. Come, old feller, don't make any unnecessary trouble, but give up; you've got to knock under.' The lieutenant said nothing, but he was a particular man, and had his own notions upon the subject, for, bidding the men give way, he coolly draws sight upon the spokesman with his rifle, and most sartin, as he was a dead shot, there would have been a vacant commission in His Majesty's Navy, hadn't the raftsman, who was frightened out of his wits, caught hold of him by the tails of his coat and dragged him into the bottom of the boat. The lieutenant drops his rifle, and catches the feller by his legs and shoulders and heaves him clear off the boat towards the skiff, while we men, dropping our oars, gave them a volley with our muskets, and then laid down to it again. We had taken them by surprise, but as we dashed along ahead, they returned our fire with interest, peppering some of our lads and killing Midshipman Hart outright, who merely uttered an exclamation as his oar flew up above his head, and fell dead in the bottom of the boat. Well, we see'd the headmost barge all ready, lying on her oars and waiting for us, and, as there was no running the gauntlet past her fire, we made for another opening from the bay as didn't appear to be obstructed, but as we nears it, and just begins to breathe free, three boats full of lobsters of redcoats shoots right across, and closes the entrance effectually on that side. We was in a regular rat-trap. We had been seen and watched from the moment we had got inside of the bay, burning the raft and all. 'Well, my lads,' says the lieutenant, 'this will never do; we must go about, hug the shore close, and try to push by the barges.' So about we went, but as we neared the shore, there was a party of them 'ere riflemen in their leggin's and hunting-shirts, all ready for us, waiting just as cool and unconsarned as if we was a parcel of Chrismas turkeys, put up for them to shoot at. 'Umph!' says the lieutenant again, ''twont do for them fellers to be cracking their coach-whips at us neither; we've nothing to do for it, my boys, but to try our luck, such as it is, with the barges.' So, as we pulled dead for the entrance of the bay, they lay on their oars, all ready for us, and as we came up they poured such a deadly fire into that 'ere yawl as I never see'd before or since. There was nineteen wounds among eight of us. The lieutenant was the only one unhurt, though his hat was riddled through and through, and his clothes hung about him in tatters. How he was presarved, is a miracle, for he was standing all the while in the starn-sheets, the most exposed of any on board. They kept firing away, as if they intended to finish the business, and gi'n no quarter, the men doing what little they could to pull at the oars; but a boat of wounded and dying men couldn't make much headway. Our men was true Yankee lads, tho', and no flinching.

"There was one man named Patterson, as pulled on the same thwart with me, and, of all the men I've ever sailed with, he showed most of what I calls real grit. At their first volley he gets a shot through his thigh, shattering the bone so that it hung twisted over on one side, but he pulls away at his oar as if nothing had happened. Presently another passes through his lungs and comes out at his back—still he pulls away and didn't give in; at last a third takes him through the throat and passes out back of his neck; then, and not till then, did he call out to the lieutenant: 'Mr. Gregory, I'm killed, sir; I'm dead; I can't do no more.' So the lieutenant says: 'Throw your oar overboard, Patterson, and slide down into the bottom of the boat and make yourself as comfortable as you can.' Well, what does Patterson do, as he lays in the bottom of the boat bleeding to death, what does he do but lifts his arm over the gunwale, and shaking his fist, cry: 'Come on, damn ye, one at a time, and I'm enough for ye as I am.' Aye, aye, Patterson was what I calls real grit. He was a good, quiet, steady man, too, on board ship; always clean and ac*ty*ve, and cheerful in obeying orders. Howsomever, his time had come, and, in course, there was an end of his boat duty in this world.

"Well, they continued to fire into us as fast as they could load, 'cause why, they was aggravated that so small a force should have fired into them; but the lieutenant takes off his hat and makes a low bow to let them know as how he had surrendered, and then directs me to hold up an oar's blade; but they takes no notice of either, and still peppered away; but just as we concludes that they didn't intend to give no quarter, but meant to extarminate us outright, they slacks firing, and, taking a long circuit, as if we'd have been a torpedo or some other dangerous combustible, pulled up aboard. There wasn't much for them to be afeard on, though, for, with the exception of the lieutenant, who was untouched, there was nothing in the boat but dead and wounded men. They took us in tow and carried us down to Kingston, and mighty savage was Sir James. He said that it was unpardonable that so small a force should have attempted resistance, and he and the lieutenant getting high, and becoming aggravated by something as was said between them, Sir James claps him in a state-room under arrest, and keeps him there under a sentry, with a drawn baggonet, for nigh on two months. After that he sends the lieutenant to Quebec, and then to England, where he remained till the close of the war; but them of us men as didn't die of our wounds was kept down in Montreal until——" Here the old man broke off abruptly, and taking another long look at the horizon, said: "If I ain't much mistaken, Master Tom, there's something a-brewing astarn there as will make this here craft wake up as if she was at the little end of a funnel with a harricane pouring through the other; and if I knows the smell of a Potomac thundergust, we'll have it full blast here before we're many minutes older."

THE PARTISAN LEGION.

OLD Kennedy quietly proceeded to make the necessary preparations to encounter the tempest. His peacoat was got out of the locker and tightly buttoned about him, and his tarpaulin well secured by its lanyard to his buttonhole. The mainsail and foresail were stowed and secured, and nothing but the jib, the bonnet of which was reefed down, was allowed to remain spread upon our dark and graceful schooner.

The cloud in the horizon began to extend itself, increasing and gradually rising and covering the sky, and the old man's prediction was evidently about to be fulfilled. A dead calm lay upon the river, and a preternatural stillness clothed in a sort of stupor the whole face of nature around us, while low muttering rolls of thunder from the dark cloud, and the frequent, sudden, crinkling lightning, glittering across its surface, warned us that we were about to encounter one of those violent and terrible thunder-storms which not unfrequently occur in this part of the country.

The distant muttering in the horizon rapidly became louder, and the perfect stillness of the forest was broken. The melancholy sighs of the coming blast increased to wails, the boughs of the trees rubbed against each other with a slow, see-saw motion, and, as the storm increased, grated with a harsh and continued groaning. The lightning became quick and incessant and blindingly vivid, and the dark gloom of the forest was rendered still darker by its rapid glare. The river itself soon was lashed into foam behind us, and in a few moments more, accompanied by huge clouds of dust, the tempest came roaring upon us. The cultivated fields and cheerful plantations which were but now smiling in quietness and repose on the other side of the

Lee. Washington. Pickens. Morgan. Sumter.
THE PARTISAN LEADERS OF THE SOUTH.

river, were now instantly shut out by the deep gloom. As the gust struck the schooner, she checked for a moment as if in surprise, and then shot forward with the speed of an arrow from the bow, swept on in the furious tempest as if she had been a gossamer or feather, enveloped in dust and darkness, the rain and hail hissing as it drove onwards, and the terrific thunder, now like whole broadsides of artillery, now quick and incessant peals of musketry, roaring with frightful violence around her, while the deep black forest, lit up by the blue lightning, bellowed incessantly with the hollow echoes. As we swept forward with frantic swiftness, a quivering white flash struck the top of an immense oak, and ere the crashing, deafening roar of the thunder followed, it was torn and splintered, shivered and burning, hurled on by the blast.

As soon as the squall struck us we ensconced ourselves below, in full confidence of our safety with Old Kennedy at the helm; and a fine subject would the old seaman have been for a painter, as he sat amid the fury of the storm, stern and erect, the tiller under the stump of his left arm, and the jib-sheets with one turn around the cleat in his right hand, the usual surly expression of his countenance increased into grim defiance, as he steadily and unmovingly kept his eyes fixed into the gloom ahead. At one time we darted by a sloop at anchor, which had let go everything by the run, her sails over her side in the water, on which, if the yacht had struck, she would have been crumpled up like a broken eggshell; but thanks to our old quartermaster's care, we dashed by in the gloom, his eyes never even for a moment turning on her as we passed.

The storm swept us on in its fury for some time, when it gradually abated in violence and began to subside. The heavy clouds, flying higher and higher in detached masses in the heavens, bye and bye lifted themselves in the western sky, and through the ragged intervals the setting sun poured his last rays over the dripping forest, bronzing the dark sides of our little schooner as he sunk and disappeared beneath the horizon. As the evening wore on, a star here and there discovered itself struggling amid the scud flying over it, and presently the moon shone out with her broad and silver light, and every vestige of the storm had disappeared.

As we glided gaily on, with a fresh, fine breeze, towards our cottage home past the deep forest, the silence was broken by a long, melancholy howl, which I supposed was that of a solitary wolf, but Smith said that it was more probably from some one of the large breed of dogs which are found on most of the plantations. Smith's mind was of a sad and pensive, although not at all of a gloomy cast; and, like most men of that character, he required strong excitement to arouse him; but when aroused, of all delightful companions that I have ever met, he was the man. The excitement of the storm had been sufficient stimulus, and, giving the reins to his wild spirits and excited feelings, he entertained us with an incessant stream of anecdote and adventure. The howl of the wolf had recalled to mind an incident in the life of his ancestor, and, in connection, he related it, with many other adventures of the celebrated Partisan Legion. I will not attempt to use his beautiful and spirit-stirring language, but will confine myself to a few disjointed anecdotes of the many which he related of the dashing corps, as they happen to recur to my memory.

The Legion, intended to act independently or conjointly with the main army, as circumstances might require, composed of three companies of infantry and three troops of cavalry, amounting in all to three hundred and fifty men, had won for itself in the Southern campaigns, and particularly in the masterly retreat of Green, before Cornwallis, the honorable distinction of being called " the eye of the Southern army." Its colonel, Green's confidential adviser and constant friend, a stern disciplinarian, was nevertheless beloved by his officers and men, and so careful was he of the interests of the latter, that while the rest of the army were suffering, the Legion by his exertions was always retained in the highest state of personal appearance and discipline. The horses were powerful and kept in high condition; indeed, he has been accused of being more careful for their

safety than for that of his men. The cavalry in the British army, mounted on inferior horses, could not stand a moment before them; and, armed with their long heavy sabres, the Legion troopers were considered full match for double the force of the enemy.

The Legion infantry were well equipped, and thoroughly disciplined men, and acted in unison with the cavalry. They were commanded by Captain Michael Rudolph, a man of small stature, but of the most determined and daring courage, and of great physical strength. He always led in person the "forlorn hope," when the Legion's services were required in the storm of posts, and he was so completely the idol of his men, that it was only necessary that he should be detailed on duty of the most desperate character, that the infantry, to a man, were anxious to be engaged in it. The leading captain of the cavalry, James Armstrong, was almost precisely his counterpart in person, in strength, in undaunted courage and heroic daring, beloved by his men, ahead of whom he was always found in the charge. O'Neal, also of the cavalry, was a bold and gallant man, who fought his way up from the ranks ; for no carpet knight had consideration in the corps. In an early part of his career he came near cutting off in the bud Cornwallis' favorite cavalry officer, Lieutenant-Colonel Tarleton ; for this officer, whatever his merits or demerits, endeavored to enter a window at which O'Neal was posted, when the latter, dropping his carabine, snapped it within an inch of his head, but the piece missing fire, Tarleton very coolly looked up at him with a smile and said, "You have missed it for this time, my lad," and wheeling his horse, joined the rest of his troop, who were on the retreat.

It were perhaps difficult to select the brave from a body of men who were all brave, but it is not invidious to say that there was not a man of more fearless courage in the corps than Lieutenant Manning of the Legion infantry. At the battle of Eutaw, commanding his platoon to charge, he rushed on in his usual reckless manner, without stopping or looking behind him, until he was brought up by a large stone-house, into which the Royal York Volunteers, under

Lieutenant-Colonel Cruger, were retiring. The British were on all sides, and no American soldier within two hundred yards of him. Without a moment's hesitation, he threw himself upon a British officer, and seizing him by the collar, wrested his sword from his grasp, exclaiming, in a harsh voice, "You are my prisoner, sir." Interposing him between the enemy and himself, as a shield from the heavy fire pouring from the windows, he then very coolly and deliberately backed out of danger. The prisoner, who was not deemed by his brother officers a prodigy of valor, pompously enumerating his rank and titles, which Manning occasionally interrupted with: "You are right—you are right—you're just the man, sir. You shall preserve *me* from danger, and rest assured I'll take good care of *you*."

Manning had retreated some distance from the house when he saw his friend, Captain Joyett, of the Virginia line, engaged in single combat with a British officer. The American was armed with a sword, while the Briton was defending himself with a bayonet. As the American approached, the Englishman made a thrust with the bayonet, which Joyett successfully parried with his sword, when both of them dropping their arms which they could not wield in so close an encounter, simultaneously clinched, and being men of great and nearly equal bodily strength, they were soon engaged in a desperate and deadly struggle. While thus engaged, an English grenadier, seeing the danger of his officer, ran up and with his bayonet made a lunge, which luckily missing Joyett's body, passed only through the skirts of his coat, but the bayonet becoming entangled in the folds, upon its withdrawal dragged both of the combatants together to the ground. The soldier having disengaged it, was about deliberately to transfix Joyett by a second thrust, when Manning, seeing the danger of his friend, without being sufficiently near in the crisis to assist him, called out, as he hurried up, in an authoritative tone, " You would not murder the gentleman, you brute!" The grenadier supposing himself addressed by one of his own officers, suspended the contemplated blow and turned towards the speaker, but before he could recover from his surprise, Manning cut him across the eyes with his sword, while Joyett, disengaging himself from his opponent, snatched up the musket, and with one blow laid him dead with the butt, the valiant prisoner whom Manning had dragged along, and who invariably asserted that he had been captured by "Joyett, a huge Virginian," instead of Manning, who was a small man, standing a horror-struck spectator of the tragedy. An equally brave man was Sergeant Ord, of Manning's company. In the surprise of the British at Georgetown, when a company of the Legion infantry had captured a house with its enclosures, the enemy made an attempt to regain it, the commanding officer calling out to his men: "Rush on, my brave fellows; they are only militia, and have no bayonets." Ord placing himself in front of the gate as they attempted to enter, laid six of them in succession dead at his feet, accompanying each thrust with, "Oh! no bayonets here—none, to be sure!" following up his strokes with such rapidity that the party were obliged to give up the attempt and retire.

But perhaps there could have been no two characters in the corps more the perfect antipodes of each other than the two surgeons of the cavalry, Irvine and Skinner, for while Irvine was entirely regardless of his person, and frequently found engaged sword in hand, in the thickest of the fight, where his duty by no means called him, Skinner was as invariably found in the rear, cherishing his loved person from the threatened danger. Indeed, he was a complete counterpart of old Falstaff—the same fat and rotund person, the same lover of good cheer and good wine, and entertaining the

same aversion to exposing his dear body to the danger of missiles or cuts; not only was he a source of fun in himself, "but he was the cause of it in others." He asserted that his business was in the rear—to cure men, not to kill them; and when Irvine was wounded at the charge of Quinby's bridge, he refused to touch him until he had dressed the hurts of the meanest of the soldiers, saying that Matthew Irvine was served perfectly right, and had no business to be engaged out of his vocation.

At the night alarm at Ninety-six, the Colonel, hastening forward to ascertain the cause, met the doctor in full retreat, and, stopping him, addressed him with: "Where so fast, doctor? Not frightened, I hope?" "No, Colonel," replied Skinner, "not frightened; but, I confess, most infernally alarmed." His eccentricities extended not alone to his acts, but to everything about him. Among other peculiarities, he wore his beard long and unshorn, and on being asked by a brother officer why he did so, he replied: "That is a secret between Heaven and myself, which no human impertinence shall ever penetrate." Like Falstaff, and with similar success, he considered himself the admired of the fair sex. "Ay," said he to Captain Carnes of the infantry; "Ay, Carnes, I have an *eye!*" Yet Skinner was by no means a man to be trifled with, for he was not devoid of a certain sort of courage, as he had proved in half a dozen duels, in one of which he had killed his man. When asked how it was, that he was so careful of his person in action, when he had shown so plainly that he was not deficient in courage, he replied: "I consider it very arrogant in a surgeon, whose business it is to cure, to be aping the demeanor and duty of a commissioned officer, and I am no more indisposed to die than other gentlemen, but have an utter aversion to the noise and tumult of battle; it stuns and stupefies me." On one occasion, when the Legion was passing through a narrow defile, the center was alarmed by the drums of the infantry beating to arms in front. Skinner, with the full sense of what was due to himself, whirled about, and giving his horse a short turn by the bridle, brought him down on his back in the middle of the defile, completely blocking it up and preventing either egress or ingress, relief or retreat. The infantry and cavalry, which had passed the gorge, immediately deployed on the hill in front, while the remainder of the Legion, galloping up, were completely severed by this singular and unexpected obstruction, until Captain Egglestone, dismounting some of his strongest troopers, succeeded in dragging the horse out of the defile by main force. It turned out that the alarm was false, otherwise the doctor's terror might have caused the destruction of one-half of the corps.

But to recur to the incident brought to mind by the howling of the wolf. When the Legion was on its march to form a junction with Marion, on the little Pedee, it one night encamped in a large field on the southern side of a stream, with the main road in front. The night passed on very quietly, until about two or three in the morning, when the officer of the day reported that a strange noise had been heard by the picket in front, on the great road, resembling the noise of men moving through the adjoining swamp. While he was yet speaking, the sentinel in that quarter fired his piece, which was immediately followed by the bugle calling in the horse patrols, the invariable custom upon the approach of an enemy. The drums instantly beat to arms, and the troops arranged for defence. The sentries, on being questioned, all concurred in the same account, "and one patrol of horse asserted that they had heard horsemen concealing with the greatest care their advance." The commander was in great perplexity, for he knew that he was not within striking distance of any large body of the enemy, and that Marion was at least two days' distance in advance; but soon a sentinel in another direction fired, and the same report was brought in from him; and it was apparent, however unaccountable, that the enemy was present. A rapid change in the formation of the troops was made to meet the attack in this quarter, but it was hardly accomplished before the fire of a third sentinel, in a different direction, communicated the intelligence of danger from another quarter. Feelings of intense anxiety were now aroused, and preparations were made for a general assault, as soon as light should allow it to be made. The pickets and sentinels held their stations, the horse patrols were called in, and the corps changed its position in silence, and with precision, upon every new communication, with the combined object of keeping the fires between them and the enemy, and the horse in the rear of the infantry.

While thus engaged, another and rapid discharge by the sentinels, on the line of the great road, plainly indicated that the enemy were in force, and that, with full understanding of their object, they had surrounded them. It was also evident that there must be a large body of the enemy, from covering so large a segment of the circle around them. It was equally apparent that they could expect no aid from any quarter, and, relying upon themselves, the corps awaited, in extreme anxiety, the scene which the day was to usher upon them.

The commander passed along the line of infantry and cavalry, in a low tone urging upon them the necessity of profound silence, reminding them that in the approaching contest they must sustain their high reputation, and expressing his confidence, that, with their accustomed bravery, they would be able to cut their way through all opposing obstacles, and reach the Pedee. His address was answered by whispers of applause, and having formed the cavalry and infantry into two columns, he awaited anxiously the break of day, to give the signal for action. It soon appeared, and the columns advanced on the great road; infantry in front, baggage in the center, and cavalry in the rear. As soon as the head of the column reached the road, the van officer, proceeding a few hundred yards, received the same account that had been given from the sentinel that had fired last.

The enigma remained unexplained, and no enemy being in view, there could be but little doubt that the attack was to be from ambushment, and the column moved slowly on, expecting every moment to receive their fire. But the van officer's attention having been accidentally attracted, he examined, and found along the road the tracks of a large pack of wolves. The mystery was now solved; it was evident that the supposed enemy was no other than the pack of wild beasts, which, turned from their route by the fire of the sentinels, had passed still from point to point in a wide circuit, bent upon the attainment of their object. A quantity of provisions had been stored some time previously on their line of march, but having become spoiled, it was abandoned in the vicinity of the night's encampment, and the wolves had been disturbed by the videttes, in the nightly progress to their regale. The agitation instantly subsided, and wit and merriment flashed on all sides, "every one appearing anxious to shift the derision from himself upon his neighbor, the commandant himself coming in for his share; and as it was the interest of the many to fix the stigma on the few, the corps unanimously charged the officer of the day, the guards, the patrols and pickets, with gross stupidity, hard bordering upon cowardice;" nevertheless, they were none the less relieved by the happy termination of an adventure attended by so many circumstances naturally alarming, and it long passed as an excellent joke in the Legion, under the title of the "Wolf reconnoiter."

The music sounded merrily, and the column marched on, elate with the fun and novelty of the adventure; and of the buglers, none blew a more cheery strain than little Jack Ellis, the bugler of Armstrong's troop. He was a fine boy, small and intelligent, as well as young and handsome, and a general favorite in the Legion. Poor little fellow! he met his death under circumstances peculiarly tragic and cruel, not long after. When the Southern army, under Greene, was slowly making its masterly retreat before Cornwallis, the Legion formed part of the rear-guard, and was consequently almost continually in sight of the van of the enemy, commanded by Brigadier-General O'Hara. The duty devolving upon it, severe in the day, was extremely so in the night, for numerous patrols and pickets were constantly required to be on the alert, to prevent the enemy from taking advantage of the darkness to get near the main army by circuitous routes, so that one-half of the troops of the rear-guard were alternately put on duty day and night, and the men were not able to get more than six hours' sleep out of the forty-eight. But the men were in fine spirits, notwithstanding the great fatigue to which they were subjected. They usually, at the break of day, hurried on, to gain as great a distance in advance as possible, that they might secure their breakfast, the only meal during the rapid and hazardous retreat. One drizzly and cold morning, the officers and dragoons, in pursuance of this custom, had hurried on to the front, and just got their corn cakes and meat on the coals, when a countryman, mounted on a small and meager pony, came galloping up, and hastily asking for the commanding officer, informed him that the British column, leaving the main line of march, were moving obliquely in a different direction, and that, discovering the manœuvre from a field where he was burning brush, he had run home, caught the first horse he could lay his hands upon, and hurried along with the information. Unwilling to believe the report of the countryman, although he could not well doubt it, and reluctant to disturb so materially the comfort of the men as to deprive them of the breakfast for which they were waiting with keen appetites, the commander ordered Captain Armstrong to take one section of horse, accompanied by the countryman, to return on the route, and having reconnoitered, to make his report.

Circumstances, however, strengthening him in the belief that the information of the countryman was correct, he took a squadron of cavalry and followed on to the support of Armstrong, whom he overtook at no great distance ahead. Perceiving no sign of the enemy, he again concluded that the countryman was mistaken. He therefore directed Armstrong to take the guide and three dragoons, and to advance still further on the road, while he returned with the squadron to finish their breakfast. The countryman, mounted on his sorry nag, protested against being thus left to take care of himself, asserting that, though the dragoons on their spirited and powerful horses were sure of safety, if pursued, he, on his jaded hack, was equally sure of being taken. The Colonel acknowledged the danger of the friendly guide, dismounted the little bugler, and giving the countryman his horse, placed Ellis upon the hack, sending him on in front to report to the commanding officer. After having returned a short distance, the squadron entered the woods on the roadside, and the dragoons leisurely proceeded to finish their breakfast; but they had hardly got it out of their haversacks when a firing of musketry was heard, and, almost immediately after, the clatter of horses' hoofs coming on at full gallop. The next moment, Armstrong, with his dragoons and the countryman, came in sight, pursued by a troop of Tarleton's dragoons at the top of their speed.

The commander saw Armstrong with his small party well in front and hard in hand, and felt no anxiety about them, as he knew that their horses were so superior to those of the enemy that they were perfectly safe, but the danger of the bugler, who could be but little ahead, immediately caused him serious uneasiness. Wishing, however, to let the British squadron get as far from support as possible, he continued in the woods for a few moments, intending to interpose in time to save the boy. Having let them get a sufficient distance, and assuring himself that there was nothing coming up to their support, he put the squadron in motion and appeared on the road, but only in time to see the enraged dragoons overtake and sabre the poor little suppliant, as he in vain implored for quarter. Infuriated at the sight, he gave orders to charge, and the English officer had barely time to form, when the squadron was upon them like a whirlwind, killing, prostrating and unhorsing almost the whole of the force in an instant, while the captain and the few left unhurt endeavored to escape. Ordering Lieutenant Lewis to follow on in pursuit, with strict orders to give no quarter, an order dictated by the sanguinary act that they had just witnessed, the commander placed the dying boy in the arms of two of the dragoons, directing them to proceed onwards to the camp, and immediately after pushed on to the support of Lewis, whom he soon met returning with the English captain and several of his dragoons, prisoners, the officer unhurt, but the men severely cut in the face, neck and shoulders. Reprimanding Lewis on the spot for disobedience of orders, he peremptorily charged the British officer with the atrocity that they had just witnessed, and ordered him to prepare for instant death. The officer urged that he had in vain endeavored to save the boy, that his dragoons were intoxicated and would not obey his orders, and he begged that he might not be sacrificed, stating that in the slaughter of Lieutenant-Colonel Buford's command he had used the greatest exertions, and succeeded in saving the lives of many of the Americans. This in some measure mollified the commander, but just then overtaking the speechless and dying boy, expiring in the arms of the soldiers, his bright and handsome face changed in the ghastly agony of death, he returned with unrelenting sternness to his first decision, and informed the Englishman that he should execute him in the next vale through which they were to pass, and, furnishing him with a pencil and paper, desired him to make such note as he wished to his friends, which he pledged him his word should be sent to the British General. The ill-fated soldier proceeded to write, when the British van approaching in sight, the prisoner was sent on to Colonel Williams in front, who, ignorant of the murder and the determination to make an example of him, in his turn forwarded him on to headquarters, thus luckily saving his life. Eighteen of the British dragoons fell in the charge, and were buried by Cornwallis as he came up, but the Americans had time to do no more than lay the body of the poor little bugler in the woods on the side of the road, trusting to the charity of the country people to inter it, when they were obliged to resume their retreat. It should be borne in mind that the commander's humane disposition could only be excited to such summary vengeance by the cruel and unwarrantable murder that they had just witnessed, and by the frequent acts of atrocity which had been repeatedly enacted by this same corps.

Perhaps the fated destiny which frequently appears to await the soldier, hanging over him like a shield while he passes through the most desperate danger, until the appointed hour arrives, was never more apparent than in the case of Lieutenant-Colonel Webster, of the British army, in this same retreat. When the rear of the American army, composed, as has been observed, principally by the Legion, had passed the Reedy Fork, the British van, under the command of Webster, endeavored to ford the river and bring them into action, a point which Cornwallis was anxious to attain, but which was entirely foreign to the plan of Greene, whose object was to wear out his pursuers. Under the cover of a dense fog the British had attained a short distance of the Legion before they were discovered. They made their appearance on the opposite bank of the river, and, after halting a few moments, descended the hill and approached the water; but, receiving a heavy fire of musketry and rifles, they fell back, and quickly re-ascending, were again rallied on the margin of the bank. Colonel Webster rode up, calling upon the soldiers in a loud voice to follow, and rushing down the hill at their head, amid a galling fire poured from the Legion troops, plunged into the water. In the woods occupied by the riflemen was an old log school-house, a little to the right of the ford. The mud stuffed between the logs had mostly fallen out, and the apertures admitted the use of rifles with ease. In this house were posted five and twenty select marksmen from the mountain militia, with orders to forego engaging in the general action, and directions to hold themselves in reserve for any particular object which might present. "The attention of this party being attracted by Webster, as he plunged into the water, they singled him out as their mark; and as he advanced slowly, the stream being deep, the bottom rugged, and some of his soldiers holding on by his stirrup-leathers, they one by one discharged their rifles at him, each man sure of knocking him over, and, having reloaded, eight or nine of them emptied their guns at him a second time; yet, strange to relate, neither horse nor rider received a single ball. The twenty-five marksmen were celebrated for their superior skill, and it was a common amusement for them to place an apple on the end of a ramrod and hold it out at arm's length, as a mark for their comrades to fire at, when many balls would pass through the apple; yet the British officer, mounted on a stout horse, slowly moving through a deep water-course, was singled out and fired at thirty-two or three times successively, and yet remained untouched, and succeeded in effecting a lodgment on the bank, where he formed his troops under a heavy fire." This gallant officer and polished gentleman, the favorite of Cornwallis, subsequently fell at the battle of Guilford Court-House, not more regretted by his brother soldiers than admired by those of the American army.

There is nothing more true than, that in war, as in love, much depends upon accident, and an alarm is frequently conveyed, and a victory won, by circumstances entirely the act of chance. As a case in point. In the retreat of the British after the battle of Monks' Corner, Lieutenant-Colonel Stuart ordered all the arms belonging to the dead and wounded to be collected, and when the retreating enemy had marched on, they were set fire to by the rear guard. As many of the muskets were loaded, an irregular discharge followed, resembling the desultory fire which usually precedes a battle. The retreating army immediately supposed that Greene was up and had commenced an attack on their rear, and the dismay and confusion was so great that the wagoners cut the traces of their horses and galloped off, leaving the wagons on the route. The followers of the army fled in like manner, and the terror was rapidly increasing, when the cessation of the firing quelled the alarm.

But the most exciting incident that our fellow voyager related, and one which would well merit the attention of the painter, was the spirited affair at Quinby's Bridge. When the British army in their turn were retreating, Sumter, Marion and the Legion frequently were able to act in concert. The 19th British Regiment, Lt. Col. Coates, having become isolated at Monks' Corner, it was determined to fall upon it, and cut it off by surprise before it could obtain relief. The British officer having taken the precaution to secure the bridge across the Cooper river by a strong detachment, it became necessary for them to make a long circuit through the deep sands, in the hottest part of the summer, before they could form a junction with Sumter, whose aid was required in the intended attack. The junction was not effected until evening, and the attack was necessarily deferred until the following morning; but about midnight, the whole sky becoming illuminated by a great conflagration, it was evident that the enemy had taken the alarm. They had set fire to the church to destroy the stores, and had decamped in silence. By the neglect of the militia, who had deserted a bridge at which they were stationed, the enemy had been able to draw off, and obtain a considerable distance in advance, before their retreat was discovered. The commander immediately followed on with the cavalry in pursuit of the main body, but was unable to come up with it, until he had arrived in the neighborhood of Quinby's Bridge, about eighteen miles from Monks' Corner. Upon its first approach, he discovered the baggage of the regiment under a rear guard of about one hundred men, advancing along a narrow road, the margin of which was bordered by a deep swamp on both sides. As soon as the cavalry came in view, the British officer formed his men across the road, which they had hardly effected, when the charge was sounded, and the Legion cavalry rushed upon them with drawn swords at full gallop. The voice of the British officer was distinctly heard "directing his men to fire," and as no charge immediately followed, the cavalry officers felt extreme solicitude, lest its reservation was meant to make it the more fatal on their near approach, for on the narrow road, and in the close column in which they were rushing on, a well-directed fire would have emptied half of their saddles; but, happily, the soldiers, alarmed by the formidable appearance of the cavalry, threw down their arms and supplicated for quarter, which the cavalry were most happy to grant them. The prisoners being secured, the main body of the cavalry pushed on under Armstrong for the bridge, which was still about three miles in front, in the hope of cutting off the enemy before they could succeed in reaching it. As Armstrong came in sight, he found that Coates had passed the bridge, and that he was indolently reposing on the opposite side of the river, awaiting his rear guard and baggage. He had, by way of precaution, taken up the planks from the bridge, letting them lie loosely on the sleepers, intending, as soon as the rear should have crossed, to destroy it. Seeing the enemy with the bridge thus interposed, which he knew was contrary to the commandant's anticipations, Armstrong drew up, and sent back word to the commander, who was still with the prisoners, requesting orders, never communicating the fact that the bridge was interposed. The adjutant soon came galloping back with the laconic answer: "The order of the day, sir, is to fall upon the enemy, without regard to consequences."

The gallant Armstrong for a moment leaned forward in his saddle, towards the adjutant, as if thunder-struck with this reflection on his courage; in the next, his sword glanced like a streak of light around his head, and shouting in a voice of thunder: "Legion cavalry, charge!" at the head of his section he cleared the bridge, the horses throwing off the loose planks in every direction; the next instant, driving the soldiers headlong from the howitzer which they had mounted at the other end to defend it, he was cutting and slashing in the very center of the British regiment, which, taken completely by surprise, threw down their arms, retreating in every direction. The horses of Armstrong's section had thrown off the planks as they cleared the bridge, leaving a yawning chasm, beneath which the deep black stream was rushing turbidly onwards; but Lieutenant Carrington, at the head of his section, took the leap and closed with Armstrong, engaged in a desperate personal encounter with Lieutenant Colonel Coates, who had barely time to throw himself with a few of his officers behind some baggage-wagons, where they were parrying the sabre cuts made by the dragoons at their heads. Most of the soldiers, alarmed at the sudden attack, had abandoned their officers and were running across the fields, to shelter themselves in a neighboring farm-house. The Colonel, by this time, had himself got up to the bridge, where O'Neal, with the third section, had halted, the chasm having been so much enlarged by Carrington's horses throwing off additional planks, that his horses would not take the leap, and seeing the howitzer abandoned, and the whole regiment dispersed, except the few officers who were defending themselves with their swords, while they called upon the flying soldiers for assistance, he proceeded to recover and replace the planks. The river was deep in mud, and still deeper in water, so that the dragoons could neither get a footing to replace the planks, nor a firm spot from which they might swim their horses to the aid of their comrades. Seeing this posture of affairs, some of the bravest of the British soldiers began to hurry back to the assistance of their officers, and Armstrong and Carrington, being unable to sustain with only one troop of dragoons so unequal a combat, they abandoned the contest, forcing their way down the great road into the woods on the margin of the stream, in their effort to rejoin the corps. Relieved from the immediate danger, Coates hastened back to the bridge and opened a fire from the deserted howitzer upon the soldiers, who were fruitlessly striving to repair the bridge, and being armed only with their sabres, which the chasm made perfectly useless, as they could not reach the enemy across it, they were also forced to give up the attempt, and retire without the range of the fire from the gun.

Marion shortly after coming up, in conjunction with the Legion, marched some distance down the banks, where they were enabled to ford the stream, and effect a passage. In the edge of the evening, they reached the farm-house, but found that Coates had fortified himself within it, with his howitzer, and was thus impregnable to cavalry. "While halting in front, Armstrong and Carrington came up with their shattered sections. Neither of the officers were hurt, but many of the bravest dragoons were killed, and still more wounded. Some of their finest fellows—men who had passed through the whole war, esteemed and admired—had fallen in this honorable but unsuccessful attempt." Being without artillery, and within striking distance of Charleston, they were obliged, fatigued as they were, to commence their retreat. Placing the wounded in the easiest posture for conveyance, and laying the dead on the pommels of their saddles, the Legion counter-marched fifteen miles; at its close, burying in sadness and grief, in one common sepulchre, the bodies of those that had fallen.

These anecdotes of the Legion are but a few of the many stirring and spirited narrations with which Smith whiled away the time, as we glided along on our return up the river. His own observations and adventures in traveling over the world were not wanting for our amusement, for, with a mind well prepared for its enjoyment, he had passed the years that had intervened, since last I saw him, in traveling leisurely over Europe and the East. With the true philosophy of life, calling all men brothers, and restrained by no narrow prejudices of country or habit, he had entered eagerly into the manners and participated in the amusements of those around him. First after the hounds in England, he shouted "tally ho!" with all the enthusiasm of the veriest sportsman in the hunt; while his voice was heard equally loud and jovial in the wild and half-frantic chorus of the drinking and smoking students of Germany. He scrupled not to wear his beard long, and partake of the hard black loaf in the cabin of the Russian boor, while, with equal equanimity, he wore his turban, and smoked his chibouque, cross-legged in the caffarets of Turkey. He climbed the huge Pyramids, and their dark and silent chambers echoed the sounds of his voice, as he called on Cheops, Isis and Orus; and, kneeling in the gorgeous mosque of Omar, he worshipped the true God, while the muzzeim from its minarets was proclaiming that Mahomet was his prophet. He had luxuriated amid the never-dying works of the great masters at Florence, and, lulled by the harmonious chant of the gondolier, had swept over the moonlit lagoons of Venice. He had whirled in all the gaiety of living Paris, and measured with careful steps the silent streets of dead Herculaneum and Pompeii. He had stood amid the awful stillness, on the glittering ice-covered summits of Mont Blanc, and looked fearlessly down into the great roaring caverns of fire boiling in the crater of Vesuvius—but now, there was a sadness about his heart which rarely lighted up, and, as I have observed, it was only under momentary excitement that he blazed into brilliant entertainment.

As the fresh breeze wafted us swiftly onwards, Venus,

amid the stars trembling in unnumbered myriads, rivalled with her silvery rays the great round-orbed moon, sailing joyously in her career high in the heavens above us, and soon the bright beacon on the plantation shore, lighted for our guidance, shone steadily over the dark water, and ere long we were all quietly seated at the supper-table, with our beatiful hostess at its head—again at Tom's cottage on the banks of the Potomac.

HUDSON RIVER.

HERE we are, met again, all booted and spurred, and ready for another journey. Come; let us make the most of our time on this mundane sphere; for, verily, we are but two of the automata of the great moving panorama so rapidly hastening o'er its surface; two of the unnumbered millions, who, lifted from their cradles, are hurrying with like equal haste towards the great dark curtain of the future, where, drawing its gloomy folds aside, they shall pass behind and disappear forever. Therefore let us hasten; for though some of us complacently imagine that we are bound on our own special road and chosen journey, yet, surely, we are but traveling the path which has been marked out for us by an all-seeing Providence; and though, like soldiers, we may be marching, as we suppose, to good billets and snug quarters, yet, perhaps, before the day's route be closed, we may be plunged into the centre of the battle-field, with sad curtailment of our history. Tempus fugit! Therefore let us hasten; for in a few short years some modern Hamlet o'er our tomb-stones thus shall moralize: " Here be two fellows tucked up right cosily in their last quarters, 'at their heads a grass-green turf, and at their heels a stone.' Hump! for all their stillness, I'll warrant me they've strutted their mimic stage, and flaunted with the best; they've had their ups and downs, their whims and fancies, their schemes and projects, their loves and hates; have been elated with vast imaginings, and depressed to the very ocean's depths; and now their little day and generation passed, they've settled to their rest. The school-boy, astride on one's memento, with muddy heels kicks out his epitaph, while the other's name is barely visible among the thistle's aspiring tops; yet both alike have rendered, with the whole human family, the same brief epitome of history. 'They laughed; they groaned; they wept; and here they are;' for such are but the features of bright, confiding youth, stern manhood's trials, and imbecile old age." And this same sage Hamlet's right; therefore, without more ado, let us get us on our travels.

Now *Westward* shall lie our course. Here come the cars. Quick—jump in! We are off. We fly over the bridges, and through the tunnels; the rail fences spin by in ribands; the mile-stones play leap-frog; the abutments dash by us. Screech! the cattle jump like mad out of our way. Already at Jersey City? We paddle across. Ay, here we are, just in time for the steamer. What a pandemonium of racket, and noise, and confusion! "All aboard!" Tinkle, tinkle. The walking-beam rises, the heavy wheels splash, we shoot out into the stream, we make a graceful curve, and, simultaneously with five other steamers, stretch like race-horses up the majestic Hudson.

How beautifully the Narrows, and the ocean, open to our view, and the noble bay, studded with its islands, and fortresses, and men-of-war, with frowning batteries and checkered sides! In graceful amity float the nations' emblems— the Tri-color, Red Cross, Black Eagle, Stars and Stripes. But we take the lead. Fire up; fire up, engineer; her namesake cuts the air not more swiftly than our fleet boat her element. Still as a mirror lies the tranquil water. The dark Palisades above us, with fringed and picturesque outline, are reflected on its polished surface; and the lordly sloops—see how lazily they roll and pitch on the long undulating swell made by our progress, their scarlet pennons quivering on its surface as it regains its smoothness.

How rich and verdant extend thy shores, delightful river! Oh! kindly spirit! Crayon, Diedrick, Irving, whate'er we call thee, with what delightful Indian summer of rustic story, of dreamy legend, hast thou invested them? Lo! as we slide along, what moving panorama presents itself! Phlegmatic Mynheers, in sleepy Elysium evolve huge smoke-wreaths of the fragrant weed, as they watch thy placid stream; blooming Katrinas, budding like roses out of their bodices, coquette with adoring Ichabods; sturdy, broad-breeched beaux, sound "boot and saddle," Roaring "Broms" dash along on old "Gun-powders." "Headless horsemen" thunder onwards through haunted hollows, heads on saddle-bow. Dancing, laughing negroes; irate, rubicund trumpeters; huge Dutch merry-makings, groaning feasts, and henpecked "Rips," pass in review before us. In the evening twilight, thy beacon, Stony Point, throws far its streaming rays o'er the darkening scenery, different, I ween, when mid mid-

STONY POINT SENTRY.

night mist and stillness, mid cannon-blaze and roar, "Mad Anthony's" attacking columns simultaneously struck the flag-staff in thy centre. The sparks stream rocket-like from our chimneys, as we enter your dark embrace, ye highlands! Hark! the roll of the drum, as we round the bend. Thy beautiful plateau, West Point, with its gallant spirits, is above us.

The thunder of thy bowling balls, old Hudson, we hear as we pass the gorges of the Catskills. Hyde Park, thou glancest by us. The villas of the Rensselaers and Livingstons flit 'mid their green trees. Thy cottages, oh Kinderhook, the Overslaugh, rush by, and now we are at Albany. Albany, Rochester, Utica, by smoking steam-car, we are delivered from you. Auburn, we breathe among thy shady walks—and now, for a moment, Buffalo, we rest with thee. All hail to thee, thou city of the Bison Bull!

NIGHT ATTACK ON FORT ERIE.

(August 14th, 1814.)

HOSTLER! bring up the horses! We will cross to the Canadian shore and ride leisurely o'er its battle-grounds. Tighten the girths, John; take up another hole. So; never mind the stirrup. Jump; I'm in my saddle. Are you ready? Aye; well broken is that gray of yours; he has a good long trot; how easy it makes your rise in the saddle, and how graceful is the gait. But here we are at the ferry. Now we cross thy stream, Niagara! Now we stand on British ground! Generous and gallant blood has deeply stained its soil! Observe these crumbling works; the old stone fort facing the river; the remains of ramparts and trenches; here a bastion, further on a redoubt; there again lines and earth-works, forming a continuous circle of defence, but all now fast sinking to their original level. These are, or rather were, the fortress and defences of "Fort Erie." When, some years since, I rode over the ground with our kind and excellent friend, the Major, I listened with great interest to his narration of the part of the campaign acted upon this spot and the adjoining country. I will repeat it to you as we ride over it. Jump your horse upon this decaying mound; it was a bastion.

Standing on this Bastion, "Here," said the Major, "we had thrown up our lines, making the defences as strong as practicable. The British had also erected formidable works about half a mile in front, (the forest intervening) composed of a large stone battery on their left, and two strong redoubts, from which they kept up an incessant discharge of shot and shells for several successive days, which was returned by us with equal vigor. At length a shell from their batteries, having fallen upon it, blew up one of our small magazines, but with trifling injury to the rest of the defences. They greatly overrated the damage, and were elated with their success. General Gaines received secret information that they intended to carry the works by storm on the following night. That night, said the Major, I shall not soon forget. It set in intensely dark and cloudy; extremely favorable to the design of the enemy. Everything was put in the fullest state of preparation to receive them. The men, enthusiastically awaiting the attack, were ordered to lie on their arms. Extended

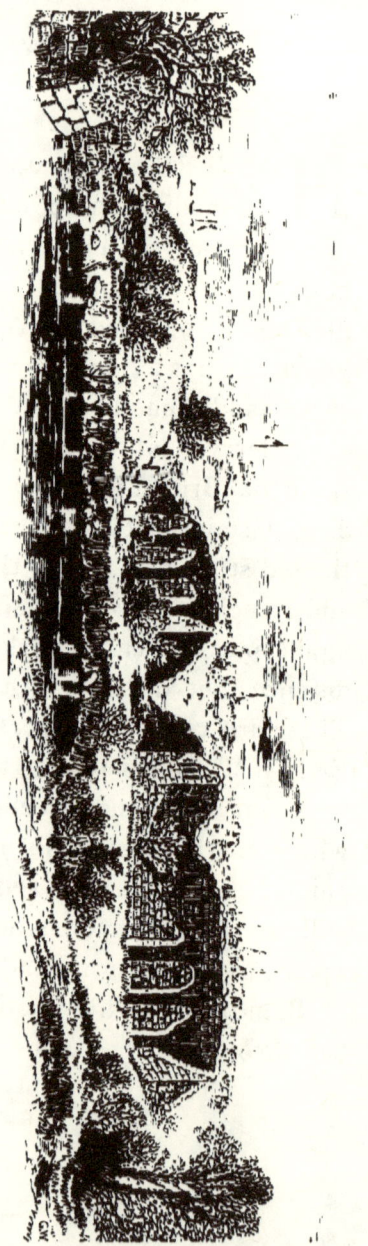

along the lines, and manning the fort and bastion, our little army, in perfect silence, awaited their coming.

"The forest had been cleared about three hundred yards in front of our works; beyond that were, as you see, the woods. As the night wore on, we listened with earnestness to every sound. A little after midnight, we heard on the dry leaves the stealthy sound of footsteps—rustle—rustle—rustle. We listened; they came nearer. A short, sharp challenge: 'Who goes there?' issued from that farther redoubt. The footsteps ceased, as if irresolute to advance or recede, and all was still. Another quick challenge, a rattle of the musket as it fell into the hollow of the hand, followed the quick reply:—' Picket guard, forced in by the enemy's advance.' 'Back, guard! back to your posts instantly, or we will fire upon you,' rung the stern voice of our commanding officer. The footsteps of the stragglers slowly receded, and entire stillness again obtained. It was as profound as the darkness; not even the hum of an insect rose upon the ear. We laid our heads upon the ramparts, and listened with all our faculties. We listened. Perhaps half an hour elapsed, when we imagined we heard the dead, heavy sound of a large body of men—tramp—tramp—tramp—advancing through the pitchy darkness. A few moments passed, a brisk scattering fire, and the pickets came in in beautiful order, under the brave subaltern in command. The measured tread of disciplined troops became apparent. Every sense was stretched to the utmost in expectancy; every eye endeavored to fathom the darkness in front, when, from Towson's battery, that towards the river, glanced a volley of musketry, and in another instant the whole line of the works, bastion, redoubt, and rampart, streamed forth one living sheet of flame. Two eighteens, mounted where we stand, were filled to the muzzle with grape, cannister, and bags of musket-bullets; imagine their havoc. The enemy came on with loud shouts and undaunted bravery. By the continued glare of our discharges, we could see dense dark masses of men, moving in columns to three separate points of attack upon our works. Our artillery and musketry

poured on them, as they advanced, a continual stream of fire, rolling and glancing from angles, bastions, and redoubts. Repulsed, they were re-formed by their officers, and brought again to the charge, to be again repulsed. At such times, hours fly like minutes. A life appears concentrated to a moment. We had been engaged perhaps an hour—perhaps three—when I heard in that bastion of the Fort, a hundred feet from me, above the uproar, a quick, furious struggle, as if of men engaged in fierce death-fight; a clashing of bayonets, and sharp pistol shots, mixed with heavy blows, and short quick breathing, such as you may have heard men make in violent exertion, in cutting wood with axes, or other severe manual labor. The conflict, though fierce, was short; the assailants were repelled. Those that gained a footing were bayoneted, or thrown back over the parapet. In a few moments, I heard again the same fierce struggle, and again followed the like result and stillness—if stillness could be said to exist under continual roar of musketry and artillery. A third time it rose, sudden and desperate; it ceased; and presently a clear loud voice rose high above the battle from the bastion: 'Stop firing in front there; you are firing on your friends.' An instant cessation followed. We were deceived. In another moment, the voice of an officer, with startling energy, replied: 'Aye, aye; we'll stop; give it to them, men; give it to them!'—and the firing, renewed, was continued with redoubled fury. The head of the centre column, composed of eight hundred picked men, veterans of Egypt, led by Lieut.-Col. Drummond in person, after three several assaults, had gained possession of the bastion, and by that ruse, endeavored to cause a cessation of the fire; a result that might have been fatal to us, had not the deception been so soon discerned. But the prize was of little value, as the bastion was commanded by the interior of the works, and the men, under cover of the walls of an adjoining barrack, poured into the gorge, that led from it, a continued storm of musketry. The firing continued with unabated fury. The enemy, repulsed with great loss in every attack, was unsuccessful on every point save that bastion, the possession of which they still retained; when I heard a groaning roll and shake of the earth, and instantly the bastion, bodies of men, timber, guns, earth and stones, were blown up in the air like a volcano, making every thing in the glare as clear as noonday. A descending timber dashed one of my artillerymen to pieces within a foot of my shoulder. Profound darkness and silence followed. Naught but the groans of the wounded and dying were heard. As if by mutual consent, the fighting ceased, and the enemy withdrew, repulsed on every side, save from the parapet which they purchased for their grave.[1] A large quantity of fixed ammunition had been placed in the lower part, and a stray wad, falling upon it, had blown them all up together; My duty required that I should immediately repair the bastion, and most horrible was the sight; bodies burnt and mutilated, some of them still pulsating with life, among them Lieut.-Colonel Drummond, the leader of the attack.[2] There he lay, in the morning light, stark and stiff, extended on the rampart, a ball having passed through his breast. His war-cry of 'No quarter to the damned Yankees'—his own death-warrant—was long remembered against his countrymen. The enemy did not resume the attack, but, retiring to their entrenched camp, strengthened their works, and prepared to make their approach by regular advances."

But come; spur on; we have far to ride; spur on. Here we are, upon their works. Here is the stone water-battery, and there the two strong redoubts, and back of them the remains of their lines, and deep intrenchments. These are the works which were carried in the memorable and desperate sortie of Fort Erie. The right by General Miller, Aspinwall and Trimble, and the left by the gallant Porter and his volunteers, under the immediate command of Davis, and the Regulars led by Gibson and Wood. "Here, on the left," quoth the Major, "fell my gallant, my accomplished friend, Lieutenant-Colonel Wood, at the head of his column. He was one of the most brilliant officers in the service, and as beautiful as a girl. I often gazed with astonishment at the desperate daring that characterized him in action; here he fell; he was bayoneted to death on the ground, on this spot"—and the Major's voice quivered, and he turned his face from me, for the cruel death of his dear friend was too much for his manhood. His body was never found. His monument rests near the flag-staff at West Point. Peace to his gallant spirit! The stars of his country can wave over no braver of her sons.

[1] The venerable Jabez Fisk, who was in the fight, in a letter to me writes: "Three or four hundred of the enemy had got into the bastion. At this time an American officer came running up and said: 'General Gaines, the bastion is full; I can blow them all to hell in a minute!' They both passed back through a stone building, and in a short time the bastion and the British were high in the air. General Gaines soon returned, swinging his hat and shouting, 'Hurrah for Little York!'" This was in allusion to the blowing up of the British magazine at Little York, when General Pike was killed.—*Lossing*.

[2] The enemy was soon repulsed in this quarter. The centre, led by Lieutenant-Colonel Drummond, was not long kept in check. It approached every assailable point of the fort at once. They brought scaling-ladders, and with the greatest coolness and bravery attempted to force an entrance over the walls. Captain Williams and Lieutenants Macdonough and Watmough, in the fort, met them gallantly, and twice repulsed them. Then Drummond, taking advantage of the covering of a thick pall of gunpowder smoke, which hung low, went silently around the ditch, and, with scaling-ladders, ascended to the parapet with great celerity, and gained a secure footing there with one hundred of the Royal Artillery before any effectual opposition could be made. Already the exasperated Drummond, goaded almost to

madness by the murderous repulses which he had endured, had given orders to show no mercy to the "damned Yankees," and had actually stationed a body of painted savages near, with instructions to rush into the fort, when the regulars should get possession of it, and assist in the general massacre. Finding himself now in actual possession of a part of the fort, he instantly directed his men to charge upon the garrison with pike and bayonet, and to "show no mercy." Most of the American officers, and many of the men, received deadly wounds. Among the former was Lieutenant Macdonough. He was severely hurt, and demanded quarter. It was refused by Lieutenant-Colonel Drummond. The Lieutenant then seized a hand spike and boldly defended himself until he was shot down with a pistol by the monster who had refused him mercy, and who often reiterated the order, "Give the damned Yankees no quarter!" He soon met his deserved fate, for he was shot through the heart, was severely bayoneted, and fell dead by the side of his own victim.—*Lossing's Hist. War of* 1812.

In the secret orders issued by Lieutenant-General Drummond, found in the pockets of Colonel Drummond, was this paragraph: "*The Lieutenant-General most strongly recommends the use of the bayonet.*" Just above this paragraph was a blood-stained fracture made by the bayonet, an inch in length and half an inch in width. There were two other copies of this order issued, one to Lieutenant-Colonel Fischer and the other to Colonel Scott.—*Lossing*.

BATTLE OF LUNDY'S LANE.

COL. MILLER AT LUNDY'S LANE.

WE cross thy tranquil plains, oh! Chippewa. Brown, Scott, Miller, Jesup, and your gallant comrades; long will this battle-ground your names remember. But far different music has resounded through these continuous woods than the wild bird's carol, the hum of insects, and the waving of the breeze that now so gently greets our ear. Aye! yonder is the white house. "There," said the Major, "as General Scott, making a forward movement with his brigade in the afternoon of the 25th of July, 1814, came in view of it, we saw the court-yard filled with British officers, their horses held by orderlies and servants in attendance. As soon as we became visible to them, the bugles sounded to saddle, and in a few moments they were mounted and soon disappeared through the woods at full gallop, twenty bugles ringing the alarm from different parts of the forest. All vanished, as if swallowed by the earth, save an elegant veteran officer, who reined up, just out of musket shot, and took a leisurely survey of our numbers. Having apparently satisfied himself of our force, he raised the plumed hat from his head, and bowing gracefully to our cortege, put spurs to his horse and disappeared with the rest. From the occupant of the house we gathered that we were about a mile distant from a strong body of the enemy, posted on the rising ground just beyond the woods in our front. General Scott, turning to one of his escort, said: 'Be kind enough, sir, to return to Major-General Brown; inform him that I have fallen in with the enemy's advance, posted in force at *Lundy's Lane*, and that in one-half hour I shall have joined battle.' 'Order up Ripley with the second brigade; direct Porter to get his volunteers immediately under arms,' was the brief reply of Major-General Brown to my message, and the aids were instantly in their saddles, conveying the orders. As I galloped back through the woods," continued the Major, "the cannon-shot screaming by me, tearing the trees and sending the rail fences in the air in their course, warned me that the contest had begun. But we are on the battle-ground. There," said the Major, "upon the verge of that sloping hill, parallel with the road, and through the grave-yard toward the Niagara, was drawn up the British line under General Riall, in force three times greater than our brigade; his right covered with a powerful battery of nine pieces of artillery, two of them brass twenty-fours.

"The *Eleventh* and *Twenty-second* regiments, first leaving the wood, deployed upon the open ground with the coolness and regularity of a review, and were soon engaged furiously in action; the fire from the enemy's line, and from the battery, which completely commanded the position, opening upon them with tremendous effect. Towson, having hurried up with his guns on the left, in vain endeavored to attain sufficient elevation to return the fire of their battery. The destruction on our side was very great; the two regiments fought with consummate bravery. They were severely cut up. Their ammunition became exhausted, and the officers, nearly all of them, having been killed and wounded, they were withdrawn from action; the few officers remaining unhurt throwing themselves into the *Ninth*, which now came into action, led by the gallant Colonel Leavenworth.

"The brunt of the battle now came upon them, and they alone sustained it for some time, fighting with unflinching bravery, until their numbers were reduced to one-half by the fire of the enemy. At this juncture, General Scott galloped up with the intention of charging the hill; but finding them so much weakened, altered his intention, entreating them to hold their ground until the reinforcements, which were hastening up, should come to their assistance. A momentary cessation of the action ensued, while additional forces hurried up to the aid of each army; Ripley's brigade, Hindman's artillery, and Porter's volunteers, on the part of the Americans, and a strong reinforcement under General Drummond on that of the British. Hindman's artillery were attached to that of Towson, and soon made themselves heard. Porter's brigade displayed on the left, while Ripley formed on the skirts of the wood to the right of Scott's brigade. The engagement was soon renewed with augmented vigor, General Drummond taking command in person, with his fresh troops in the front line of the enemy. Colonel Jesup, who had at the commencement of the action been posted on the right, succeeded, after a gallant contest, in turning the left flank of the enemy, and came in upon his reserve, 'burdened with prisoners, making himself visible to his own army, amid the darkness, in a blaze of fire,' completely destroying all before him. The fight raged for some time with great fury, but, it became apparent, uselessly to the Americans, if the enemy retained possession of the battery, manifestly the key of the position.

"I was standing at the side of Colonel Miller," said the Major, "when General Brown rode up and inquired whether he could storm the battery with his regiment, while General Ripley supported him with the younger regiment, the *Twenty-third*. Miller, amid the uproar and confusion, deliberately surveyed the position, then, quietly turning, with infinite coolness replied, '*I'll try, sir.*' I think I see him now," said the Major, "as he turned to his regiment, drilled to the precision of a piece of mechanism; I hear his deep tones, '*Twenty-first*—attention! Support arms; double quick; march!' Machinery could not have moved with more compactness than that gallant regiment followed the fearless stride of its leader. Supported by the *Twenty-third*, the dark mass moved up the hill like one body; the lurid light glittering and flickering on their bayonets, as the combined fire of the enemy's artillery and infantry opened murderously upon them. They flinched not; they faltered not, as the deadly cannot-shot cut yawning chasms through them. Within a hundred yards of the summit a volley, sharp, instaneous as a clap of thunder; another moment, rushing under the white smoke, a short furious struggle with the bayonet, and the artillerymen were swept like chaff from their guns. Another fierce struggle; the enemy's line was forced down the hill, and the victory was ours; the position entirely in our hands; their own pieces turned and playing upon them in their retreat. It was bought at cruel price, most of the officers being either killed or wounded. The whole tide of the battle now turned to this point. The result of the conflict depended entirely upon the ability of the victorious party to retain it. Major Hindman was ordered up, and posted his forces at the side of the captured cannon, while the American line correspondingly advanced. Stung with mortification, General Drummond concentrated his forces, to retake, by a desperate charge, the position. The interval amid the darkness was alone filled by the roar of the cataracts, and the groans of the wounded. He advanced with strong reinforcements, outflanking each side of the American line. We were only able, in the murky darkness, to ascertain their approach by their heavy tread. 'They halted within twenty paces; poured in a rapid fire, and prepared for the rush.' Directed by the blaze, our men returned it with deadly effect, and after a desperate struggle the dense column recoiled. Another interval of darkness and silence, and again a most furious and desperate charge was made by the British, throwing the whole weight of their attack upon the American centre. The gallant *Twenty-first*, which composed it, received them with undaunted firmness; while the fire from our lines was 'dreadfully effective.' Hindman's artillery served with the most perfect coolness and effect. Staggering, they again recoiled. During this second attack, General Scott in person, his shattered brigade now consolidated into a single battalion, made two determined charges upon the right and left flank of the enemy, and in these he received the scars which his countrymen now see upon his manly front. Our men were now almost worn down with fatigue, dying with thirst, for which they could gain no relief. The British, with fresh reinforcements, their men recruited and rested, after the interval of another hour, made their third and final effort to regain the position. They advanced, delivered their fire as before, and although it was returned with the same deadly effect, steadily pressed forward. The *Twenty-first* again sustained the shock, and both lines were soon engaged in a 'conflict, obstinate and dreadful beyond description.' The right and left of the American line fell back for a moment, but were immediately rallied by their officers. 'So desperate did the battle now become, that many battalions on both sides were forced back,' the men engaged in indiscriminate melee, fought hand to hand, and with muskets clubbed; and 'so terrific was the conflict where the cannon was stationed, that Major Hindman had to engage them over his guns and gun-carriages, and finally to spike two of his pieces, under the apprehension that they would fall into the hands of the enemy.' General Ripley at length made a most desperate and determined charge upon both of the enemy's flanks; they wavered, recoiled, gave way; and the centre soon following, relinquished the fight and made a final retreat. The annals of warfare on this continent have never shown more desperate fighting. Bayonets were repeatedly crossed, and after the action many of the men were found mutually transfixed. The British force engaged was about five thousand men; the American, thirty-five hundred; the combined loss in killed and wounded, seventeen hundred and twenty-two, officers and men. The battle commenced at half-past four o'clock in the afternoon, and did not terminate till midnight. We were so mingled," said the Major, "and so great the confusion in the darkness, that as I was sitting with a group of officers in the earlier part of the night, on horseback, a British soldier came up to us, and recovering his musket, under the supposition that he was addressing one of his own officers, said, ' Colonel Gordon will be much obliged, sir, if you will march up the three hundred men in the road to his assistance immadiately, as he is very hard pressed.' I called him nearer, and pressing his musket down over my holsters made him prisoner. 'What have I done, sir,' said the astonished man, ' what have I done?' and to convince British officers, as he supposed, of his loyalty, exclaimed, 'Hurrah for the King, and damn the Yankees.' As he was marched to the rear, the poor fellow was cut down by a grape shot. In another part of the field, an American aid pulled up suddenly on a body of men under full march. In reply to his demand, 'What regiment is that?' he was answered, 'The Royal Scots.' With great presence of mind, he replied, ' Halt! Royal Scots, till further orders,' and then, turning his horse's head, galloped from their dangerous proximity. It was a horrid conflict. Humanity sighs over the slaughter of the brave men that fell in it."

But here we are, at the grave-yard, with its drooping willows and flowering locusts. Still—still—and quiet now.

No armed men now disturb its calmness and repose; no ponderous artillery wheels rudely cut its consecrated mounds; no ruffian jest; no savage execration; no moan of anguish break now upon its hallowed silence. The long grass and blossoming heather wave green, alike o'er the graves of friend and enemy. The marble tells the story of the few; the many, their very parents know not their resting place. See this broken wooden slab; it has rotted off even with the ground, and lies face downwards, the earth-worm burrowing under it, in this neglected corner. Pull the grass aside; turn it over with your foot. What is the nearly effaced inscription?

"Sacred
TO THE MEMORY OF
CAPT'N —— BROWN,
OF THE
21st Regiment,
WHO DIED OF WOUNDS RECEIVED IN ACTION, WITH THE ENEMY,
ON THE 25TH OF JULY, 1814."

And this is honor! This is fame! Why, brave man! e'en now I read the tribute to thy bravery in the bulletin of the action. Thou had'st comrades—father—mother—sisters—to mourn thy loss; and *now*, the stranger's foot carelessly spurns thy frail memento; nor father, mother, sisters, nor human hand can point to the spot where rest thy ashes. Peace to thy manes! brave countryman, where'er they sleep.

See from this point how gently and gracefully undulates the battle-field; the woods bowing to the evening breeze, as the soft sunlight pours through their branches, show not the gashes of rude cannon shot; the plain, loaded and bending with the yellow harvest, betrays no human gore; yon hill—scathed, scorched and blackened with cannon flame, the very resting-place of the deadly battery—no relic of the fierce death-struggle, as, covered with fragrant clover and wild blue-bell, the bee in monotonous hum banquets o'er it. Nought mars the serenity of nature as she smiles upon us. Yet, burnt in common funeral pyre, the ashes of those brave men, of friend and foe, there mingle in the bosom whence they issued. The frenzied passion passed, the furious conflict o'er, they have lain down in quiet, and, like young children, sleep gently, sweetly, in the lap of that common mother who shelters, with like protection, the little field-mouse from its gambols, and the turbaned Sultan sinking amid his prostrate millions. Shades of my gallant countrymen!—Shades of their daring foes!—farewell. Ne'er had warriors more glorious death-couch; the eternal cataracts roar your requiem.

NOTE.—The reader is referred, for further information, as to these battles, to Lossing's excellent History of the War of 1812, a work not in existence when these sketches were written.

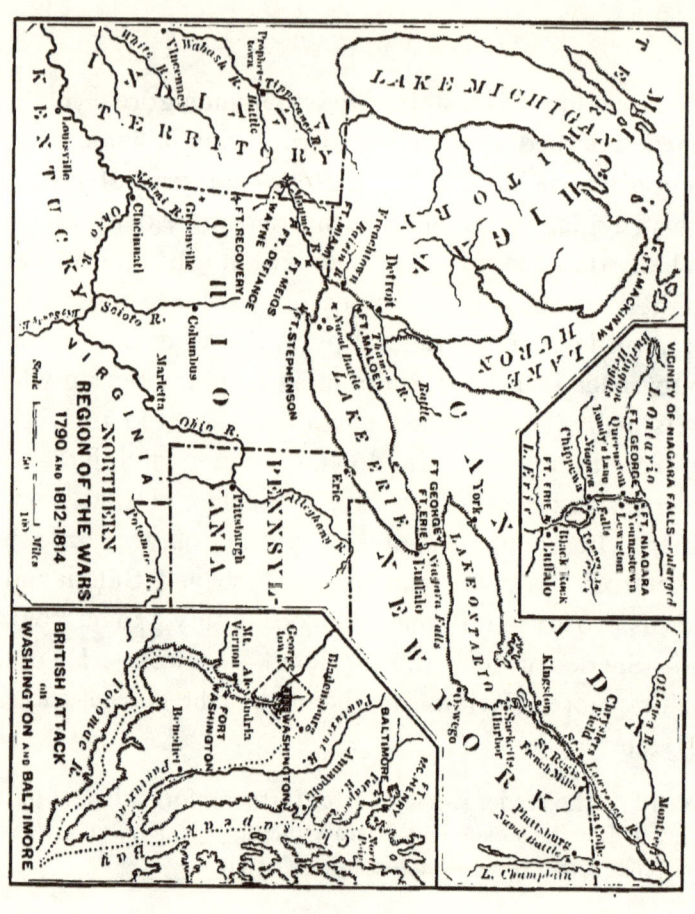

LAKE GEORGE AND TICONDEROGA.

THE Sun of Morning hurls himself in blazing splendor o'er thy crystal waters, beautiful Horicon! as we float upon thy placid bosom; not as of yore, in feathery canoe, but in gaily-colored bark, drawn by Steam Spirit. As he vainly strives to break his fiery prison, see how he puffs and pants in the fierce embrace of the glowing element, in furious efforts dragging us onward with frantic swiftness, e'en as the frightened steed, the vehicle wildly bounding after him; as the valve of safety opens, hear the shriek of mad delight with which exultingly he proclaims his freedom; now, the iron portal closed, how like Sampson in the Prison Mill, struggling, giant-like, he again applies him to his toil. Imprisoned Spirit! there is no help for thee. Sweat thou must, and pant, and groan, till—like thy fellow-laborer, man, released from fire fetter, as he of earth—resolved to pure ether, thou shalt float again free and delighted in the clear elements above!

Ho! brother spirit, tarry, tarry; wait thou a little till I join thee; then how gallantly we'll ride! Couched on summer clouds, lazily we'll float; or, glancing on sun rays, shoot, swift as thought, 'mid the bright worlds rolling in sublimity above us. We'll bathe in the Moon's cold splendor, fan in the sultry heat of crimson Mars, slide upon Saturn's eternal snows; or, joyously gamboling along the Milky Way, we'll chase the starry Serpent to his den. Ho! brother spirit;

but we must bide our time ; madly now, in wild career, thou sweep'st the placid lake from under us.

But whom have we here? A sturdy hunter in home-spun clad, with his long rifle ; his broad-chested hounds in quiet, sleeping at his feet; our fellow-passenger till, landed on some mountain-side, he follows his sylvan war. Clear animal health and vigor shine from each lineament. With what open, unsuspicious manhood, what boundless freedom, he comports himself. Ha! what is it, hound? What is it? Why dost shake thy pendant ears and gaze so keenly in the distance ; and why that plaintive howl? Ay, ay, hunter, thy practised eye hath caught it. On yon wooded island to the windward ; a noble buck with graceful form and branching antlers. He sees us not, but the dog's quick senses have caught his scent upon the passing wind. Still, boy, still! Pilot, put her a little more under the island. Hunter, lend me thy rifle; launch the canoe. Come, hunter; peace, hounds; keep the dogs on board; paddle for yonder point. Now we shoot upon the pebbly beach ; now make her fast to this dead log. We'll steal gently through the woods and come upon him unawares. Softly ; press those vines away ; whist! avoid the rustling of the branches ; here, creep through these bushes ; tread lightly on the fallen leaves ; you'll mire upon that swampy bottom. Hush, hush ; tread softly—that crackling branch ! He lifts his head ; he looks uneasily about him. Stand quiet! Now he browses again ; get a little nearer ; we are within distance. I'll try him—click. Back go the antlers ; the cocking of the rifle has alarmed him— he's off. Here goes!—crack! He jumps ten feet in the air. I've missed him ; he bounds onward ; no—yes—by Jove ! he's down — he's up again — he plunges forward —

falls again—he rises—falls—he struggles to his knees—he—falls! Hurrah! he's ours—quick—quick—thy *couteau' chasse;* we'll make sure of him. Stop; stop! Poor deer! and *I* have murdered thee—for my *sport,* have murdered thee; have taken from thee the precious boon of life; with cruelty have broken the silver chord, which the beggar's blunt knife can sever, but not the jeweled fingers of the monarch again rejoin. There, there, thou liest, true to the Great Master's picture:

> "The big round tears course down thy innocent nose in piteous chase,
> And thy smooth leathern sides pant almost to bursting."

Thy life blood flows apace—e'en now thy large soft eye dims in the sleep of death—and *I* have slain thee. Thou had'st nought other enemy than the gaunt coward wolf, or fanged serpent; him, with light leaping bounds, thou laugh'st to scorn, as his long howl struck on thy quick ear and the sullen rattler, with many blows of thy tiny polished hoof thou dash'st to pieces, ere from his deadly coil, his flattened head, with glistening tongue and protruded fangs, could reach thee. Oh! I shame me of my miscreant fellowship. E'en the poisonous serpent, with quick vibrating tail, did give thee warning; *I* stole upon thee unawares. Hunter! take again thy weapon; for thee; 'tis thy vocation; perhaps 'tis well; the game is thine. I entreat of thee, let not my innocent victim again reproach my eye-sight. So! here is the canoe; we again embark; we rock against the steamer's side; and now again rush onward in our swift career. Islands glide by us in countless numbers. The frightened trout scales in quick alarm from the splashing water-wheels, while echo, mocking their watery clamor, wakes the old mountains from their sleepy stillness, who again, like drowsy giants, relapse into repose as we leave them far behind us.

RUINS OF FORT TICONDEROGA.

Ticonderoga, we approach thy shore. Ay, true to appointment, here are the horses. Mount—on we go, over hillock and valley, through brake, through briar, through mud, through water, through swamp, through mire; we gallop over the broad green peninsula; leap the entrenchments; thread the lines. Here is the citadel; descend the moat: the wild dank weeds and furze o'ertop our heads. Ay—here's a chasm, a breach in the ancient walls; spur up; spur up; now we draw rein within the very centre of the blackened ruins. How lovely the view, from the soft undulating promontory: the lake bathing its sides; Horicon's mountains o'erlooking it on this; the stalwart yeomen of the verdant State, free as the winds, on that! Oh! Ticonderoga, 'midst these uncultivated wilds; these silent mountains; various and eventful hath been thy history.

Ho! Old Time—how calmly strok'st thou thy long grey beard, as, seated on the broken ruins, thou ponderest their past! Come! come, old father! ascend this crumbling battlement—lean on my shoulder—I, as yet, am straightest,—I will hold thy scythe. Now point to me the drama which past generations have acted upon this green peninsula.

"What do I see?" I see the savage life; the light canoe floating on the blue lake; painted warriors spearing the salmon, chasing the deer upon the plain, dragging the surly bear in triumph; I see the swift paddle chase; I hear the laugh of children; the voice of patient squaws; the distant yell, as, rounding the point, the returning braves bemoan the dead left on the war-path, and, as the shades of evening close, the sun in golden radiance retiring o'er the mountains, I see them congregate in wigwams in the cove. The blue smoke rises gently o'er the tree-tops, and all is still; quiet and serenity obtain; the whip-poor-will, and cricket, amid the drowsy hum of insect life, keep melancholy cadence.

"Stranger! venture not near them—the peace is treacherous; no civilized challenge shall give thee warning, but the cruel war-shriek wildly ring o'er the insensate brain as the light tomahawk trembles in thy cloven skull."

Wild mist rolls onward; I hear sounds of distant music; the mellow horn, the clashing cymbals break from its midst. Ah! it rises. A gallant army, in proud array, with flags and banners; bright glittering arms, and ponderous artillery. With alacrity they effect their landing. They fraternize with the red-skinned warriors. Their military lines run round like magic. I feel, e'en where we stand, huge walls, grim towers rise, and bastions springing up around us; the spotless drapeau blanc, high o'er our heads, floats in the breeze; wild chansoms of love, of war, of la belle France, mix with mirth and revelry.

"Stranger, 'tis the quick 'Qui Vive' that doth arrest thy footstep."

Ay—now, Old Time, the mystic curtain again rolls upwards. "What do I see?"—Red-coated soldiers advancing in proud battalia through the forest glades, the sunbeams dancing on their bayonets. I hear the sound of bugles, the clamorous roll of drums, the groaning jar and creak of heavy-wheeled artillery. Spread along the lines, covered with sharp abattis and water moat, I see the impatient Gaul, with savage ally, in ambushment, await their coming; they advance with desperate valor; they ford the ditch, hew the sharpened trees with axes. In vain; the balls, like hail, from unseen foes murderously destroy them. Their leader falls; hark! the bugle with melancholy wail sounds their retreat.

Again, Old Time, an interval; again red-coated soldiers! again groaning artillery! Look up! the drapeau blanc has vanished; the meteor flag streams proudly from the flagstaff.

"Stranger, 'tis the Anglo-Saxon's rough challenge that gruflly breaks upon thy ear."

Long peace and silence, old father, now obtain; the sentry sleeps upon his post; women and children play upon the ramparts; but hark! what is it far in the distance that I hear? The sound of battle! the fusilade of musketry, the roar of cannon! I see Bunker's Hill from light barricade sweep down her thousands; I see hurrying forward the hardy

husbandman with hastily-caught musket; the robed divine; the youth; the old man, cheered on by mothers, sisters, tender wives, to strike

"For their altars and their fires,
God, and their native homes."

BATTLE OF BUNKER HILL.

I see new Nation's symbol—Stars and Stripes;—and—watch—Now, in the midnight darkness, through the fortress moat—how advance that fearless band of men! Lo! in silence they penetrate the fortress' centre. Hark! what voice rouses the astonished officer, as, starting from his slumbers, he meets, close at his throat, the bayonet's threatening point? "Surrender!" "To whom?" "The Great Jehovah, and the Continental Congress!"

ETHAN ALLEN AT TICONDEROGA.

Now floats the spangled banner proudly o'er the citadel; patriotic men assemble; armies make temporary resting place; invalid soldiers breathe the health-restoring air, and age wears on. Ha! was that a meteor, flashing from Defiance Mountain summit? And there, another? Plunge! plunge! Cannon shot! screaming, yelling, bounding i' th' very centre of the fortress.

" 'Tis the Englishman with his artillery."

Quick, quick! St. Clair, withdraw the army; the position is no longer tenable. Strike not the flag! let it shake defiance to the last! Quick, the magazine—the train! Ha, hah! Ætna, Vesuvius like, the explosion.

Hallo! Old time! Ho! thou of the scythe! What! hast gone? Am I?—ay, I am—alone! Nought but the blackened ruins, and the crumbling ramparts, in silence surrounding me.

MONTREAL.

NOW, in steam palace, we shoot in swift career o'er thy tranquil surface, Lake Champlain; thy rolling mountains, in wavy outline, accompanying us in our rapid progress. Vast primeval forests sleep in stillness along thy borders. Their sylvan patriarchs, reigning for centuries, untouched by woodman's axe, stretch proudly their far-reaching branches, till ancient Time, pointing with extended finger, the wild spirit of the winds breathes on them as he passes, and they succumb, with sullen uproar, long with mock semblance retaining form and length, as if deriding the puny offspring shooting up around them; bestowing sore fall, I ween, and tumble on adventurous hunter, as stumbling through the undergrowth he plunges prostrate o'er them.

Forests immense cover the mountains, gorges, valleys, reigning in stern solitude and silence, save where the fierce fire-god, serpent-like, pursues his flaming journey. There, followed by wreathing smoke columns, forward he leaps, with fiery tongue licking up acres, while the waterpools, hissing in mist, join in his escort, and the wild game, with frantic swiftness, strive to escape the hot destruction of his embraces. With steady, noiseless progress, the white villages appear and disappear beside us. Rouse's skeleton Tower looms largely in the distance;—now, 'tis passed.

Thy military works, and crimson flag, Isle Aux Noix, town of St. Johns, Richelieu, La Prairie; we pass ye all; and advancing in soft summer atmosphere, Chambly, we behold thy mountain ramparts filling the far distance. St. Lawrence,—majestic river, stretched like sheet of polished steel, as far as eye can reach—we stand upon thy level shores. Rapid, wide, rushing expanse of waters, with what glorious brightness thou look'st upon thy verdant shores, covered with continuous lines of snow-white cottages, and listenest to the soft music of the religious bells of the kind-hearted, cheerful habitans, as, with rude painted cross upon their door-posts, they scare away the fiend, and joyously intercommune, in honest simple neighborhood. La Chine, we speed o'er thy surface with race-horse swiftness; and now *Montreal!* beautiful—most beautiful, couched at the foot of emerald mountain, liest thou upon the river's margin, thy spires, roofs, cupolas, glittering in the sun-beams with silver radiance; thy grand cathedral chimes floating onwards till lost in dreamy distance. We land upon thy granite quay, measure the extended esplanade, now climb thy narrow streets and alleys. Almost we think we tread one of thy antique cities, ancient France: alleys narrow; dark and gloomy courts; grim inhospitable walls; in place of airy casement, gratings and chained iron portals, military barracks, nunneries, prisons, fantastic churches, and Notre Dame's cloud-piercing towers, in huge architectural pile, looming high above all. Noisy, chattering habitans, in variegated waist-belts and clattering sabots, rotund dark-robed priests, lank voyageurs, red-coated soldiers and haughty officers, jostle each other on the narrow trottoir; but, mark! the sullen, down-cast Indian, in blanket robed, with gaudy feathers and shining ornaments, his patient squaw, straight as an arrow, her piercing-eyed papoose clinging to her shoulders, silently following him in noiseless mocassins, moves along the *kennel.* Verily, poor forest child, it hath been written, and Moslem-like, thou to thy destiny must bow; the fire-water and the Christian will it; fold thee closer in thy blanket robe, and—die. See yon Indian girl standing at the corner; with what classic grace the blue fold drapery, thrown o'er her head, descends her shoulders, as, fawn-like, she stands, avoiding the rude passer's stare.

Hardy ponies, in light calash, dash through the narrow streets, of passengers' safety regardless; or, tugging at great trucks, strive, in renewed exertion, to vociferous cries and exclamations of the volatile Canadian. How well these Englishmen sit their horses. See that gentleman; with what delicate hand he reins his fiery blood that treads as if on feathers, and how picturesque appear, amid the motley throng, these red-coated soldiers.

Come! here stands one at the Champ de Mars; how martially he deports himself; his exactly poised musket and his brazen ornaments, how bright! Inscribed upon his gorget are the actions which have signalized his regiment—"Badajos," "Salamanca," "Vittoria," "Waterloo." We will address him. Soldier, your regiment was at Salamanca? "*S-i-r.*" By the inscription on your gorget, your regiment distinguished itself at Salamanca; "scaled the imminent deadly breach" at "Badajos;" stood the Cuirassiers' wild charge amid the sulphurous smoke at Waterloo? "Don't know, indeed, s-i-r." And this is the gallant soldier! Why, for years, under the menace of thy sergeant, thou hast scoured that gorget to regulation brightness; for years hast marched under thy regimental colors emblazoned with those characters; and still, in ignorance need'st a Champoillion to decipher them. Verily thy daily wage of sixpence and thy ration are full compensation for thy service.

THE NUN.

NOW as we pass, look up! How minute appears the colossal statue of "Our Lady" in its niche on the vast front of the cathedral. And the nunneries; self-constituted prisons for those whom God hath born to freedom; how like birds of evil omen they do congregate. Here is that of the Grey Order. Ring at the gateway; we will enter. Here we pass the courtyard; how still, how gloomy, and how prison-like! This is their hospital. Piteous collection! The blind, the halt, the maimed, the hideously deformed, consumption, palsy, the wrecks of fevers! See, with what continued torture that wretched being writhes in her fixed position. This is the small spark of good amid the brands of evil. These orphan children are kindly cared for, but where the child-like joy and mirthful freedom! With what stealthy step the officials move about their duties along the silent corridors! and, aye! here is the chapel, with its gilded altars, its ornaments, its embroideries, its bleeding hearts, its sacred symbols. See with what gentleness the "*Lady*" performs the servile duties of the sanctuary! with what humility she bends before the altar. How beautiful that cheek of tint of Indian shell; those dark romantic eyes with their long pensile lashes; that nose of Grecian outline; the small vermilion mouth; the throat and neck of snow, and the glossy raven tresses escaping in rich luxuriance from the plaited coif as they fall upon her sloping shoulders. Mournful seems her devotion; now rising, she stands before the Mater Dolorosa; now wistfully gazes down the dark long corridor in sorrowful meditation. Hush! be silent. I will steal gently near her. Lady! Turn not; 'tis thy kind spirit whispers. Art thou content? Does thy young active soul find employ congenial in these gloomy mysteries? Does thy springing, youthful heart, sympathize in these cold formalities; this company of grim-visaged saints and bearded martyrs; with joy enchain thee? Does the passionate imagination and deep feeling flashing in those dark eyes; the already hectic kindling of that cheek, look with pleasure to long years; a life of cold monotonous routine; of nightly vigils; fastings; of painful mortifications? Lady! listen. They chain thy soul. Break thou away. Quick, in thy youth, fly from them, fly! One moment. Speak not. See'st thou yon cottage peering from its green shades and graveled walks; its parterres of the myrtle and the lily, its diamond lattice enwreathed and almost hidden in the embrace of sweet-smelling honeysuckles and clustering roses; and its interior with its simple yet delicate refinements? See'st thou in snowy dishabille the lovely woman? with what heart-felt glee the frolicking, half-naked child, with chubby arms, almost suffocates in its little embrace her neck; its golden ringlets mingling like streams of light 'mid her dark tresses; with what ecstasy she enfolds him in her embraces, with maternal lips pressing in exquisite delight the plump alabaster shoulders? Lady, such scenes, not gloomy walls, invite thee. Nay, 'tis not the voice of the Tempter; 'tis not, as they will tell thee, the poisonous breath of the many-colored serpent stealing o'er thy senses. Let bearded men, wrecked on their own fierce lawless passions, seek these dark cells, these painful vigils, these unmeaning mortifications. They are not for thee. The world awaits thy coming. The pawing steed, throwing the white froth flakes o'er his broad chest, impatiently awaits thee. Fly, dear lady, fly! The joyous, carroling birds, the dew-spangled meadows cry, Come! The green, green trees; the bubbling water-falls; the soft summer breezes; the rosy tinted East; the gorgeous drapery of the West—cry to thee, Come! The voice of thy lover, frantic at thy self-sacrifice; the voice of him who in the fragrant orange bower encircled thy slender waist, whilst, with heightened color and downcast eyes, thou listen'd to his rapid vows; the voice of him, who with thy glossy raven tresses floating on his shoulder, and thy warm, sweet breath, mingling with his, lavished soul, existence, all, on thee,—in agony cries, Dearest, dearest, come! Nay, nay, 'tis but for *thy* happiness,—I leave thee—exclaim not—I am gone.

CATARACTS OF NIAGARA.

INDIAN LIFE.

NOW—on, on, over the Chute, and down the Rapid; leaping the Saults; through the rivers, over the islands; we glide, we glide, we rush, we fly. Ho! Ariel, beautiful spirit, riding on thy rainbow, shoot not thy silver arrows at us as we pass. Tricksy spirit, fare thee well;—now —far in the distance,—fare—thee—well! Ha! Ha! Old frolic Puck, sweating, panting, holding thy lubbard sides; we race, we race, we pass thee, too; in vain thou strugglest to o'ertake us. Farewell, farewell! Go pinch the housemaids, tickle with straws the snoring herdsmen, tumble about the dusty mows, sprinkle sweet hay before the ruminating cattle, clutch by the tail the cunning fox, as stealthily he crawls within the hen-roost; and anon, rub thy hands in glee o'er the embers on the capacious kitchen hearth, and on all-fours cut antics with the glowering cat, as, with bowed back and shining eyes, she watches thee i' th' corner. Peer into the kettles and into jars, see whether the barm rises, whether the yeast doth work; till with clash—clatter, the metal lid slips from thy fingers on the hearth-stone, and villain-like, thou shoot'st up the chimney, with "Ho! ho! ho!" laughing at the sleepy yeoman, as half covered, with oaken cudgel grasped, shivering, he peers through the door-crack the cause o' th' uproar. Farewell, farewell, mirthful goblin—farewell —farewell. Ontario, we waft across thy surface. Queenstown, thy sanguinary heights, crowned with brave Briton's monument, we pass; and now, the rising mist-wreaths warn us of thy approach, Niagara. Huzza! huzza! now for a bath under the roaring Cataract! In what wild chaos of waters the clamorous rapids, as if from the horizon, rush down upon us; jumping, leaping, boiling in fierce confusion: and this frail bridge, how it groans and shakes in the torrent's sweep! A slip from Mahomet's sword-edge, o'er the awful Hades, would not consign us to more inevitable destruction, than would a treacherous plank or rotten beam from this shaking platform. We tread the deep green woods of Goat Island, their mossy trunks covered with love-marks of Orlandos and Rosalinds; and, amid the roar, descend the great Ferry stair-case. Stop a moment at this landing; step out. How the solid earth shakes, jars and vibrates! How the wild winds rush by us, as the huge fluid arch stretches over with continuous plunge; and see that group of wild flowers, scarlet, green and purple, smiling in beauty byond the reach of human hand, glistening in moisture midst the very spray in the rock cleft. But haste, haste! Here is the boatman. Leap in, leap in! Now how, in our little cockle-shell bark, we whirl and sport in the eddies, o'er the fathomless depths below, like wing-born insects playing over the abyss.

We land; ascend the heights; we pass the sentry. At the tiring-house. We robe ourselves for the enterprise; tarpaulin coats, hats bound with old rope, trowsers of tow cloth, shoes of cowhide; ha! ha! But quick! descend the long spiral stair-case. Now, Guide; we follow. Beware you fall not on these sharp, slippery rocks. We approach. The Table Rock hangs o'er us. In grandeur the solid fluid mass falls precipitate. Prepare. Turn as you enter; hold down your head; repress your breath:—are you ready? Rush! We are beneath the yawning chasm; soaked in an instant. Like furious rain-storm, and wind, and tempest all combined, this wild, frightful roar. What? Scream louder, louder! Hold firm by the guide; a slip from this narrow ledge, and, whew—splash—dead in our faces,—almost suffocated. Turn to the dripping rock wall, and catch your breath till the wind-rush again lifts the watery curtain. Slimy eels glide by; darkness deep above, dim light strives to reach us through the cataract sheets. We are at the extreme verge. Guide, guide; ha! what indicates that motion of thy lips? closer,—close in my ear. "Termination rock." Turn, turn—splash—swash—drenched, suffocated; return, return. We see again the light. Rush! We stand once more in the clear open sunlight. Whew! puff—dripping—dripping, a shower-bath worthy of old Neptune. How delightfully our nerves spring under its exhilarating influence. Take care; again these slippery stones. Beware! beware! here we ascend again the stair-case. In the attiring-room. Towels, brushes; Christains once more.

Come; come! Now to the Table Rock. See with what treacherous glitter the wide Niagara stretches in perfect smoothness far towards Chippewa, till, descending upon us, it shoots the rapids o'er their rocky beds like things of life, and with wild rush around the island, sweeps resistless o'er the awful cataracts, a roaring hurricane of waters. Give me your hand—lean forward; look into the abyss; careful! Evil spirits take us at advantage at such times, and whisper us to leap forward. How lashed in milky whiteness the huge gulf boils and foams as the waters plunge fractured, disjointed, tumbling in masses; and the wild birds, how fearlessly they skim amid the white mist rising from its surface. How the earth shudders and trembles around us. You are already dizzy. Come back from the edge. How awful; how terribly sublime! How tame, how useless, helpless, description! Would that I, with voice of inspiration, could command language adequate to portray the grandeur of the scene under stern Winter's reign! Transcendantly beautiful! A thaw and rain, followed by sudden chill and cold, clothes all the forest; every hedge and shrub, with transparent coat of ice. Gnarled oaks, from massive trunk to their extremest twigs, become huge crystal chandeliers; the evergreen pines and hemlocks, with long lancing branches, great emeralds; lithe willows, sweeping, glassy cascades; the wild vines, stiff in silvery trellises between them; the undergrowth, with scarlet, blue and purple berries, candied fruits; the pools of frozen water at their feet, dark sheets of adamant; and ever and anon, as the north wind passes o'er them, the forest becomes Golconda, Araby —one Ind of radiant gems, quivering with diamonds, rubies, sapphires, in glittering splendor, pearls, emeralds, hyacinths, chrysolites, falling in showers, as, fractured from their crackling branches, they strew the snowy bed stretched smooth around them; that wide, smooth river, far above the Rapids, ice-chained, a solid snow-white bed, gleaming in the mid-day sun; yon Tower, misshapen giant phantom, ice God, in frozen shroud and winding-sheet, firmly fixed 'mid the swift running waters—huge stalactite icicles, Winter's hoary beard, hanging in fantastic curtains from each rock ledge, pinnacle, projection; while on the black rapids, the vast ice-fields, breaking in masses, pile in wild confusion, grinding and swaying on their treacherous holds, till, gathering momentum, with slide and plunge, submerged, they sweep onward 'mid the wild roar of the Cataracts, which, with stern, resistless power, hold their terrific course; those huge sheets, those watery arches, those green beryl masses, plunging in resistless fury, unabated vastness, with desperate leaps into the foaming abyss below, the spray falling in silver showers, pierced by the sun's rays dancing around them in countless rainbows; while the ice avalanches, breaking from their grasps on the surrounding rocks and precipices, with booming plunge and uproar, fall crashing, buried in the dark whirlpools, boiling in the fathomless depths below; the dark river, in torrents of copperas-hue, whirling in eddies, rushing o'er its deep rocky bed, in savage contrast with the snow-covered precipices that chain it to its course. Deep, resistless sweep of waters! black as despair—Sadoc here were to thee the waters of Oblivion—here that Lethe, which, till other worlds received thee, should blot existence from keenest memory.

The voice of the Unseen addressed the afflicted Patriarch from the whirlwind's midst; us does it warn from this chained whirlwind of the waters. Sublime, terrible, indescribable, as is this scene by human tongue, how tamely all its grandeur sinks beneath the catastrophe which the being of future ages shall survey, or would, if with eagle's wings he could soar high in the clouds above it; when the narrow rock-belt which Niagara for by-gone centuries has been slowly wearing, severed, the light tract alluvial crumbling —the whole chain of inland oceans—Huron, Erie, Michigan, with awful wildness and destruction, sweep in second deluge o'er this outlet; the adamantine rocks sinking like snow-wreaths from their beds; all principalities, kingdoms, states, whate'er they shall be, between the Atlantic and the Alleghanies, the Labrador and Mexico, swept from existence, and in their place a heaving surge, wild waste of waters. Fool! revolve this scene terrific in thy heart; ponder it well; then, if thou canst, say, indeed, there is no God! Thy life, at best a flickering taper, shall soon meet extinguishment. Then shall there be an eternity to convince thee.

MOUNT HOLYOKE.

HERE we are, in the middle of the month of August. The "world" have long since fled the hot walls and blazing pavements of old Gotham, and even the very school-boys are let loose from their pale-faced pedagogues, to frolic like young colts in the country. Come, let us not remain in the sweltering city. Throw a few things in your carpet-bag; that is sufficient. Make me the guide. We will leave Saratoga and Newport to their flirtations; another field is before us. Now, Eastward ho! shall lie our course. Distance and time are left behind us; already we are ensconced at the Mansion House in this most lovely of villages, Northampton.

Well does it deserve the name. Come one moment to the corner of this piazza. Look down the long avenues. See the verdant arches, formed by the boughs of the antique elms, bending toward each other in loving fraternity; and the snow-white houses at their feet, their court-yards smiling with flowers; and the still more smiling faces that glance behind their transparent windows. That will do; you have stared long enough at the demure beauty behind the green blinds. Truly it seems, as it mostly is, the abode of retired gentlemen: a very Decameron sort of a place in this working-day world of ours. But are we not Americans? *Why* should we rest? To breakfast; behold, a regular Yankee feast. Snow-white bread and golden butter; chickens that one short hour since dreamed of bins of corn and acres of oats, on their roosts in the lofty barn; steaks, pies, tea, preserves, the well-browned cakes, and last, not least, the sparkling amber cider. Blessings on the heart of the nice-looking damsel at the coffee urn, with her red cheeks and neat check apron. But, egad! my dear friend; prudence! hold up; we have to ascend the mountain, and you will not find the feast that you are stowing away with such Dalgetty industry, likely to improve your wind. That last hot roll lengthens our ascent just one-quarter of an hour. There! the horses are neighing and impatiently champing the bit at the door. Are you ready? Come then. Look out, lest that fiery devil throw you on the bosom of our common mother, earth! Your bones would find her a step-dame; those flaming nostrils are sworn enemies to your long spur gaffs. But here we go! How balmy and delightful the cool air of the morning; the verdant grass rises gracefully; the wild flower shakes its tiny bells, and drinks the dewy diamond glittering on its lips, as it waves gently o'er them. The rich yellow sun mocks the trees, as it rolls out their broad shadows on the velvet turf beneath; while from knoll and waving mullen stalk, the meadow-lark, with outstretched neck and piercing eye, utters his notes in almost delirious rapture. We clear the broad meadows. Our very horses, with ears erect, gather speed with every bound, and seem ready to cry, ha! ha! We are the fabled centaurs of old.

The heavy morning mist, rising in huge volumes, reluctantly bares the forest on the mountain-side; it curls and breaks in vast masses; it slowly rolls off to the eastward. Aye! there he stands; there stands old *Holyoke*, with his cragged coronal of rocks, a gigantic Titan, bidding defiance to time and tempest. Gallop, gallop; we are within two hundred feet of the summit. This precipice—its dark sides frowning and grim, the velvet moss, and little clusters of scarlet and yellow flowers peeping from its crevices, where the rippling brooklet scatters its mimic showers over them, wreathed fantastically with vines and gnarled branches from its clefts—we must climb on foot. Rest a moment. How perfectly still the dense forest extends around us. Nought breaks the silence, save the querulous cry of the catbird, as it hops from branch to branch, the mimic bark of the squirrel, or the distant hollow tap of the woodpecker. Now, a little more climbing; take care of those loose stones; a few steps additional ascent; give me your hand; spring! here we are on the rocky platform of its summit. Is not the scene magnificent? We stand in the centre of an amphitheatre two hundred miles in diameter. See! at the base of the mountain curls, like a huge serpent, the Connecticut, its sinuosities cutting the smooth plains into all sorts of grotesque figures; now making a circuit around a peninsula of miles, across whose neck a child might throw a stone; here stretching straight as an arrow for a like distance; and there again returning like a hare upon its course. See the verdant valleys extending around us, rich with the labor of good old New England's sons, and far in the distance—the blue smoky distance—rising in majesty, God's land-marks, the mountains. See the beautiful plains, the prairies beneath us, one great carpet of cultivation; the fields of grain, the yellow wheat, the verdant maize, the flocks, the herds, the meadow, the woodland, forming beautiful and defined figures in its texture, while the villages, in glistening whiteness, are scattered, like patches of snow, in every part of the landscape; and hark! in that indistinct and mellow music we hear the bell slowly tolling from yonder slender spire. Oh! for a Ruysdael, to do justice to the picture.

Surely God did not intend that we should sweat and pant in cities, when he places such scenes before us. How like the fierce giants of old the lofty mountains encircle it, as a land of enchantment. See! see! the clouds, as they scud along in the heavens, how they throw their broad shadows, chasing each other on the plains below. Imagine them squadrons, charging in desperate and bloody battle. But no; widows' and orphans' tears follow not *their* encounters: rather the smiles of the honest, hard-handed yeoman, as he foresees his wains groaning with the anticipated harvests; his swelling stacks; his crowded granaries. Here, for the present, let us recline on the broad and moss-covered rocks, while, with the untutored Indian, its rightful owner, in silent admiration we worship the Great Spirit, whose finger moves not, save in beauty, in harmony and majesty.

WHITE MOUNTAINS.

KNOCK! knock! knock! W-e-l-l. Thump! thump! thump! Who's there? What do you want? "Passengers for the White Mountains, sir; time to get up; stage ready." Is it possible? three o'clock already? W-e-l-l, I'll get up. Call the gentleman in the next room. My friend, how are you, after your trip of yesterday to Mount Holyoke? A little stiff in the knees and ankles, eh! But come; the stage is at the door. Waiter, hold the light. How forlorn look the heavy muddy vehicle, and half-waked horses, by the dim light of the stage-lamps. That's right, my good fellow; throw those carpet-bags inside. Shut the door. All ready. Driver, go ahead! "Aye, aye! sir." Hey! Tchk! tchk! Crack! crack! crack! off we go. The steady clatter of the horses' hoofs, the jingling of the harness, the occasional roll as we pass over the boards of some bridge, and the intejectional whistle of the driver as he encourages the horses, are the only things that break the silence for the next hour. The morning light begins to dawn. Whom have we here? Only two fellow travelers:—an honest, clean-looking countryman, snugly fixed in one corner, with his night-cap pulled over his eyes, and his mouth wide open, as if admiring the melody that his nose in bugle strain is enacting just above it; and opposite to him a gross fat man, of rubicund visage, his eyes ensconced in goggles, who nods, and nods, and nods; and now his head bobs forward into his neighbor's lap. How foolish he looks as he awakes to consciousness. It is broad daylight. Let us get up with the driver on the outside, and enjoy our cigars and the scenery together.

Here we go, through the Connecticut River Valley, famous for its scenery and its legends; the region of bright eyes and strong arms; the land of quiltings and huskings; of house-raisings and militia trainings; and the home of savory roast pigs and stuffed turkeys, of fat geese, of apple sauce, and pumpkin pies; the Ultima Thule to the Yankee's imagination. Now we are at Deerfield. While they are about our breakfast, we will run across the road, and see the old Williams Mansion. A hundred years since, it was surrounded by Indians, and its occupants, the clergyman and his family, carried off captives to Canada. Here is the very hole cut in the front door by their tomahawks, and here the hacks of the hatchets. Through this hole they ran their rifles, and fired into the house, killing a man confined to his bed by sickness; and here is the ball, lodging to this day in the side of the wall;—and this occurred one hundred years ago! Say you, that the people that treasure up these legends, and retain these memorials untouched, have no poetry in their souls? But there goes the stageman's horn! Our breakfast finished, we resume our places at the side of our good-natured driver, and on we roll. We pass Battleboro', snugly ensconced in its mountain eyrie, and Hanover, with its broad parade, its flourishing colleges, and its inhabitants that never die—save from old age.

With teams of six and eight horses, we speed over hill, over dale, over mountain, over valley, ascending and descending the mountains in full run; our gallant horses, almost with human instinct, guiding themselves. Snorting leaders, swerve not aside in your career; linch-pins, do your duty; traces and breeching, hold on toughly; or, "happy men be our dole." Hah! Wild Amonoosac, we greet thy indeed wild roar. How it sweeps the fallen timber in its boiling eddies! The huge logs slide dancing onwards with the velocity of the canoes of the Indian; or, caught by envious projection, or uplifting rock, form dams and cascades, till the increasing and cumbrous masses, gathering momentum, plunge forward, sweeping all before them—and—but whist! Step into the shade of this tree; look into the dark pool beneath those gnarled roots; how beautifully the gold and purple colors glitter; how motionlessly still is the head; how slight and tremulous the movement of that fin, the wavy motion of the tail! A two-pounder, as I am a Christain! Whist! whist! See that dragon-fly, gently sailing o'er the surface; he rests a moment on it. Watch! the head slowly turns; the fins move decidedly; ay, now, one rapid whirl of the tail, an electric leap to the surface. Poor fly, thy history is written; and well for thee, thou greedy trout, that no barbed hook suspends thee in mid air, struggling in beauty, though in death, the prize of exulting angler. And thou, too, art there, savage *Mount Franconia*, with thy fantastic and human outline! Old Man of the Mountain!* with what grim stoicism thou lookest down upon the busy miners, as, with picks and powder-blast, they rive the sullen mineral from thy vitals. Ay! watch thou by the lurid glare the sweating, half-naked forgemen, as they feed with thy forests the roaring furnaces. Watch the molten ore, slowly running in glittering streams, with fiery showers of scintillations, into the dark earth-troughs below, while, with ceaseless din, the ponderous trip-hammers, and clanking machinery, break the, till now, Sabbath stillness of thy dwelling-place. But fare thee well, thou imperturbable old man; fare thee well; for now we enter the dense continuous forest, through which the busy hand of man has, with unwearied industry, cut the avenue. How deliciously the aroma of the gigantic pines mingles with the pure elastic air of the mountains. See the thick undergrowth; the dogwood with its snowy blossoms, the scarlet sumac, the waving green briar profuse with delicate roses, the crimson raspberry loaded with its fruit.

* Profile of the Mountain.

millions of bushes, the yellow sensitive plant, the dancing blue-bell, and, rising through the entangled mass of verdure and beauty, see the luxuriant wild grape, and clinging ivy, joyously climbing the patriarchs of the forest, encircling their trunks, and hanging their branches in graceful festoons and umbrageous bowers. No human foot, save with the aid of pioneer, can penetrate its matted wildness; nought, save those huge patriarchs rising above it, as they grow old and die, and fall with crashing uproar, as into flowery sepulchre, intrude upon its solitude. Then, indeed, in heavy booming plunge and rush, they seem to wildly sing, like their painted children, their death-song. But whence that wild and dissonant shriek, that rings upon the ear? Ah! yonder, erect and motionless, he sits, upon the towering oak, with haughty eye and talons of iron, screaming his call of warning to his partner slowly circling in graceful curves high in the blue ether above him.

But see, where, as the dense forest stretches onward, the casual spark, dropped by the hand of the woodman, spreading into flame, and gathering in mighty volumes of fire, has swept onward in its roaring, crackling, destroying progress, leaving nought behind it save these grim and blackened skeletons and dead plains of ashes. See what darkness and desolation, and apparent annihilation, extend around you; but yet, silently and quietly, ere long, shall the germ of life which can never die rise from those ashes, and verdure and beauty reign again, as was their wont. Even so the solitary mourner, when death strikes down at his side his dearest ones, stands helplessly encircled by solitude and desolation; but soon all-pervading benevolence causes the green germ of the soul to rise from the ashes, and his heart again expands with tenderness and sympathy.

The scene of desolation is passed! and now, lest the Lord of fire should reign uncontrolled, lo! where the spirit of the whirlwind has swept in his wild tornado. Lo! far as your vision can command the circle—where, rushing from the mountain gorges, his chariots have whirled along in their fierce career of destruction. In mid height, the lofty trees are snapped like pipe-stems, and prone, like the field of grain laid by the hand of the reaper, lie huge trunks with the moss of centuries—not here and there one solitary, but for miles the whole vast forest prostrate—never again to rise.

But speed! speed! the mountain passes are before us! See the huge rock ramparts shooting their peaks upward, their frowning sides trickling and discolored with the corroding minerals in their bowels; the stunted pines and evergreens clinging like dwarf shrubs in their crevices. See the huge slides—they have swept whole torrents of rocks, of earth, in promiscuous destruction, from their summits upon the valley below; the river, filled and turned from its course in their path; the very forest itself, the loftiest trees torn up, their branches, their trunks, their upturned roots, ground and intermixed with rock and earth, and splintered timber, swept on in wild, inextricable confusion; and here! where, starting from their slumbers, the devoted family rushed naked and horror-stricken to meet one in mid career. Well might the Puritans of old deem these deserts the abode and haunts of the evil one.

But on, on; how toilsome the ascent! Long since have we passed the region of vegetation: the dry and arid moss, clinging to rock and stone, is alone around us. Drink of that spring, but beware its icy coldness; not summer alters its temperature. Behold, in the clefts and gorges, the never-melting snow-wreaths! The flaming suns of summer pass over, and leave them undiminished. Courage! we climb; we climb. Courage, my friend! We ascend, we ascend; we reach the top; now panting, breathless, exhausted, we throw ourselves upon the extreme summit.

Gather your faculties; press hard your throbbing heart. Catch a view of the scene of grandeur around you, before the wild clouds, like dense volumes of steam, enclose us in their embrace, shutting it from our vision;—mountains—mountains—rolling off as far as eye can reach in untiring vastness; a huge sea of mountains held motionless in mid career. How sublime! how grand! What awful solitude! what chilling, stern, inexorable silence! It seems as if an expectant world were awaiting, in palpitating stillness, the visible advent of the Almighty; mountain and valley in expectant awe. O man! strutting in thy little sphere, thinkest thou that adoration is confined alone to thy cushioned seats, thy aisles of marble; that for devotion the Almighty looks to nought but thee? Why, look thou there!—beneath—around—millions, millions, millions of acres teeming with life, yet hushed in silence to thy ear—each grain the integer and composite of a world; the minutest portion a study, a wonder in itself—lie before thee in awful adoration of their Almighty Founder. Well did the Seers of old go into the mountains to worship. O, my brother man!—thou that dost toil and groan and labor in continual conflict with what appears to thee unrelenting fate; thou to whom the brow-sweat appears to bring nought but the bitter bread and contumely and shame; thou on whom the Sysiphean rock of misfortune seems remorselessly to recoil—ascend thou hither. Here, on this mountain-peak, nor king nor emperor are thy superior. Here, thou *art* a man. Stand thou here; and while with thy faculties thou canst command, in instant comprehension, the scene sublime before thee, elevate thee in thy self-respect, and calmly, bravely throw thyself into the all-sheltering arms of Him who watches, with like benevolence and protection, the young bird in its grassy nest, and the majestic spheres, chiming eternal music in their circling courses!

BASS FISHING OFF NEWPORT.

HERE we are, at Newport! What a little gem of an island, rising, like emerald on sapphire, from the surrounding ocean! We will walk up to the Mall. Ay, here, with its green blinds and scrupulously clean piazza, is old Mrs. E———'s, and they are at tea already. Come, take your seat at table.

With what serene dignity and kindness the old lady, in her nice plaited cap, her spotless kerchief, and russet poplin dress, her pin ball, with its silver chain, hanging at her waist, presides at the board, crowded with every imaginable homely delicacy, from the preserved peach and crullers made by herself, to the green candied limes brought home by her grandson from his last West India voyage. See the antique furniture, with its elaborate carving; the mahogany-framed looking-glasses; and, in the corner, on the round stand, the large Bible, carefully covered with baize, surmounted with the silver spectacles. No place this for swearing, duel-fighting, bewhiskered heroes; but just the thing for quiet, sober folk, like you and me. What sayest thou, Scipio, thou ebon angel—that the ebb sets at five i' the morning, and that old Davy, the fisherman, will be ready for us at the Long Wharf at that hour? Well, get yourself ready, and go along with us. Call us in season. Ay, that will do; the roll of those eyes, the display of that ivory, to say nothing of the scratch of that head and the sudden displacement of that leg, sufficiently evince thy delight.

So, so; here we are, punctual to the hour. Ay, yonder he is, in his broad strong fishing-boat; yonder is old Davy, as he was twenty years ago; the same tall gaunt figure, the same stoop in the shoulders, bronzed visage, and twinkling gray eyes; the same wrinkles at the side of his mouth, though deeper; the same long, lank hair, but now the sable silvered; the same, the same that he was in the days of my boyhood. He sees us. Now he stretches up to the wharf. Jump in; jump in! Be careful, thou son of Ethiopia, or thy basket will be overboard—sad disappointment to our sea-whet appetites some few brief hours hence. All in. We slide gently from the wharf. The light air in the inner harbor here barely gives us headway. Look down into the deep, still water, clear as crystal; see the long seaweed wave below; see the lithe eels coursing and whipping their paths through its entangled beds; and see our boat, with its green and yellow sides, its long flaunting pennant, its symmetrical white sails, suspended, as if in mid-air, on its transparent surface.

How still and tranquil lies the quiet town, as the sun gilds its white steeples; and how comfortable look the old family mansions rising from the green trees. How beautifully the yellow sun casts his shadows on the undulating surface of the island, green and verdant; the flocks of sheep, and browsing cattle, grouped here and there upon its smooth pastures. We float past Fort Wolcott; its grass-grown ramparts surmounted by dark ordnance, and its fields cheerful with whitewashed cottages and magazines.

Ay! now it breezes a little; now we gather headway, and

now we pass the Cutter. See her long, taper, raking masts, her taut stays and shrouds; and hear, as the stripes and stars are run up to her gaff, the short roll of the drum, the "beat to quarters." Hah! Davy, old fellow, dost remember that note last war? How many times, at midnight, we've sprung from our beds as that short, quick 'rub-a-dub" warned us of the approach of the blockading frigates, as they neared the town. But no, no, old tar; I recollect that thou then wast "captain of thy gun," on board the dashing *Essex*. Ay! well now do I remember, brave old sailor, thy conduct in her last desperate battle. Eighteen men hadst thou killed at thy single gun. I think I see thee now, as, grimed with powder, spattered with blood, thou didst advance, through fire and smoke, and approach thy saturnine commander on the quarter-deck. I hear thy brief, business-like request: "A fresh crew for Number Three, Second Division. All my men are killed!" And the short, stern response, "Where is your officer?" "*Dead*—swept overboard by cannon-shot." And well I see the momentary play of anguish round his mouth, as, resuming his hurried walk, he gloomily replies: " I have no more men; you must fight your gun yourself!" Ay; and as thy proud ship a helpless target lay, for twice superior force, I hear poor Ripley, thy brave comrade, severed almost in twain by cannon-shot, crying, with short farewell " Messmates, l am no longer of use to myself or country," as he throws himself, his life-blood gushing, overboard.

But now the wind freshens, the smooth surface darkens, the sails belly out in tension, and the white ripples gather under our bows. We round the point; Fort Adams, we pass thy massive walls, thy grim "forty-twos" glaring lik wild beasts chained, ready to leap upon us from their case ments. Ay! now we run outside; now it freshens; now it breezes; she begins to dance like a feather. There it comes stronger! see the white caps! There she goes, scuppers under! swash, swash, swash; we jump from wave to wave, as we run parallel with the shore, our pennant streaming proudly behind us. Here it comes, strong and steady! there she takes it—gunwale under; luff, old fellow! luff up, Davy, or you'll give us all wet jackets. Ay! that will do; she's in the wind's eye. How the waves tumble in upon the land! see the Spouting Rock; see the column of white foam thrown up as, repulsed, the waves roll out again from the rocky cavern. We near the Dumplings, and—Round to! round to! here are the lobster-pots; haul in; tumble them in the bottom of the boat; ay, there's bait enough. Now we lay our course across to Beaver Light; we slide, we dash along, springing from wave to wave—dash, dash—no barnacles on her bottom at this rate, Davy. Ay, here we are; a quick run—a good, quick run. Anchor her just outside the surf; ay, that will do; give her a good swing; let her ride free; she rolls like a barrel on these long waves. Look to your footing, boys—steady, steady. Now then, for it. Davy, you and Scip will have as much as you can do to bait for us. All ready? Here goes then; a good, long throw; that's it—my sinker is just inside the surf. What! already? I've got him; pull in, pull in. See, my line vibrates like a fiddle-string! Pull away; here he is— *Tautaug*—three-pounder! Lie you there! Ay, slap away, beauty; you've done forever with your native element. There, again! off with him. Again—again—again. This is fun to us, but death to you, ye disciples of St. Anthony!

Give me a good large bait this time, Scipio; that will do; now, whis—whis—whis-te—that's a clean, long throw. By Jupiter! you have got a bite with a vengeance. Careful—give him more line—let it run—play him—ease, ease the line around the thole-pin; he'll take all the skin off your fingers else. Pull away gently; there he runs. Careful, or you lose him; play him a little, he begins to tire; steady, steady; draw away. Now he shoots wildly this way; look out! There he goes under the boat; here he is again. Steady; quick, Davy, the net! I've got it under him; now then, in with him! Bass! twenty pounds, by all the steelyards in the old Brick Market! Ay, there they have got hold of me; a pull like a young shark; let it run; the whole line is out; quick, quick—take a turn round the thole-pin; snap! There, Davy; there goes your best line, sinker, hooks and all. Give me the other line. Ah, ha! again, again, again. This is sport. One, two, three—nine bass and thirty Tautaug. So, the tide won't serve here any longer; we will stretch across to Brenton's Reef, on the other side. Up anchor; hoist away the jib. Here we go, again coursing over the blue water. How the wind lulls! Whew, whew, whew; blow, wind, blow! Put her a little more before it; that will do. Hallo, you, Scipio! wake up, wake up! Here we are, close on the reef; give her plenty of cable. Let her just swing clear, to lay our sinkers on the rocks. That will do. How the surges swell and roar, and, recoiling, rush again boiling on the rocks! So—so, they don't bite well here to-day. The tide comes in too strong flood; well, we can't complain; we have had good sport even as it is. Come, Africa, bear a hand. Let's see what you have got in that big basket. Come, turn out; turn out!

Ham, chicken, smoked salmon, bread and butter ; and in that black bottle ?—ay, good old brown stout. Pass them along, pass them along; and wo be unto thee, old fellow, if thy commissariat falls short!

BRENTON'S REEF.

WITH what sullen and continuous roar the ocean waves heave in upon this inhospitable reef. See, as they recede, how the long, slimy rock-weed hangs dripping, and how deeply the returning surge buries it again. Oh, never shall I forget a scene upon this horrid reef. A dark, portentous day in autumn, was followed in the evening by a terrific storm. Low, muttering thunder, which had been growling in the distant horizon, as the night set in, grew louder. The perfect stillness which had obtained, as if in preparation, was broken by long moaning sighs; the lightning became quick and incessant, and ere long the tempest, like an unchained demon, came bounding in from Ocean. The lightning, intensely vivid, accompanied by crashing and terrific thunder, illuminated the surrounding coast with glittering splendor; the islands, the rocks, and yon beacon tower, now exposed to brightness surpassing noon-day, and now plunged into blackest darkness. The ocean appeared a sea of molten fire. Rain—hail—dashed hissing by, and mid the screaming of the blast, and the torrents rushing from the skies, the huge waves plunged, and roared, and, lashed in milky whiteness, broke mast-high upon these horrid rocks. While the fishermen in their cottages were thanking their stars that they were snug and safe on shore, was heard, in the temporary lulls of the howling storm, signal-guns of distress. The neighboring inhabitants were soon upon that point, and, by the glittering flashes, within musket shot of the shore discerned a Spanish ship on the very ridge of the frightful reef; the stumps of her masts alone remaining; the surf running and breaking in a continual deluge over her, while in her fore-shrouds were congregated the unhappy crew. She was so near that they could almost see the expression of agony in their countenances as, with extended hands, the crew piteously shrieked for help. Their situation was hopeless. Nothing could be done for them. No whale-boat could have lived for a moment, the surf rolled in with such resistless violence. They could only listen in silent horror. They heard the very grinding of her timbers, as shock on shock hastened her dissolution; and amid the fury of the storm and their frantic cries for aid, in the momentary lulls, the sickening, continuous wail of a young boy lashed in the mid-rigging; his supplicating exclamation, "Ai Jesus! Ai Jesus!" Often, years after, in their dreams, did they hear those plaintive cries, and see that young boy's face turned imploringly to Heaven, while that "Ai Jesus! Ai Jesus!" rang wildly in their ears. But a short time could human fabric sustain the ceaseless plunge of the foaming elements. By the lightning flashes the number of the sufferers was seen to lessen, as, relaxing their hold, they dropped off exhausted one by one; swept into the rocky caverns below; until, a longer interval of darkness—a more intense flash of lightning—and all had disappeared. Nought was left but the white foam, as it rushed tumultuously boiling and coursing over the long reef. It was so brief, so hurried—the appearance of their fellow creatures in their agony, and their disappearance so sudden—that it seemed a feverish dream. But the dead, mutilated bodies, ceroons of indigo and tobacco, and broken planks, swept along the shore on the following morning, convinced them of its sad reality.

The corse of the young boy, ungashed by the ragged rocks, was found and buried apart from the rest in the church-yard, for it appeared as if there was, in his childish helplessness, a claim for protection. That expression of agony I ne'er heard since, save once, and that— But, Davy, we have had all the sport we are like to have to-day; get up the anchor, and we will fan along up to the harbor. So—let her jibe; now put her before it; ay, that will do. As I was saying: Shortly after the close of the last war, buoyant with youth and hope, I made—what was then not so common as now—the tour of Europe, lingering long in old Spain, fascinated with the romantic character of the countrymen of Cervantes, of the gallant Moors, of the Alhambra and the Cid. It chanced one evening, strolling about the streets of Madrid in pursuance of adventure, that, passing through one of the most unfrequented squares, I was attracted by lights shining through the long Gothic windows of a large chapel or cathedral. I approached, and entering with some curiosity, found it entirely silent. No living soul was present within its walls. The lofty chancel and altars were shrouded in mourning. By the wax candles on the altars I could see the fretted arches, the shrines and monuments along the walls, and the family banners wreathed in gloomy festoons above them. I wandered about, alone and uninterrupted. Nought moved, save the old blood-stained flags, as they fitfully waved to and fro in the wind. I gazed around me in admiration on the rich shrines and their appropriate pictures. Here, with her offerings of flowers, the wax candles burning bright and clear, was the Madonna, her lovely countenance beaming with celestial sweetness, as she looked down upon the infant Saviour nestling in her arms, the Baptist standing at her knee pressing the plump little foot to his lips. And there, John in the island of Patmos, his emaciated limbs staring from their scanty covering of sackcloth, and his gaunt features glowing with inspiration, as from among the cloud of scattered grey hair and venerable beard, with upturned face he received from the flame-encircled trumpet above him the Holy Revelation. Here, armed *cap-a-pie*, the chivalrous Knights of the Temple consigned their slain brother to his rocky sepulchre, as, with grim, stern, averted countenances, they watched the fierce conflict and assault of the daring Infidel upon their Holy City. And there, the cross of Constantine richly emblazoned on its altar, was the *Crucifixion*, the Saviour extended on the cross, the thieves on each side of him, the head just bowed—and the awful *"It is finished!"* announced to the nations in frightful phenomena; the sun, turned to blood, throwing a lurid and unnatural glare on the assembled multitude; the war-horses, riderless, rearing and plunging with distended nostrils; rolling in convulsions, the solid mountains; the affrighted soldiery, horror-stricken, wildly lifting their hands to ward off the toppling crag, which, torn from its foundation by the earthquake, was in another instant to grind them to powder; while the Roman centurion, with curling lip, holding tighter in his grasp the crimson flag, the "*S. P. Q. R.*" shaking fiercely in the wild wind, seemed to deride the Jew, even in that dread moment, with his abject slavery. And here was San Sebastian, his eyes streaming with martyr tears;—

The tinkling of a small bell struck upon my ear; boys clad in scarlet swung their censers to and fro, and the incense floated high above them to the vaulted arches.

A train of monks, in purple robes embroidered with white crosses, appeared in procession, slowly advancing on the tesselated pavement, bearing on tressels, covered with dark pall, a corse, by the muffled outline, of manly stature. Two female figures, grave servitors with deep reverence supporting them, followed close the dead. The deep thunder tones of the huge organ swept upward as they entered, wild, grand and terrible, as if touched by no earthly hand; scarce audible sounds floating from the smallest pipes would catch the ear; then bursts, like the roaring whirlwind, pouring in the whole mass of trumpets, rolling, and rising, and falling; the most exquisite symphonies floating in the intervals until, fainter, fainter, the heart sickened in efforts to catch their tones. Dead silence followed; the corse was deposited in the chancel, the dark black pall slowly withdrawn, and the noble figure of a cavalier in the bloom of manhood, pallid in death, lay exposed before us. Clad in sable velvet, his rapier rested on his extended body, the jeweled cross-hilt reverently enclosed in his clasped hands, as they met upon his broad chest, while the luxuriant raven hair, parted on the high forehead, the dark arched eyebrow, and the glossy moustache curling on the lip, added deeper pallor to what appeared deep, deep sleep. The servitors withdrew, and the mother and the daughter advanced to the last sight of him that was so generous, so kind, so beautiful, —their all. The thick veil, thrown hastily aside, discovered the furrowed, time-worn, grief-worn features of the mother, convulsively writhing and working, as, sinking at its head, her lips pressed in uncontrollable agony the damp, cold white forehead. The sister, clad in robes of purest whiteness, her golden ringlets dishevelled and floating around her, and in their rich luxuriance almost hiding her graceful form, bent o'er him; and, as her gaze met not the answering smile of kindness and protection to which from infancy it was wont, but the stern, calm, sharpened features, in their icy stillness, then—as with frantic sobs her exquisitely feminine, almost childish, countenance, streaming with tears, was lifted upwards, and her hands wringing with anguish—uttered in deep convulsive bitterness, that *"Ai Jesus!"* in smothered tones again struck upon the startled ear. Long silence followed, unbroken save by sobs, as, sunk by its side, they embraced the still, unconscious ashes. Slowly the deep grave voices of the monks rose in solemn tones, and as their mournful chant sank into deep bass, at intervals was it taken up by a single female voice in the choir, which, high above the organ tones, with surpassing sweetness ascended higher, higher, until every nook in the lofty arches above appeared filled and overflowing with the rich melody; then, descending lower, lower, lower, the imagination wildly sought it in the passing wind. The monks drew near with uplifted and extended hands, muttering in low tones their benediction; then crossing themselves, encircling the corse on bended knees, with eyes lifted up to heaven, uttered, in loud voices:

"Ora pro illo—mater miserecordiæ,"
"Salvator Hominum—Ora pro illo"——

"Ora pro illo," again rose like a startled spirit from the choir, that single female voice rising with an intensity that made the old walls re-echo the petition, and then, de-

scending like the fluttering of a wounded bird, it became less, less, and all was still.

After a brief interval, leaning in apparent stupor upon the arms of the affectionate retainers, the ladies, slowly withdrawing, passed again the chancel's entrance, and the sacred procession raising the body, with melancholy chant bore it to the lower part of the chapel. I heard the clank of iron as the rusty portal of the family sepulchre reluctant turned upon its hinges; and then rested from its human journey that corse forever. I made inquiries, but could learn nought about the actors in the scene other than that they were strangers—a noble family from the Havana; that the father, invalid, had died in crossing the sea, and the usual story of Spanish love, and jealousy, and revenge, had consigned the son and brother, in the bloom of his days, by duel, to his grave; and subsequently, that the mother and sister had closed the history of the family, dying, broken-hearted, in the convent to which they had retired.

But, here we are, at the wharf. Our rapid journey approaches now its termination. A few short hours, and we shall again be merged in the ceaseless din of the city; the fair and tranquil face of nature change for the anxious countenances of our fellow men; the joyous carol of the birds, the soft forest breeze, and the sea-beach ripple, for paved streets and our daily round of duty and of labor. We have found "a world beyond Verona's walls." Perhaps at future time we may again travel it together. Till then, thanking you for your "right good and jollie" company—Farewell!

OLD TRINITY STEEPLE.

(Broadway, near the Bowling-Green.)

GROUND *covered with ice—Furious storm of snow and sleet—Two gentlemen becloaked and bemuffled, hurrying in different directions, come in full contact, and, mutually recoiling, hasten to make apology.*

My dear sir, a thousand pardons! "No, indeed, sir; 'twas I—I was the offending party." No, I assure you; I —I— Eh! is it? It is!—my old friend, the reader. Why, my dear friend, you came upon me as if you had been discharged from a catapult; a Paixhan shot was nothing to you! But where so fast in the fury of the storm; not to Union Square? Heavens! man, you will never reach there living; why, in this horrid cold the spirits of Nova Zembla and Mont Blanc are dancing in ecstasy about the fountains in the parks, and the very cabs are frozen on their axles! Never think of it. Come, come with me to my rooms hard by in State Street, and, on the word of a bachelor and a gentleman, I'll promise to make you comfortable. Come, take my arm; whew! how this northwester sweeps around the Battery! Here we are; this is the house; a real aristocratic old mansion; is it not? Enter, my dear friend; run up the stairs. ˙Holloa! ho! Scip, Scipio, Africanus, Angel of Darkness, come forth, come forth! Ay! here you are. And you, too, shaggy old Neptune, your eyes sparkling with delight, and your long tongue hanging out over your white teeth; down, you old rascal; down, sir; down! Now, is not this snug and comfortable; a good roaring fire of hickory? None of your sullen red-hot anthracite for me! How the cold wind howls through the leafless trees upon the Battery! Draw the curtains, Scip; come, bear a hand, take the reader's hat and coat. Invest him with the wadded damask dressing-gown that Tom sent home from Cairo; and the Turkish slippers; so, so, now bring me mine; place the well-stuffed easy chairs; roll the round table up between us; bring in the lights. Now, reader, at your elbow, lo! provision for your wants, material and mental, genuine old Farquhar and amber Golden Sherry; the Chateaux I got years since from Lynch; and just opened is that box of genuine Regalias. Only smell! "Fabrica de Tabacos, Calle-a-Leon, En la Habana, No. 14." Is it not Arabia's perfume? Ha! give me your smoking Spaniard in his sombrero; e'er any a half-naked Bedouin of them all; or if indeed you do prefer it, there stands the chibouque coiled up in the corner, and the metaphysical German's meerschaum on the shelf. There are biscuit and anchovies, and olives, "old Cheshire," and other inviting things for your wants physical; and for your mental, lo! uncut and damp from the publishers with the regular new-book smell—the North American, Old Blackwood, the Quarterly, the Edinburgh Review, and other Maga's; and by a slight curve of thy vertebræ cervical, behold, shining through yon glazed doors, glowing in gold, dross to the gold within, the great master bard of England; Cervantes, the chosen spirits of Italia and Gaul; Irving, worthy to be called Washington; and Halleck, genuine son of the voyagers in the Mayflower; and of literature much other goodly store.

Now, Scip! Lord of the Gold Coast, throw more wood upon the fire. Ay! that will do, my good old faithful servant, that will do. Now take that pepper and salt head of thine down to the kitchen hearth, there to retail thy legend and goblin story, or ensconce thee in the corner at thy will; Ah! hah, old Neptune, snug in thy place upon the hearth-rug, thy nose lying between thy outstretched paws as thou lookest intently in the fire, bless thine honest heart! thinking, I warrant me, of the beautiful child whom thou didst leap the Battery bridge to save. How bravely thou didst bear the little sufferer up on the fast rushing tide. The grateful father would have bought thee for thy weight in gold, as thou didst lie panting and half exhausted; but look not so wistfully, my dog; a sack of diamonds could not purchase thee. No, never do we part till death steps in between us—and, by my faith, an' thou goest first, thou shalt have Christain burial.

Now, dear reader, as thou reclinest comfortably in that big arm-chair, thy feet in Ottoman slippers resting on the fender, the blue smoke of thy cigar wreathing and curling around thy nose as it ascends in placid clouds and floats in misty wreaths above thy forehead, the glass of Chateaux, like a ruby resting upon its slender stem of light, quivering at thy elbow, and that open Blackwood upon thy knee, dost not,— confess it!— dost not feel more kind and charitable than if, with benumbed fingers, thou wert following a frozen visage to thy distant mansion in the great city's far purlieus?

But, heaven guard us! how savagely the tempest roars and howls around the chimney-tops. Good angels preserve the poor mariner as he ascends the ice-clad rigging, lays out upon the slippery yard, and handles with frost-benumbed fingers the rigid canvas folds. Ah! I recollect, it was in just such a night as this, a few years since, years that have rolled past into retrogade eternity, that I was seated in that same arm-chair, in the same bachelor independence, the fire burning just as brightly; the curtains as snugly drawn; my beautiful Flora looking down with the same sweetness from her frame above the mantle; my snow-white Venus between the piers; the Gladiator stretching forth his arm in just such proud defiance from his pedestal; my Rembrandt, Claude and Rubens flickering in softness in the fire-light; the Fonarina and St. Cecilia, with vase of incense clasped and upturned eyes of deep devotion, hanging in the same placid stillness between their silken tassels, and that Æolian harp chiming just such wild and fitful strains; 'twas in just such a cold and inhospitable night, that, sitting with my legs extended upon the fender, I fell into a train of rather melancholy musings.

The clock of St. Paul's slowly doled out the hour of midnight, and it seemed as if, in the responsive a-l-l-'-s w-e-l-l of the watchman, rendered indistinct by the distance, the spirit of the hour was bewailing in plaintive tones the annihilation of its being. Time's brazen voice announced to unheeding thousands, "Ye are rushing on eternity." I thought of my friends who had dropped off, one by one, from around me; youth and old age had alike sunk into the abyss of death; consumption, fever, palsy, had done their work; the slight ripple of their exit had subsided, and all was still, as quiet and as beautiful as if they had never been. Among others, was poor Louisa S——, in the prime of her youth and the bloom of her beauty. But one short week, she was the pride of her friends, the idol of her husband; in another, the slow toll of the village bell announced her funeral. I shall never forget the scene. The soft yellow light of the declining sun was streaming through the lofty elms which bordered the rustic graveyard, painting their broad shadows on the velvet turf, as the procession of mourners slowly wended their way among the mounds which covered the decaying remnants of mortality. Leaning upon a tomb-stone near the fresh dug grave, I had awaited its arrival. The bier was placed upon the ground, the coffin-lid thrown open, and friends looked for the last time upon the beautiful face, pallid and sharp in death. Her dark hair was parted upon her forehead, but the dampness of death had deprived it of its lustre, and her soft eyes were closed in the slumber from whence they were never again to wake. I gazed long and painfully upon that face, which appeared to repose only in serene and tranquil sleep, while the sobbing group reached forward to catch a last and parting glimpse of it in its loveliness. I could not realize that the lovely form was still forever. The coffin-lid was replaced in silence, a suppressed whisper from the sexton, a harsh grating of the cords, and the gaping pit received its prey. While the clergyman, in his deep and gloomy voice, was pronouncing the burial service of the dead, I looked around upon the uncovered group; the mother and sister in unrestrained sobs gave vent to their anguish, but the husband stood, his eyes fixed upon the grave, in deep and silent agony. He moved not, but when the dead heavy clamp of earth and stones fell upon the coffin, which contained the remains of all that was dear to him, he gave a gasp, as if he had received a death-wound, but that was all; the thick, convulsive breathing, and the swollen arteries upon his temples, showed that his was the bitterness of despair. Ere long, his wasted form, beneath its own green hillock, rested at her side.

I had sat some time, thinking " of all the miseries that this world is heir to," when gradually my room became mazy, the tongs and fender were blended into one, the fire slowly disappeared, and, to my utter horror and astonishment, I found myself swinging upon the weather-cock of Trinity Church steeple. How I came there I could not tell, but there I was. Far, far below me, I saw the long rows of lamps in Broadway and the adjoining streets shining in lines of fire ; while here and there the glimmer of those upon the carriages, as they rolled along, resembled the ignis fatui in their ghostly revels upon the morass. The bay lay in the distance, glittering in the moonlight, a sea of silver, the islands and fortresses like huge monsters resting upon its bosom. All nature appeared at rest. An instant, and but an instant, I gazed in wild delight upon the scene ; but, as the novelty vanished, the dreadful reality of my situation became apparent. I looked above me—the stars were trembling in the realms of space. I looked below, and shuddered at the distance. I tried to believe that I was in a dream ; but that relief was denied me. I grew wild with fear ; I madly called for help ; I screamed, I yelled, in desperation. Alas! my voice could not be heard one-half the distance to earth. I called on angels, Heaven, to assist me ; but the cold wind alone answered, as it rushed around the steeple in its whistle of contempt. As my animal spirits were exhausted, I became more calm. I perceived that the slender iron upon which the weather-cock was fixed was slowly bending with the weight of my body, already benumbed with cold. Although it was madness, I ventured a descent. Moving with extreme caution, I clasped the spire in my arms, I slid down inch by inch. The cold sweat poured off my brow, and the blood, curdling in my veins, rushed back in thick and suffocating throbs upon my heart. I grasped the steeple tighter in my agony, my nails were clenched in the wood, but in vain; slip, slip, the steeple enlarged as I descended; my hold relaxed; the flat palms of my hands pressed the sides, as I slid down with frightful rapidity. Could I but catch the ledge below! I succeeded—I clutched it in my bleeding fingers; for a moment I thought that I was safe, but I swung over the immense height in an instant; the wind dashed me from side to side like a feather. I strove to touch the sides of the steeple with my knees. I could not reach it; my strength began to fail; I felt the muscles of my fingers growing weaker. The blackness of despair came over me. My fingers slid from the ledge; down, down, I plunged—one dash upon the roof, and I was stretched motionless upon the pavement.

A crowd collected around me. I heard them commiserating my fate. They looked at me, and then at the steeple, as if measuring the distance from whence I had fallen; but they offered no assistance. They dispersed. I slowly raised myself on my feet; all was cold and still as the grave. Regions of ice, an immense transparent mirror, extended on every side around me. The cold, smooth plain was only measured by the horizon. I found myself on skates; I rushed along, outstripping the winds; I ascended mountains of ice; I descended like a meteor; Russia, with her frozen torrents, Siberia, with its eternal snows, were behind me; miles and degrees were nothing; on I rushed; Iceland vanished; with the speed of a thunderbolt I passed Spitzbergen; days, weeks expired, but still I sped forward, without fatigue, without exhaustion. How delightfully I glided along; no effort, no exertion, all was still, cold and brilliant. I neared the pole; the explorers were slowly wending their tedious way; they hailed me, but I could not stop; I was out of sight in an instant. I saw an immense object swinging to and fro in the distance; it was the great and mighty pendulum. As I neared it, a confused noise of voices broke upon my ear; mathematical terms echoed and re-echoed each other like the hum of a bee-hive. I was surrounded with winged chronometers, barometers and magnets; plus (+), minus (—) and the roots ($\sqrt{}\sqrt{}$) were flying around me in every direction, jostling each other without mercy. Every instrument of science appeared collected in solemn conclave, for great and mighty purpose; but soon all was hubbub and confusion. But amid the uproar, the giant pendulum still swung forward and backward with the noiseless motion of the incubus; I neared it and saw that the top of the huge rod was riveted by the pole star, which shone with the intensity of the diamond. But, but—

I saw the ship approaching among the distant icebergs, the great lordly icebergs; how they rolled and roared and ground against each other in the heavy surge! their huge sides now shining great sheets of silver; now glancing with the deep blue of the precious sapphire; now quivering in the sun's rays, with all the hues of the grass-green emerald and blazing ruby. Ha! I saw her; I saw the gallant ship threading her way among them, as their castellated sides towered mountain-like above her. I made one spring, one gallant spring, and, catching by her top-mast, slid down in safety to her decks. Her sails were spread widely to the winds, and recklessly we ploughed our course onward through the icy flood; but now her speed diminished, now we scarcely moved. The rudder creaked lazily from side to side, and the long pennant, supinely resting on the shrouds, languidly lifted itself as if to peer into the dark flood, and then, serpent-like, settled itself again to its repose. A sullen distant roar began to break upon my ear; it increased; our before quiet bark, hastening, rushed onwards as if ashamed of her dull reverie; but still there was no wind; the sea was smooth and placid, but the swelling surge was thrown forward from her bows by the increasing velocity with which we dashed along. The rushing noise of waters increased, and sounded like distant thunder; the white surges showed themselves in the distance, leaping and jumping with frightful violence. I approached the captain; his gloomy brow, the ghastly paleness of the crew, as with folded arms they stood looking in the distance, alarmed me. I eagerly asked the cause of the appearances before me. He answered not. He stood immovable as a statue. But, in a cold unearthly voice, a scar-marked sailor groaned, "We are food for the Maelstrom!" Can we not, I frantically exclaimed, oh! can we not escape? Bend every sail, ply every oar— "Too late, too late," echoed again the gloomy voice; "our doom is sealed." The finger of the speaker pointed to a fiendish figure at the helm, who, with a low hellish laugh, was steering for the midst. The raging waves boiled and roared around us; our fated ship plunged forward; a steady resistless power sucked us in; on we were hurried to our frightful goal. The whale, the leviathan, swept by us; their immense bodies were thrown almost entirely in the air; their blood stained the foaming brine; they roared like mad bulls. The zig-zag lightning in the black canopy above us was reflected in fiery showers from the spray; the thunder mingled with the yells of the struggling monsters; their efforts were vain; more power had infants in giants' hands; the devouring whirlpool claimed us for its own. On we were borne in unresisting weakness; faster and faster; circle after circle disappeared; we were on the edge of the furious watery tunnel; we were buried in its depths; the long arms of the loathsome polypi stretched forward to seize us in their foul embrace—but an unseen hand raised me.

Green woods, gardens, fountains and grottoes were around me. Beautiful flowers, roses, hyacinths, and lilies clustering in immense beds, covered the ground with one great gem'd and emerald carpet. The gorgeous tulip, the amaranthus and moss rose vied with each other in fragrant rivalry, and the modest little violet claimed protection in the embraces of the myrtle. Fountains poured mimic cataracts into their marble basins, or, spouting from the mouths of sphinxes and lions, ascended in crystal streams, irrigating with copious showers the party-colored beds beneath. The long vistas were shaded with the magnolia and flowering almond, while snow-white statues watched the beautiful picture of happiness around. Birds of variegated color and splendid plumage were flying from tree to tree, and it appeared as if in their sweet notes, and the fragrance of the flowers, nature was offering up her incense to the Creator.

I was invigorated with new life; I ran from alley to alley; delicious fruits tempted my taste; the perfumes of Arabia floated in the earthly paradise; music floated around;

trains of beautiful girls moved in graceful ballets before me; their slender forms were clad in snow-white robes; their girdles gemmed with diamonds; their alabaster necks twined with wreaths of roses. A joyous laugh burst from them, as they danced, now in circles, now advancing, now retreating. The circle opened; a veiled figure was in the midst; I approached; the fairies disappeared; the veil was slowly lifted, one moment; my Cora! we were alone; we wandered from bower to bower; her small white hand, with electric touch, was within my delighted grasp; her golden ringlets mingled with my raven locks; her dark eyes melted into mine. I fell upon my knee; a cold and grizzly skeleton met my embrace; the groups of houris were changed into bands of shriveled hags; in place of wreaths of roses, their shriveled necks were covered with the deadly nightshade and dank mandragora; forked adders and serpents twined upon their long and bony arms; I shuddered; I was chained in horror to the spot; they seized me; they dragged me downward to the dank and noisome vault. 'Twas light as day; but 'twas a strange light, a greenish haze, sickly and poisonous as if the deadly miasma of the fens had turned to flame. The dead men with burning lamps were sitting on their coffins, their chins resting upon their drawn-up knees, and as I passed along the extended rows, their eyes all turned and followed me, as the eyes of portraits from the canvas. Ha! what cadaverous unearthly stare met me at every turn; I looked on all sides to avoid them, but still, where'er I turned, the ghastly muffled faces, with their blanched lips, and deep sunken eyes livid in their sockets, surveyed me with frightful interest; and that fierce old hag, how she preceded me, step by step, her finger pointing forward, while her Medusa head was turned triumphantly over her shoulder, with its infernal leer upon my cowering form. Worlds would I have given to have been out from among the ghastly crew, but a spell was on me, and I hurriedly made the circuit of the vault, like a wild beast in his cage. But the old knight, sitting grim and ghastly as if by constraint, in the lone corner, his long grizzly beard flowing o'er his winding-sheet — how his cold grey eye glanced at his long two-handed sword before him, as I passed, as if to clutch it! I plucked the old grey beard for very ire; ha! what a malignant and discordant yell did then salute my horror-struck senses! I gave one bound of terror, and burst the prison door, and—and—

My noble white charger leaped clear of the earth, as he felt my weight in the saddle. I was at the head of an immense army; my bold cuirassiers formed a moving mass of iron around me. The bugle sounded the signal for engagement; peal after peal of musketry flashed from the dark masses; the rattling reverberating roar rolled from right to left; the gaping throats of the cannon announced in broad flashes the departure of their messengers upon the journey of death. On we rushed, battalion on battalion; we stormed the redoubt. "Charge!" I shouted, "charge the villains! men of the fifth legion, follow your leader; hurrah! they bear back." I seize the standard from a fallen soldier; I plant it upon the blood-stained parapet; horrible confusion! the trenches are choked with dead. Hah! brave comrade, beware! his bayonet is at thy shoulder—'tis buried in thy heart. I will avenge thee! I dashed upon him; we fought like tigers; we rolled upon the ground; I seized my dagger; the bright steel glittered; thousands of deep hoarse voices wildly roared: "The mine, the mine! beware, beware!" Flash! roar! bodies, earth, rocks, horses, tumbrils, all descending, covered me; and—and—

I awoke; the fender and fire-irons upset with horrid din and clatter; the table, its lights and tea-set hurled around; and myself, with might and main striving with mighty effort to get from beneath the prostrate wreck, which in my terror I had dragged above me. Old Neptune, aghast, howled in consternation, from the corner, while a group of fellow-boarders, half dead with laughter and amazement, were staring through the open door in wonder at such unusual uproar from the lodger in quiet "No. VI."

OLD SCIPIO.

BUT hark! Old Scipio is fast asleep and snoring like Falstaff behind the arras. Now that old negro is as assuredly dreaming of witches, or wrecks, or pirates, or ghosts, that have been seen flitting about the burying-grounds and country church-yards at midnight, as he sits there. He is somewhere between eighty and one hundred, he does not exactly know which; but as your negro keeps no family record, it is safe to allow a lee-way of some ten years in the calculation of his nativity. Of his genealogy though, he is quite sure, for he proves beyond a doubt, that he is the son of Job, who was the son of Pomp, who was the son of Caleb, who was the son of Cæsar, who was the son of Cudjoe, who was caught in Africa. His whole life has been passed in and about the shores of Long Island Sound, and he is not only a veritable chronicle of the military adventures that have been enacted upon its borders in the American wars, but his head is a complete storehouse, stuffed to overflowing with all sorts of legendary lore of wrecks, of pirates, of murders and fights, and deeds unholy, of massacres, bombardments and burnings, all jumbled up in such inexplicable confusion, history and legend, truth and fiction, that it is almost impossible to divide the one from the other. Sometimes in the cold winter nights, when the storm is howling, as it does now, I put him upon the track, and upon my word, the influence of his gossip told in drowsy undertone is such, that I find it a matter of serious question, whether the most monstrous things in the way of the supernatural, are by any means matter of wonderment; and fully concede, that men may have been seen walking about with their heads under their arms, vanishing in smoke upon being addressed; that old fishermen have sculled about the creeks and bays in their coffins, after they were dead and buried; that gibbets are of necessity surrounded by ghosts, and that prophecies and predictions, and witchcraft are, and must be, true as holy writ.

Indeed, with all the sad realities of life about me, I find it refreshing to have my soul let loose occasionally, to wander forth, to frolic and gambol, and stare, without any conventional rule, or let, or hindrance to restrain it. In how many adventures has that good old negro, quietly sleeping in the corner, been my guide and pilot. In our shooting, and fishing and sailing excursions, the shores of the Sound became as familiar to us as our own firesides, and the dark black rocks, with their round and kelp-covered sides, as the faces of old friends and acquaintances.

At a little village upon the western borders of Long Island Sound I passed my school-boy days, and there it was that the old negro, formerly a slave, but long liberated, and in part supported by my family, had his hut. There it was that under his influence I thoroughly contracted the love of adventure which, in the retrospect, still throws a sort of world of my own around me. All sport, whether in winter or summer, night or day, rain or shine, was alike to me the same, and sooth to say, if sundry floggings, for truant days, had been administered to Old Scip instead of me, the scale of justice had not unduly preponderated; for his boats, and rods, and nets, to say nothing of his musket which had belonged to a Hessian, and the long bell-mouthed French fusee, were always sedulously and invitingly placed at my control. The old negro was sure to meet me as I bounded from the school-room with advice of how the tides would serve, and how the game would lie, and his words winding up his information in a low confidential undertone still ring upon my ear, " P'rhaps young massa like to go wid old nigger."

His snug little hut down at the creek-side was covered, and patched, and thatched, with all the experiments of years to add to its warmth and comfort: its gables and chimney surmounted with little weathercocks and windmills spinning most furiously at every whiff of wind, its sides covered with muskrat and loon skins nailed up to dry, and fishing-rods and spears of all sizes and dimensions piled against them, the ducks and geese paddling about the threshhold and his great fat hog grunting in loving proximity to the door-way: while its interior was garnished with pots and kettles and other culinary utensils, the trusty old musket hanging on its hooks above the chimney place, the fish-nets and bird-decoys lying in the corners, and the whitewashed walls garnished and covered with pictures and colored prints of the most negro taste, indigo and scarlet, naval fights, men hanging on gibbets, monstrous apparitions which had been seen, lamentable ballads, and old Satan himself in veritable semblance, tail, horns and claws, precisely as he appeared in the year Anno Domini 1763; and under the little square mahogany framed fly-specked looking-glass, his Satanic Majesty again in full scarlet uniform as British Colonel with a party of ladies and gentlemen playing cards, his tail quietly curled around one of the legs of his arm-chair, and the horse-hoof ill disguised by the great rose upon his shoe. But Scip was safe against all such diabolical influence, for he had the charmed horse-shoe firmly nailed over the entrance of his door.

How often have I silently climbed out of my window and stealthily crept down the ladder which passed it, long and long before the dawn, with my fowling-piece upon my shoulder, and by the fitful moonlight wended, half scared, my way through the rustic roads and lanes, leaping the fences, saturated with the night-dew from the long wet grass, the stars twinkling in the heavens, as the wild scudding clouds passed o'er them, and nothing to break the perfect stillness. How often at such times have I stopped and stared at some suspicious object looming up before me, till, mustering courage, I have cocked my piece and, advancing at a trail, discovered in the object of my terror a dozing horse, or patient ox, or cow quietly ruminating at the road-side.

How often have I sprung suddenly aside, my hair standing on end, as a stealthy fox or prowling dog rushed by me into the bushes, and felt my blood tingle to my very fingers' ends, as some bird of prey raised himself with an uneasy scream and settled again upon the tree-tops, as I passed beneath. How I used to screw my courage up as, with long strides and studiously averted eyes, I hurried past the dreaded grave-yard; and as I came upon the borders of the winding creek, and walked splashing through its ponds and shallows, how would I crouch and scan through the dim light to catch a glimpse of some stray flock of ducks or teal, that might be feeding upon its sedges. How would I bend and stoop as I saw them delightfully huddled in a cluster, till getting near I would find an envious bend of long distance to be measured before I could get a shot. How patiently would I creep along, and stop, and crouch, and stop, till getting near, and nearer, a sudden slump into some unseen bog or ditch would be followed by a quick "quack," "quack," and off they'd go, far out of reach of shot or call. But all would be forgotten when I reached the old Negro's hut. There a hot corn-cake and broiled fish or bird was always on the coals to stay my appetite, and then off we'd sally to the bar to lie in wait for the wild fowl as they came over at day-break. The snipe in little clouds would start up with their sharp "pewhit" before us, as we measured the broad hard flats left damp and smooth by the receding tide; the Kildare with querulous cry would wing away his flight, and the great gaunt cranes, looming, spectre-like, in the moonlight, sluggishly stalking onwards, would clumsily lift their long legs in silence as we advanced, and fan themselves a little farther from our proximity.

Arriving, we would lay ourselves down, and on the stones await the breaking of the dawn, when the wild fowl feeding within the bay arise and fly to the southward over it. Dark objects, one after another, would glide by us, and in silence take their places along the bar, bent on the same sport that we were awaiting, and nothing would break the stillness save the gentle wash and ripple of the waves upon the sands, or the uneasy and discordant cry of the oldwives, feeding on the long sedge within the wide-extended bay. The stars would ere long begin to fade, the east grow gray, then streaked with light, and every sportsman's piece be cocked with eager expectation. A flash, a puff of smoke at the extreme end, showed that a flock had risen, and simultaneously birds would be seen tumbling headlong. As the astonished flock glanced along the bar—flash—flash—puff—bang, would meet them, their numbers thinning at each discharge, till, passing along the whole line of sportsmen, they would be almost annihilated; or, wildly dashing through some wider interval in the chain of gunners, they would cross the bar and escape in safety. Then as the light increased followed the excitement; the birds getting up in dense flocks, all bent in one direction, a complete *feu-de-joie* saluted them—flash—flash—flash—the reports creeping slowly after, the wild fowl tumbling headlong, some into the water, and some on the sportsmen; while here a gunner, dropping his piece, might be seen rushing in up to his neck recklessly after his victim, and there some staunch dog's nose just above the surface, unweariedly pursuing the wing-broken sufferer, which still fluttered forward at his near approach. Ah, ha! that—that was sport. Hundreds of wild fowl, from the little graceful teal to the great fishy loon and red-head brant, were the fruits of the morning's adventure. And what a contrast the sparkling eyes and glowing faces of the elated sportsmen to the city's pale and care-worn countenances. They were a true democracy, white man, and black, and half-breed, the squire and the plowman, all met in like equality.

THE PEQUOT.

AMONG the sportsmen on the bar at the season that I have just described there was always found a tall, gaunt, taciturn old Indian, who passed among the people by the name of "Pequot." His hut was about a mile beyond Scipio's, on the same creek, and, like him, he obtained his support mainly by the fruits of his hunting and fishing. Now and then, in the harvest, or when the game was scarce, he would assist the farmers in their lighter work, receiving, with neither thanks nor stipulation, such recompense as they saw fit to make; and sometimes, in the cold depths of winter, he would appear, and, silently sitting at their firesides, receive as a sort of right his trencher at their tables. He was so inoffensive to all around him that he was always sure of welcome. But there was a feature in his character unusual to the Indian's nature, which was his dislike to ardent spirits. He was a great deal at Scipio's hut, and I was struck with the harmony which subsisted between two characters so apparently dissimilar, the sullen, haughty Indian and the light-hearted, laughter-loving negro; but there was a sort of common sympathy, of oppression, I suppose, between them, for they always assisted one another, and sometimes were gone for days together in their fishing expeditions on the Sound. All the information that Scipio could give about him was that he was supposed to have come in from some of the Western tribes, and that from his haunting a great deal about a neighboring swamp, where the gallant tribe of Pequots had long years before been massa cred by fire and sword, the people had given him the name of Pequot. Whatever he was he was a fine old Indian. The poetry of the character was left, while contact with the whites and the kind teachings of the Moravians had hewn away the sterner features of the savage. Even old Scip showed him habitual deference, for there was a melancholy dignity about him. I recollect once being taken aback by the display of a burst of feeling which let me into his ideal claims and pretensions.

There was a good-natured old Indian by the name of Pamanack, belonging to one of the tribes which still clung to Long Island in the vicinity of Montauket, who occasionally made his appearance off old Scip's hut, in the Sound, in his periogue, accompanied by some half dozen long-legged, straight-haired, copper-colored youths, his descendants. They every now and then came cruising along the various fishing-grounds, and always, when in the vicinity of Scip, the old Indian would pay him a visit and receive a return for the hospitality paid to the black man when in his similar excursions he got as far eastward as Montauket. On the particular occasion to which I have alluded old Pamanack had drank more than was good for him, when the Pequot presented himself silently at the door of old Scipio's hut, and leaning upon his long ducking-gun looked in upon the group. After a few words of recognition passed between them Pamanack held out his black bottle and invited the visitor to drink. Pequot drew himself up, and for a moment there was a mingled expression of loathing and ferocity flashing from his countenance that showed his Indian's nature in a blaze; but it was only momentary, for in another the expression vanished from his countenance, the habitual melancholy resumed its place upon his features, and the words fell slowly from his lips: "The fire water, the fire water; ay, the same—the Indian and his deadly enemy." Then, looking steadily at Pamanack as he held the bottle still toward him: "Pequot will not drink. Why should Pamanack swallow the white man's poison and with his own hands dig his grave? Pamanack is not alone. His squaw watches at the door of his wigwam as she looks out upon the long waves of the ocean tumbling in upon the shores of Montauket. His young men gather about him and catch the tautog from its beetling rocks and tread out the quahog from its muddy bed. His old men still linger on the sandy beach, and their scalp-locks float wildly in the fresh sea-breeze. Pamanack has yet a home; but Pequot, he is the last of his race. He stands on the high hills of Tashaway and sees no smoke but that from the wigwams of the Long Knives. He moves in silence along the plains of Pequonnuck, but the fences of the pale faces obstruct his progress. His canoe dances at the side of the dripping rocks, but the cheating white men paddle up to his side. His feet sink in the plowed field, but it is not the corn of the red man. His squaw has rolled her last log and lies cold in her blanket. His young men—the fire water and fire dust have consumed them. Pequot looks around for his people; where are they? The black snake and muskrat shoot through the water as his moccasin treads the swamp where their bones lie, deep covered from the hate of their enemies. Pequot is the last of his race. He cannot drink the fire water, for his young men have sunk from its deadly poison as the mist-wreath in the midday sun. The good Moravians have told him that it is bad, and Pequot will drink no more, for his race is nearly run. Pequot will sit on the high rocks of Sasco, and his robe shall fall from his shoulders as his broad chest waits the death arrow of the Great Spirit. There will he sit and smoke in silence as he looks down upon the deserted hunting-grounds of his fathers. Pequot's heart is heavy." As he finished the last words he abruptly turned, and was soon far distant on the sands, moving toward the high hill of which he had spoken. The Great Spirit was kind to him, for a few years after he was found stark and stiff, frozen to death on the very rocks to which he had alluded. As for old Pamanack, he did not appear to hold the fire water in such utter abhorrence; for, taking a long swig at the bottle, his eye following the retiring form of the Pequot, he slowly muttered: "Nigger drink, white man drink; why no Indian drink too?"

CAPTAIN KIDD.

BUT the Sound! the Sound! How many delightful reminiscences does the name bring to my recollection! The Sound, with its white sand-banks and its wooded shores; its fair broad bosom covered with fleets of sails scudding along in the swift breeze in the open day, and its dark waves rolling and sweeping in whole streams of phosphorescent fire from their plunging bows as they dash through it in the darkness of midnight. The Sound! redolent with military story. The Sound! overflowing with legend and history. Reader, if you had been cruising along its shores from infancy, as I have; if you had grown up among its legends and luxuriated in its wild associations; if you had spent whole days on its broad sand-beaches, watching the gulls as they sailed above you, or the snipe as they ran along on the smooth, hard flats; if you had lain on the white, frozen snows on its shore in the still nights of midwinter, your gun by your side, gazing till your soul was lost in the blue spangled vault as it hung in serene and tranquil grandeur above you, your mind, in unconscious adoration, breathing whole volumes of gratitude and admiration to the great God that gave you faculties to enjoy its sublimity, and in the stillness, unbroken save by the cry of the loon as he raised himself from the smooth water, seen in every sail moving in silence between you and the horizon the "Phantom Ship," or some daring buccaneer, and in every distant splash heard a deed of darkness and mystery—then could you enter into my feelings.

To me its black rocks and promontories and islands are as familiar as the faces of a family. Are there not the "Brothers,"* unnatural that they are, who, living centuries together, never to one another have as yet spoken a kindly word, and the "Executioners,"* and "Throgs,"* and "Sands,"* and "Eatons,"* all throwing hospitable lights from their high beacon towers, far forward, to guide the wandering mariner; and the "Devil's Stepping-stones,"* o'er which he bounded when driven from Connecticut; and the great rocks, too, inside of Flushing bay on which he descended, shivering them from top to bottom as he fell. And are there not the "Norwalk Islands," with their pines; "Old Sasco," with her rocks; "Fairweather," with the wild bird's eggs resting on her sands, and the far-famed fishing-banks off the "Middle ground." Is it not from the whirlpools of the "Gate" to "Gardiners," and the lone beacon tower of "Old Montuket," one continuous ground of lore and adventure? In her waters the "Fire ship" glared amid the darkness, her phantom crew standing at their quarters, as, rushing onwards in the furious storm, she passed the shuddering mariner. Beneath her sands the red-shirted buccaneers did hide their ill-gotten, blood-spotted treasure, and 'twas on her broad bosom that, with iron-seared conscience, sailed that Pirate, fierce and bold, old Robert Kidd; to this very day his golden hoards, with magic mark and sign, still crowd her wooded shores.

How, were he waking, old Scipio's eyes would upward

* Rocks and Light Houses.

roll their whites, if he did but hear that name so dread and grim! If, from very eagerness, he could utter forth his words, he would give whole chapters, ay! one from his own family history, for it is said Kidd's men caught old Cudjoe, his great ancestor, clamming on the beach off Sasco, and without more ado carried him aboard. As the old negro was sulky, they tumbled his well-filled basket into the galley's tank, and incontinently were about to run him up to dangle at their long yard-arm, when Kidd, who was taking his morning "drink of tobacco" on his poop, roared out in a voice of thunder: "Ho! Scroggs, boatswain, dost hang a black-a-moor at my yard-arm, where so many gentlemen have danced on nothing? In the foul devil's name, scuttle the goggle-eyed fiend to the sharks overboard," and overboard he went, but, diving like a duck, he escaped their firelocks' quick discharge, and reached the shore in safety.

And his deep buried treasures! Where went the gold dust from the coast of Guinea? the gems from Madagascar? the dollars and doubloons pirated from the Spanish galleons? the broken plate and crucifixes from the shores of Panama? and where the good yellow gold, stamped with the visage of his most gracious majesty? Where? where, but on the haunted borders of this very Sound. Why, the very schoolboys, playing in the woods upon its shores, know, when the earth doth hollow sound beneath their feet, that Kidd's treasure's buried there. Do they disturb it? No, not they; they know too well the fierce and restless spirit that guards the iron pot. Didst ever hear the brave old ballad, "*As he sail'd, as he sail'd?*" It's a true old ballad, a time-honored old ballad; it gives his veritable history. It has been sung time out of mind, been chanted by the old tars in the sultry calms of the tropics, and the greasy whalers have kept time to it over their trying kettles on the smooth Pacific. It has been sung amid the icebergs of Greenland, and heard on the coast of New Holland; the spicy breezes of Ceylon have borne it among the sleeping tigers in their jungles, and the Hottentots pulled tighter their breech-cloths as they have listened to its tones. The Chinese, and the Turks, and the Dutchmen, and the Danes, and everything human within the smell of salt water, have heard it, and that too in the rich manly tones of the English and American sailors. Ho! Scip! wake from out thy corner, and give us the old ballad. Shades of red-capped buccaneers! fierce negro slavers! spirits of the gallant men who fought the British on her shores! desperate old Kidd in person! we conjure you, we conjure you, arise and hover around us, whilst we chant the lay. Ho! Scipio! the old ballad, as it stood, smoke-blacked and grimed, upon thy cabin's walls; ay! that is it, and in tones which chime in unison with the dreary storm and howling blast without—

"Yᴇ LAMENTABLE BALLAD, AND Yᴇ TRUE HISTORIE OF CAPTAIN ROBERT KIDD, WHO WAS HANGED IN CHAINS AT EXECUTION DOCK, FOR PIRACY AND MURDER ON Yᴇ HIGH SEAS."

He calleth upon the captains:

You captains bold and brave, hear our cries, hear our cries,
You captains bold and brave, hear our cries,
You captains brave and bold, tho' you seem uncontroll'd,
Don't for the sake of gold lose your souls, lose your souls,
Don't for the sake of gold lose your souls.

He stateth his name and acknowledgeth his wickedness:

My name was Robert Kidd, when I sail'd, when I sail'd,
My name was Robert Kidd, when I sail'd,
My name was Robert Kidd, God's laws I did forbid,
And so wickedly I did, when I sail'd.

He beareth witness to the good counsel of his parents:

My parents taught me well, when I sail'd, when I sail'd,
My parents taught me well, when I sail'd.
My parents taught me well to shun the gates of hell,
But against them I rebelled, when I sail'd.

He curseth his father and his mother dear:

I cursed my father dear, when I sail'd, when I sail'd,
I cursed my father dear, when I sail'd,
I cursed my father dear and her that did me bear,
And so wickedly did swear, when I sail'd.

And blasphemeth against God:

I made a solemn vow, when I sail'd, when I sail'd,
I made a solemn vow, when I sail'd.
I made a solemn vow to God I would not bow,
Nor myself one prayer allow, as I sail'd.

He burieth the Good Book in the sand:

I'd a Bible in my hand, when I sail'd, when I sail'd,
I'd a Bible in my hand when I sail'd,
I'd a Bible in my hand by my father's great command,
And I sunk it in the sand, when I sail'd.

And murdereth William Moore:

I murdered William Moore, as I sail'd, as I sail'd,
I murdered William Moore, as I sail'd,
I murdered William Moore, and left him in his gore,
Not many leagues from shore, as I sail'd.

> And being cruel still, as I sail'd, as I sail'd,
> And being cruel still, as I sail'd,
> And being cruel still, my gunner I did kill,
> And his precious blood did spill, as I sail'd.

And also cruelly killeth the gunner.

> My mate was sick and died, as I sail'd, as I sail'd,
> My mate was sick and died, as I sail'd,
> My mate was sick and died, which me much terrified,
> When he called me to his bedside, as I sail'd.

His mate, being about to die, repenteth and warneth him in his career.

> And unto me he did say, see me die, see me die,
> And unto me did say, see me die,
> And unto me did say, take warning now by me,
> There comes a reckoning day, you must die.
>
> You cannot then withstand, when you die, when you die,
> You cannot then withstand, when you die,
> You cannot then withstand the judgments of God's hand,
> But bound then in iron bands, you must die.

> I was sick and nigh to death, as I sail'd, as I sail'd,
> I was sick and nigh to death, as I sail'd,
> I was sick and nigh to death, and I vowed at every breath
> To walk in wisdom's ways, as I sail'd.

He falleth sick, and promiseth repentance, but forgetteth his vows.

> I thought I was undone, as I sail'd, as I sail'd;
> I thought I was undone, as I sail'd,
> I thought I was undone, and my wicked glass had run,
> But health did soon return, as I sailed.
>
> My repentance lasted not, as I sail'd, as I sail'd,
> My repentance lasted not, as I sail'd,
> My repentance lasted not, my vows I soon forgot,
> Damnation's my just lot, as I sail'd.

> I steer'd from Sound to Sound, as I sail'd, as I sail'd,
> I steer'd from Sound to Sound, as I sail'd,
> I steer'd from Sound to Sound, and many ships I found,
> And most of them I burn'd, as I sail'd.

He steereth thro' Long Island and other Sounds.

> I spy'd three ships from France, as I sail'd, as I sail'd,
> I spy'd three ships from France, as I sail'd,
> I spy'd three ships from France, to them I did advance,
> And took them all by chance, as I sailed.

He chaseth three ships of France.

CAPTAIN KIDD

<small>And also three ships of Spain.</small>

I spy'd three ships of Spain, as I sail'd, as I sail'd,
   I spy'd three ships of Spain, as I sail'd,
I spy'd three ships of Spain, I fired on them amain,
   Till most of them were slain, as I sail'd.

<small>He boasteth of his treasure.</small>

I'd ninety bars of gold, as I sail'd, as I sail'd,
   I'd ninety bars of gold, as I sail'd,
I'd ninety bars of gold, and dollars manifold,
   With riches uncontroll'd, as I sail'd.

<small>He spyeth fourteen ships in pursuit, and surrenders.</small>

Then fourteen ships I saw, as I sail'd, as I sail'd,
   Then fourteen ships I saw, as I sail'd,
Then fourteen ships I saw, and brave men they are,
   Ah! they were too much for me, as I sail'd.

Thus being o'ertaken at last, I must die, I must die,
   Thus being o'ertaken at last, I must die,
Thus being o'ertaken at last, and into prison cast,
   And sentence being pass'd, I must die.

<small>He biddeth farewell to the seas, and the raging main.</small>

Farewell the raging sea, I must die, I must die.
   Farewell the raging main, I must die,
Farewell the raging main, to Turkey, France, and
     Spain,
   I ne'er shall see you again, I must die.

<small>He exhorteth the young and old to take counsel from his fate:</small>

To Newgate now I'm cast, and must die, and must die,
   To Newgate now I'm cast, and must die,
To Newgate I am cast, with a sad and heavy heart,
   To receive my just desert, I must die.

To Execution Dock I must go, I must go,
   To Execution Dock I must go,
To Execution Dock will many thousands flock,
   But I must bear the shock, I must die.

Come all you young and old, see me die, see me die,
   Come all you young and old, see me die,
Come all you young and old, you're welcome to my
     gold,
   For by it I've lost my soul, and must die.

<small>And declareth that he must go to hell, and be punished for his wickedness.</small>

Take warning now by me, for I must die, for I must
     die,
   Take warning now by me, for I must die,
Take warning now by me, and shun bad company,
   Lest you come to hell with me, for I must die,
   Lest you come to hell with me, for I must die.

SPIRITIANA—No. I.

HYDRACHOS.

Cleopatra—Hast thou the pretty worm of Nilus there,
That kills and pains not?
Clown— Truly I have him ; but I would not be the party that should desire you to touch him, for his biting is immortal ; those that do die of it, do seldom or never recover.
Cleopatra—Get thee hence ; farewell.
Clown— I wish you all joy of the worm.
Cleopatra—Farewell.
Clown— You must think this, look you, that the worm will do his kind.
Cleopatra—Ay—ay, farewell.
Clown— Look you, the worm is not to be trusted but in the keeping of wise people; for, indeed, there is no goodness in the worm.
Cleopatra—Well, get thee gone; farewell.
ANTHONY AND CLEOPATRA.

SCENE.—*Hendrick's Cottage on the Heights at the Narrows. The Ocean opening out to the horizon. Staten Island, with its woods, green hills and fortifications, on the right; Fort Hamilton, New Utrecht, and the fair farms of Long Island on the left. On the rustic piazza, o'ershadowed by two giant hemlocks and the sweeping foliage of old willows, are seated, in luxuriant arm-chairs, with their legs well rested on stools in front, two gentlemen. (Between them, a round table, on which, half filled with rich purple, rests a crystal pitcher of "Chateau Margaux," a diamond cut goblet of "golden Sherry," a dusty, cobwebbed bottle with a label, on which, dimly, is to be seen the word "Farquar," sundry condiments, fruits, old Cheshire, biscuits, et id omne genus, and a cedar box, the lid half off,* "RE-

GALIA, 1840.") *One, tall and slender—the* "TALL SON OF YORK." *The other in dressing-gown and slippers—ejus nomen* HENDRICK. *The blue smoke of their Regalias rises in light clouds, and wreathes and floats gracefully above their heads, while the drowsy note of the locusts in the o'erhanging trees, and the busy hum of the bees diving into the honey-suckles and flowering vines, indicate the dreamy quiescence of a summer's afternoon.*

THE TALL SON* (*loquitur*).—By Jupiter! Hendrick, but this is a beautiful scene that Nature has so lavishly spread before you. No wonder that your bays leave punctually at three to carry you from the heated walls of Old Gotham. A magnificent prospect! How grandly old Ocean stretches onward to the embrace of the distant horizon! The ships, with their bellying canvas, seem like things of dreams, sleeping upon his broad bosom. And see! the fleecy clouds now hurrying on, and now hanging motionless in the blue canopy above. These shores, too, with their undulating hills, green forests and lordly villas! it's a scene worthy the pencil of a *Ruysdael*. Yonder massive forts appear, with their engines of destruction so grimly crouched in their embrasures, the guardians of this peaceful scene. By the blood of old Eclipse!† (a health to the veteran) By the fair form of the goddess sprung from the light foam of yonder sea! (a glass to the fair Cytheria) I admire your taste. This snug little Dutch cottage of yours, my dear boy, with its flowering walks, and roses, and honey-suckles, is perfect-

* The *soubriquet* by which the Editor of the "Spirit of the Times" was known to his correspondents.

† A celebrated race-horse.

ly delightful, and but that you are a bachelor, I should set you down as a happy man.

HENDRICK.—Married or unmarried, bachelor or Benedict, right happy am I, my dear "Spirit," to welcome you within its walls.

> "Now is the winter of (*my*) discontent, made glorious by summer
> By this (tall) "*Son of York*,"
> And all the clouds that lowered about our house
> (Need not go far to find themselves)
> In the deep bosom of the ocean buried."

But Egad! my dear boy, what a pair of beauties you have got in your traces. What blood! what muscle! what necks! what shoulders! Their nostrils are fire, and their eyes shame the gazelle—

> "With champing bits, and arching necks,
> And eyes like listening deer,
> And spirits of fire, that pine at rest,
> And limbs that mock at fear."

Old Scip', who was born in a stable, and expects to be buried under a manger, who looks upon himself as first cousin to horse-flesh, stands with arms a-kimbo and eyes wide open, in speechless astonishment in the carriage-house, where he has taken them under cover.

SPIRIT.—They *are* horses—"Taking them for all in all, we ne'er shall see their like again." Five years old, blood as pure as the Bourbons, match to the curl of a fetlock, do their "*two-thirty*" without laying a hair, and so delicate on the ribbons, that the little finger of a girl of fifteen can turn them in a circle. The "*Avenues*"* glory in the light tap of their hoofs, and "*Cato's*"* and "*Burnham's*"* are vociferous

* Stopping places on the avenues.

in their praise. But, by the mare of Mahomet, Hendrick, this road of yours is infernally heavy. I've had a halo of dust three feet in diameter around my wheels all the way down from the ferry. Your sandy desert may be very well for your "Araby's Daughter," but it's the devil and all on horseflesh with four wheels behind it. But, Hendrick, though this cottage of yours is unexceptionable, and the scenery beautiful, your wine exquisite in its bouquet, and your "Regalias" in their flavor, and everything so comfortable, even to the old Newfoundlander there, dreaming of whole lagoons of wild-fowl and avalanches of mutton bones, don't you find, my dear fellow, that you want excitement—don't you feel a little Robinson Crusoeish now and then?

HENDRICK.—Not a whit, not a whit. I have, you know, sufficient business for employment, plenty of books, salubrious air—as you say, beautiful scenery, my nags, my rod, my gun, my dogs (Soho! you villains, come up and show yourselves; there's a pair of game ones for you), a crack at the deer and wild-fowl in the fall, an occasional scamper about the country when the humor seizes me, and, thank heaven, a tolerably contented mind. I envy no man his greatness, and wish well to all of Adam's race, both small and great. I look above, and around, and about me, and in everything, the sea, the air, the earth, behold indicated the finger of benevolence and goodness. I find study and employment in every object of Nature, from the small and delicate flower opening its petals at my feet, the minute insect hurrying through its brief and ephemeral existence (type of our own) to Old Ocean, rolling his "ceaseless dashings" to my cottage door, and the great glorious constellations sweeping onwards in silent sublimity above its lowly roof.

Spirit.—All very true, Hendrick, by my faith! All very true; very fine philosophy, and still finer poetry; but I know you of old, my boy. A pretty woman in your path sends all this philosophy to the devil; you're destined yet to have that old bachelor's coat of yours pulled over your ears. Sings:

> "The village maid steals through the shade,
>   Her shepherd's suit to hear,
> To beauty shy, by lattice high,
>   Sings high born Cavalier.
>
> The star of Love, all stars above,
>   Now reigns o'er earth and sky,
> And high and low the influence know,
>   But *where* is County Guy."

Hendrick.—Out upon thee, profane wretch! Being bachelor incorrigible, schoolst thou me? Out upon thee! But be that as it may, do I not see that empty crystal on its delicate stem casting reproachful glances on thee? Fill it! fill it to the brim with golden sherry, and touch it to thy lips in token of reconciliation. What a man now wert thou with a bottle of that under thy waistcoat, and thy nags before thee on a two mile stretch of clear road! The clatter of their hoofs were like the roll of a drum. There were nothing then could overtake thee, save the great "Hydrarchos."

Spirit—The great what?

Hendrick—The great Hydrarchos.*

Spirit—What i' the name of the bottomless pit is that?

Hendrick—Why, the great serpent exhumed in Missouri! Mouth six feet wide, with teeth to match; ribs twelve feet in diameter, and length from his snakeship's snout to the end of his diabolic tail about one hundred and fifty feet—the

*Subsequently found to be a deception.

representative of the incarnate fiend that lay "chained to the burning lake," he snap't you up a pair of elephants as a cat does a mouse—cousin germain to him that

> "Swallowed a church and a steeple
> And all the good people."

Spirit—Egad! what a favorite he would be in "Old Virginy," that home of snakedom, of whom it is written: "If truth is not, then there's no snakes in Virginy."
(*Dinah's voice is heard singing in the kitchen.*)

> "Snake baked a hoe cake,
> Asked de frog to mind it.
> De frog he fell asleep,
> And de lizard came and stol'd it.
> Chorus—Ruberree—ceder bree—heigho Juba!
>
> De snake began to beat de lizard,
> De lizard he denied it,
> And de frog said ye did, for
> I seed ye when ye stol'd it.
> Chorus—Ruberree—ceder bree—heigho Juba!
> Alligator in de swamp, catching de old gander."

Hendrick—Ha! ha! Truly you have woke up "Old Vairginy" herself; but, joking aside, it is a great curiosity, and well worth seeing, whether it be Behemoth, Leviathan, Kraken, Sea Serpent, or that enormous snake represented by Placide "who never saw the end of his tail;" it is the remains of a stupendous animal. Apropos of snakes, in one of your late "Spirits" I saw a communication relative to the fascinating power of serpents in which the writer urges that the influence lies not in "the bright and glittering eye," but in the poisonous and noxious effluvia emitted by the reptile. I agree with him, the more particularly that it calls to mind a case that came under my observation in

South Carolina a number of years since. A gentleman was traveling through a forest on a warm summer morning, when his attention was excited by the faint cry of a cat-bird that was hopping about in a sort of maze in the path a few yards in advance of him. It uttered a ceaseless, weak, but evidently distressed cry, and appeared to be attracted by some object a little in advance of it. He halted his horse and gazed around him to ascertain the cause, and after looking attentively a minute or two perceived a large black-snake coiled up a short distance from the bird, its head elevated a few inches, but perfectly motionless, and its bright and piercing eye fixed with deadly malignity on its victim, while its tongue, like a little flame, silently played in and out of its mouth. Both animals were too much engaged to notice him, and he remained a few minutes an interested spectator of the scene, the bird becoming evidently more weak and helpless, when he began to perceive an unpleasant odor, which was soon followed by nausea and slight faintness. Divining or imagining the cause, he dismounted, and breaking a stout switch approached, and with two or three well-directed blows dispatched the serpent, perceiving as he did so the peculiar effluvia more strongly. The bird stood in a sort of stupor for a few seconds after he had killed its foe, but gathering strength it lifted itself upon its wings and flew weakly and slowly to a neighboring thicket, where it was soon lost to his view. He felt convinced, upon revolving the theory in his mind, that the popular idea with regard to the fascination was incorrect, and that the poisonous effluvia emitted by the snake was the cause of the stupefaction of its victim.

SPIRIT—Now you speak of it, I think that I have myself

occasionally perceived about snakes an unpleasant odor such as you describe. By-the-bye, your story reminds me of Monk Lewis's "Anaconda," the story of an Englishman that was besieged in his summer-house in Ceylon by an enormous boa, and the effect upon his senses of the deadly effluvia emitted by the monster. You recollect it?

HENDRICK—Perfectly well. I read it in my boyhood, and a most thrilling tale it was. The Englishman letting slip his dog with a note describing his situation tied around his neck, and the monster's snapping him up like lightning before he had got ten feet from the door—of the discovery by the people on the plantation of his situation, and their driving a herd of cattle toward the serpent to divert him from his prey—of his springing upon the headmost bullock, lashing him to a tree, breaking every bone in his body in his coils, lubricating and then swallowing him; his consequent helplessness—their dispatching him with clubs and axes, and the release of the poor Englishman, who subsequently died of his terror and the effects of the effluvia. I recollect it well.

SPIRIT—It was well told. Speaking of Lewis, I came across, the other day, for the first time, the novel from which he received his sobriquet, "the Monk." It is a most exciting story and written with great power. But he presents vice, notwithstanding the attendant horrors, in such captivating colors that I am not sure but that the devil who finally flew away with the monk from the dungeons of Madrid had also a fair right to fly away with the author.

HENDRICK—Yes, he was of the Byronic-diabolic school. But to return to the snakes; I knew a case where a child was apparently under the influence of fascination, whatever might be the cause. It was in a farm-yard in a village in an adjoining State. The child, about four years old, was observed standing perfectly still, gazing intently upon a stone fence a short distance in front of it. It was called repeatedly by its nurse, but paying no attention she went to bring it in. As she approached she noticed that the child was trembling from head to foot, its finger pointing to the wall in front. As she took its hand her eye followed the direction of its finger, and she saw a "copper-head" glide off the stones down into the wall. This snake, which was afterwards killed, called in that part of the country the "rattlesnake's cousin," is exceedingly venomous and more dangerous than the rattlesnake, inasmuch as, devoid of rattles, it gives no warning. The child, when recovered from its agitation, said that she saw beautiful ribbons and colors playing before her on the wall.

SPIRIT—I should think that that could hardly come under the name of fascination, as the natural colors of the snake would have been sufficient of themselves to attract the child's attention; but its terror would seem to sustain the idea that there is an intuitive dread in the human family to the serpent tribe.

HENDRICK—It is the common opinion with regard to black-snakes that they will not attack a human being unless previously assaulted, although there are said to be instances where they have attacked children. But in the same part of the country in which the incident that I have just related of the child occurred there was an instance to the contrary. A farmer by the name of Birdsey was in the woods felling timber. Being seized with a hemorrhage from the nose he laid down his ax, and seating himself upon a rock on the edge of a small brook near by, leaned his head upon his hand, his elbow resting on his knees, letting in that position the blood drop into the water. Whilst thus seated he felt a blow across his back which he thought was from the decayed branch of some overhanging tree falling upon him, but in an instant he was undeceived by finding his elbow tied to his knee and both arms bound tight to his body by the coils of a huge black-snake, whose hissing head, with its glistening eyes and forked tongue, was darting threateningly within a couple of inches of his face. After the paralysis of a moment's fear he succeeded in introducing the fingers of his right hand into his jacket pocket, got out his knife, opened it with his teeth, and succeeded in relieving himself from its horrid embrace only by cutting the serpent into half a dozen pieces.

SPIRIT—There is an astonishing tenacity of life in snakes, as you may have observed when you have cut them in two with a spade or ax. The species called "racers"—black-snakes with a white ring around their necks—are said sometimes to attack people. I recollect that I was once out in the open fields, in the vicinity of a forest, when one started close at my feet. I immediately leveled my piece, when he turned, and with head erect made dead for me. I let him have both barrels, one after the other, and then, laying down my gun, battered him with stones till, as I supposed, life was extinct; but conjecture my surprise when, passing the same place an hour or two after, I found that he had disappeared.

HENDRICK—If it had remained you would have found it swarming with insects and vermin devouring it. How interesting it is to observe the same overruling hand always at work in carrying out its laws, whether great or small! The instant the dissolution of animal life takes place, whether in the mastodon or man, the reptile or the minute insect, these Nature's scavengers rush in from a thousand quarters to their appointed task. Without them the world were soon one noisome charnel-house.

SPIRIT—Ay! a great arena, where the conflict between "life and its arch-enemy, death," is incessant. However brave the resistance, the grim monster invariably conquers, and the corpse, hurried off the stage, makes way for other struggles, other conflicts and other actors on the scene. But what a wondrous mystery lies concealed under its opposite, Life (if, indeed, there is anything *not* enveloped in mystery). The Greek word for *life* is *Bios*, and *Bia* means *violence*. Bichat defines organic life as "*the sum of the functions that resist death;*" in other words, the final result of that circle of natural causes which, surrounding it from its inception, eventually ends in its inevitable extinction. It reminds one of the Italian state prisoner who finds to his horror, as time progresses, that the iron chamber in which he is confined is jointed, and that slowly, silently and surely it is contracting to crush him out of existence. But this *organic* life, though doomed, does not appear to surrender, even after the spirit has withdrawn from it, without a struggle; for soon after the *apparent* death there supervenes a resistance called the *rigor mortis*—a general stiffening of the whole body to such an extent that it can be lifted by the shoulders and stood upright like a statue. This *rigor* lasts for several hours, sometimes a couple of days, when finally, the laws of chemistry obtaining the ascendant, the organic particles gradually soften, lose cohesion, disintegrate, and, dissolving, change into four or five gallons of water and four or five handfuls of lime, which sink into the earth from whence they came, the gases ascending into the atmosphere. Thus resolved, they again commence the eternal circle of re-creation, according to the fiat which has been appointed for them, whether into prince or peasant, mountain or valley, mastodon or insect, forest tree or delicate flower, without destruction or change of their original elements. There can be no stronger logical argument for the *immortality of the soul* than this non-destructibility of matter; for, so far as human reason can judge, it cannot be possible (probable, if you please) that base matter, made use of by the Spirit as its servant and slave, can survive its more noble and ethereal lord.

HENDRICK—The same wood where Birdsey was attacked was a perfect paradise for the poet or the sportsman. The giant patriarchs of the forest, their trunks bearded with the moss of centuries, towering high and grandly into the blue heavens, their broad branches spreading out their green leaves joyously to the blue ether and genial shower, while the summer breezes, sweeping among them, sent forth solemn hymns of harmony to Him who had raised them from the minute seed. The squirrel and the rabbit gamboled undisturbed on the fine greensward spread out at their feet, which was clear from undergrowth and smooth as a park, save where here and there a swampy bottom, loaded with vines and glistening with wild flowers, gave variety to the scene and cover to the game. Through it coursed a lovely little rivulet, which swept smoothly along around the roots of the alders and old trees, attended by the dragon-fly and many-colored birds and insects in its course, though now and then bubbling and disputing for the mastery with some envious rock or pertinacious log, in whose eddies the trout were quietly sleeping or playing among the bubbles. You could hardly advance a dozen yards, in the season, without having the blood started to your cheek by the sudden *w-h-ir* of the partridge or the quiet spring of the woodcock getting up at your feet.

SPIRIT—Ah-ha! Hendrick, ah-ha! are you there? are you there, my boy? "Take heed, dogs," take heed! Care, Sancho!—Dash, take heed! See!—tails and noses straight as a line—stiff as a ramrod. *Whir—whir*—bang—bang—one, two, th-r-e-e; bring 'em in, boys—bring 'em in. Load and on, ah-ha! Spirit of Nimrod! how delicious at the evening supper those delicate white breasts, scored with the gridiron, sprinkled knowingly with pepper and salt, flanked with the white bread and golden butter, the honest mealy potatoes bursting from their russet jackets, and the dark brown Mocha swimming with cream, sending forth its rich aroma.

HENDRICK.—Ay, ay—but the trout, too, the trout, my Spirit. Quick! look into this deep pool here, just out of the eddy. Whist! here, here, in the shade of this oak. Peer down into the deep, dark hollow at its feet, around its gnarled and fantastic roots; do you see him? do you see? How beautifully the gold and purple colors glitter! how motionlessly still is the head, the slight movement of the fin. the wary motion of the tail—a three-pounder, by the Goddess Diana! Hist, hist! throw your fly lightly over him; let it fall quietly on the surface; ay! now he rushes from his reverie, the head slowly turns, now the fins move more decidedly; now, now—one rapid whirl of the tail, and, ha-ha! —he rests on the earthen platter at the other end of the table. Allow me to help you, my dear fellow, to—egad!

we are at a regular Barmecide's feast; this will never do—a glass of "Chateau" with you in reality, my boy.

SPIRIT (*smacks his lips*)—There's no Barmecide in this, though, Hendrick.

HENDRICK—True for you, my Spirit. But "those same men in Buckram"—I have got more to say about those same snakes. When the western States began to be settled, the New Englanders, as usual, were foremost among the pioneers. There was a man in the same village that we have been speaking of, who pulled up stakes in the autumn, shouldered his ax and rifle, and, with his wife and baby, trudged off to Ohio. He settled upon the "grant," and, building a shanty, proceeded incontinently to level the forest around him. Now, in his economy of labor, he had erected his cottage against the side of a large rock, where, by leaving a hole in his roof, he saved the trouble of building a chimney; but, unconsciously and unfortunately for him, a certain colony of sage rattlesnakes had their den under, and held the same rock, by right of prior occupancy. As the weather was cool, they remained very quiet in their den, the fire of the woodman, for his cooking, being built upon the stones outside of the cottage door; but as it became cold, one night, in the absence of her husband, the wife built a fire against the side of the rock, and retired to bed with her child. Something aroused her from sleep, when, rising to look around, she saw the whole floor of the hut covered with the reptiles, awakened from their dormancy by the heat of the fire, writhing and hissing and crawling about with frightful vivacity; and what was worse, between her and the door, and some already crawling up upon the bed. Fortunately, there was a small attic cockloft above her, into which, by the aid of a ladder leading to it, she was able to crawl, where, with her child in her arms, she watched the scene below in comparative safety. But here a new cause of alarm seized her: should her husband return, as she expected, he would enter the cabin, and, before he was aware of the new denizens, be stung to death. She succeeded, however, in making a hole through the logs of the roof, and, patiently waiting his return, was able to give him, from the prison, a timely caution as to the state of affairs in the home department. The honest woodman ascended the roof of the shanty, and soon, with his axe, relieved his wife from her confinement, and then, setting fire to the hut, destroyed its meager contents and the snakes together.

SPIRIT—Well, for my part, I would as lief take the devil by the tail as a snake, but I have seen those Southern boys catch them as they ran, as they would a whiplash, and snap off their heads.

HENDRICK—So would I. I abhor the very sight of a snake, and had I any doubts as to my legitimate descent from Mother Eve, they would be dissipated by my innate antipathy to the reptile race.* But speaking of catching snakes reminds me of a good story that my friend D—— tells of himself. He was at the time, in his vocation as engineer, employed in the construction of the South Carolina Railroad. One day, in Charleston, a naturalist, showing him his collection, among other specimens of the serpent

---

* Nevertheless, it is a fact equally humiliating and true, that the idolatrous worship of this loathsome reptile has always obtained in enormous proportions in the human family. His temples were cylindrical, and were called OB–EL–IS–KA, or *The Temple of the Serpent God*, hence our word *obelisk*.

tribe, pointed to one of a very venomous character, which he said he was anxious to obtain alive, as he wished to make a drawing of it before the colors faded (as they do immediately after the life is extinct), at the same time begging D——, should he fall in with it in the woods, to capture and bring it in to him unhurt. D—— very naturally suggested that a serpent of that character was more to be admired than handled. But the doctor, himself an enthusiast in his profession, assured him that nothing was more easy than to secure him. He had simply to cut a forked stick, and placing its crotch over the snake's head, take him by the neck just behind, in which position he would be perfectly harmless. D——, a few days after, in the woods, came across the snake in question, and proceeded straightway to follow the doctor's directions; cut the forked stick, and, approaching the sleeping reptile, placed the crotch over his head, and then, putting down his thumb and finger, secured him, *secundum artem*, as the doctor had suggested. Letting go the stick, the snake was in an instant coiled around his arm, so tight as to be absolutely painful, but at the same time, it must be acknowledged, effectually prevented from biting. A moment's reflection was sufficient to show D—— that he was in a very respectable fix—that he had got to hold on to his snakeship till death did them part, or run the chance of making his exit from this sublunary sphere with the only consolation

> "As up to Heaven he went
> Of crying—'cru*el*, cru*el*, cru*el* sar*pent*.'"

So he turned about, commenced trotting as fast as he could (for he was on foot) three miles back to Charleston, to deliver to his friend, the Doctor, his much-desired specimen.

The upshot of the business was, that by the time he had got to town, what with eagerness to secure the prize and trepidation lest he should be stung, the miniature representative of Satan was choked to death, and my friend pretty effectually cured of any more snake captures.

[SCIPIO *and* DINAH *seen looking around the corner of the piazza, gazing intently at* "THE SPIRIT."]

SPIRIT—
> "Hah!
> By the pricking of my thumbs,
> Something wicked this way comes."

SCIPIO to DINAH—I say, Dinah! dat's him as Massa Hendrick calls "de Spirit." Golly! Dinah, he no more like de spirits in old times, than nothing at all. *Whar* he big horns? *Whar* he claws? *Whar* he long tail? and *whar* he great flaming eyes? And see, Dinah, he smoke 'bacca 'stead o' brimstone!

SPIRIT (*suddenly turning, descries the negroes; throws himself into an attitude*)—
> "Angels and ministers of grace *defend* us,
> Be ye spirits of health, or goblins damned,—
> Bring ye airs from Heaven, or blast from Hell,—
> *Why* come ye in such questionable shape?
> Say, *why* is this? *Wherefore?* What should we do?

SCIPIO—Golly! Massa?

SPIRIT—
> "Avaunt and quit my sight—
> ————There is no speculation in those
> Eyes of thine. Thy bones are marrowless.
> Avaunt, I say."

SCIPIO—Hi! Dinah. (*Exit precipitately Scipio and Dinah*).

SPIRIT (*laughing*)—Ha—ha—ha!

> "So, being gone,"
> "Richard is himself again."

HENDRICK—Ho, ho, ho! Egad, you have frightened half a dozen years out of the blacks.

SPIRIT—Well, Hendrick, there's an end to all things, white and black. One more glass, my boy, and I must be off.

HENDRICK—Never think of it, my dear fellow; you don't stir. We must make a night of it. There's a capital bed and an indifferent good supper for you within.

SPIRIT—I cannot, Sachem, I cannot. I must be at the Opera to-night, "come what, come may," and I have just one hour to do ten miles and dress before the curtain rises.

HENDRICK—Well, if you must, you must. "Welcome the coming, speed the parting guest." But one more toast before you go. No heel taps; fill with old " Farquar," to the brim, boy, to the brim! Here's to the " Bayonets and Boarding pikes"—the gallant boys of the Army and Navy—health and success to them!

SPIRIT—With all my soul, not forgetting the Dragoons, "with their long swords, saddles, bridles," (*tossing off his wine*). Holloa! Scip'! you image of Satan, bring round those horses. Ay! you are there, you black villain, are you? Ah, ha! my beauties. (*Ascends the box, takes the ribbons, gives a flourish with his whip, the extreme length of the lash coming round with peculiar grace upon the rear of Scipio, who jumps up, clapping his hand to the aggrieved part, but catches with a broad grin with the other, the half dollar tossed in the air.*) Good bye, Hendrick, I'm off. Hey! babies! (*the horses spring forward.*)

HENDRICK—There he goes, off like a whirlwind. Good bye, old fellow! How the sand flies! One hundred to one he shows his back to everything on the road. Ay, ay! he's a right good fellow; no cant and no humbug.

[*Exit Hendrick.*]

SPIRITIANA.—NO. II.

WINTER.

By my faith! 'tis a good world, and a brave world, and a jolly world; and they be knaves and varlets that say it be not.—*Master Peter.*

HENDRICK'S *Cottage at the Narrows, Long Island. Ground covered with snow; a handsome light blue sleigh, with voluminous wolf and buffalo robes filling the interior and falling out over the sides and runners, and four beautiful bloods in the traces; bays with coal-black leaders, covered with foam, at the door. Seated within it, muffled in furs, the one holding the ribbons tall and slender, and the other with the never-failing cigar in his mouth, broad-shouldered and manly, the* " TALL

Son" and "Tom Jones" *bound and accoutered for a sleigh ride; the former, rising on his feet, hails the house.*)

Tall Son—Hilla—ho!—house—ho—house! Wake up, Hendrick! Hilla—ho! Scip! you black old rascal, crawl out here—crawl out!

(*The door suddenly opens; a black face projects itself for an instant and as suddenly withdraws, the door closing after it, and Scipio runs hastily to Hendrick's study with—*)

Scipio—"Golly! Massa. Here's Massa "Spirit" and another gemman at the door in dere sleigh, der noses as red as roses and de horses all in a lather!

Hendrick—The deuce they are! (*Jumps up, kicks over the stool on which his legs are resting, throws his book upon the table and incontinently places himself at the door.*) Ah! ha! "Spirit"—Tom! boys, I am right glad to see you. Come—get out and warm yourselves. Let Scipio take the horses round to the stable out of the cold. Come in, boys; come in!

Spirit—Can't, Hendrick; can't, 'pon my honor. We are bound on a tour of observation. Going to wake up K—— at the Fort down here, and then round by New Utrecht and Bath and Flatbush home. You see old Sol yonder is throwing sidelong glances at us even now; he is so impatient at this season of the year to get on his night-cap. For a gentleman that has so much to do he gets up confoundedly late and goes to bed unreasonably early.

Hendrick—Come in, a few minutes at least, and let your horses have a chance to breathe.

Spirit—Well, we'll spare a few moments; come, Tom.

Hendrick—That's right. Scipio, throw blankets over the horses. Come, come in here, into my study—warm and snug. Throw off your caps and overcoats. There you are —a pair of beautiful Caryatides to my fire-place. " May your shadows never be less." Tom, my dear boy, I'm right glad to see you!

TOM—Glad to see *you*. (*Puff—puff—puff.*)

SPIRIT—*Entre-nous*, Tom is somewhat silent. He took a pretty stiff tankard of hot whisky punch coming down, and the effect of the unusual potation in the cold weather is, I fear, a decided inroad on his pia mater. He has been very taciturn for the last half hour.

HENDRICK—Well, isn't this a glorious scene around? Old Winter in all his rigor and all his savage beauty.

SPIRIT—Yes, " by the frosty Caucassus!" Summer's gone—its leaves and its flowers, its birds and soft breezes— and old Dame Nature, like a true Chinese, has donned her robes of *white* mourning for her.

TOM—Do your Chinese wear black of white color?

SPIRIT—Even so, great Thomas. We, the " outside barbarians," alone use the sombre in token of our grief.

TOM—Well, well; I say nothing. I can smoke, though; they can't object to that?

SPIRIT—No! by the flaming nostrils of Fashion! no, Tom—that they cannot. Your Turk and your Arab, your American Indian and your New Hollander, your Englishman and your Frenchman, alike enjoy the fragrant weed; all smoke. " Vanity of vanities," saith the preacher ; nevertheless, all smoke. (*Spies a sealed envelope lying on the table, addressed to* " THE SPIRIT.") Egad! Hendrick, what's this? Shall I be my own post-boy and pocket it, " postage free?"

HENDRICK—E'en as you like. It's only a sketch I was about sending you for a corner of " The Spirit."

Spirit—" Business before pleasure," as " Mad Anthony" used to say to his soldiers. " Wax! by your leave." Tom, I'll read this *here;* 'twill save the necessity of doing it next week. (*Reads.*)

> I pass like night from land to land,
> I have strange power of speech;
> So soon as in his face I see,
> I know the man that must hear me,
> To him my tale I teach.
> —*Rime of ye Ancient Mariner.*

COTTAGE AT THE NARROWS.

Start not, my dear " Spirit," at the heading of this communication. But here I am in some measure embargoed in my snug little cottage. The snow is piled in drifts around my windows; the old willows are bending under their hoary loads; the ocean, dark and gloomy, roused by the tempest, is lashing himself into fearful wrath; and the vessels, like frightened birds, with reefed sails, are scudding in every direction for a harbor. The blacks are nodding a dreary dialogue over the dying embers on the kitchen hearth. The Newfoundlander, with nose between his paws, at my feet, is fast asleep, unconscious alike of all ills that do afflict the family, canine or human. The horses, in their warm, well-littered stalls in the stable, are contentedly munching at their oats, while the little terrier, with eyes like blazing coals, is standing guard over a new-found rat-hole, whereupon, if his ratship pops his head, he will i' the instant be " dead for a ducat—dead." And here am I, before my cheerful fire, lolling in my great arm-chair, suddenly aroused by the notion that to drive away *ennui* I'll seize my pen and give you

A PEEP OVER THE BLUE RIDGE.

> LEP.—"You have strange serpents there?
> ANT.—"Ay, Lepidus.
> LEP.—Your serpent of Egypt is bred now
> Of your mud, by the operation of your
> Sun! So is your crocodile."—*Ant. and Cleo.*

WHOA, my beauties!—soh, boys, soh! Them there's what we call *mountains*, in old Virginy," exclaimed the good-natured stage-driver, as he pulled up his leaders on the summit of a pass on the road.

It was in the decline of a summer's afternoon in the month of June, that we thus halted for a moment on the top of one of the high hills, in the vicinity of the *White Sulphur Springs*, of Virginia, to catch a glimpse of the Alleghanies, as they rolled away like waves of verdure in the distance, their huge masses melting in the horizon like dark clouds, while the atmosphere above and around them hung still and breathless, and pure as the sapphire. We gazed upon the scene, and with reluctance tore ourselves from the view, as the snorting leaders, "touched up," sprang forward again on their journey. A few miles further, suddenly turning an abrupt precipice in a valley of great elevation, between the mountains, but still below us, burst on our view the little fairy, "*White Sulphur*"—the Saratoga of the South and the West, the place of our destination. On four sides of a hollow square, of perhaps the eighth of a mile in length, the rows of cottages (or cabins, as they are called) were glistening cheerfully in the evening sun, in bright relief against the dark background of forest, which in their rear immediately overhung them. Connected by long piazzas, they looked out upon the square, which was laid out in a verdant lawn, divested of trees, save here and there some of the old patriarchs of the forest, huge oaks and chestnuts, left for shade or ornament, and under whose shade were lounging groups of visitors. At the extreme end, under its canopy, rested the Spring, the health-restoring waters that furnish us its great attraction (an idea of the taste and smell of which any of your sporting readers may have, by washing his gun-barrels and smelling the contents), while in the center was the great dining-hall and ball-room. The line of cottages were so arranged that at intervals a higher edifice with columns added to the architectural effect. The rows connected by piazzas were designated by various names. There was "*Alabama Row*," where might be seen the bachelors and men without encumbrance, indulging themselves, indolently reclining with their cigars or their books, while beyond was "*Paradise Row*," specially designated for the ladies, with or without, as might be, their lords paramount, husbands, or brothers. *Louisiana Row*, *New York*, *Pennsylvania*, and *Georgia*, with other States, were duly represented, while far off in one corner was "*Wolf Row*," a sort of Alsatia, where the " roaring boys," the " babes of grace," and the " sporting men " (as the *gamblers* are called at the South) were quartered. Some of the stories that they told of the " carryings on " in that part of the premises evinced a queer state of morals, and to the actors in the scenes might have been, one would think, more exciting than agreeable ;

as, for instance, one drunken gambler going into the cabin of his next-door neighbor, with whom he had quarreled in the night, and pinning him to the pillow with his bowie-knife, calling for his "boy" to bring a light that "he might despatch the scoundrel." However, at the time we were there, the desperate characters had been driven from the place, and, inclosed with a fence, were two of the cabins which were leased to a leading gambler (who ran the risk of the law) and whose interest it was to keep off all of the same vocation as himself. There, if you chose, you might, under proper (?) introduction, be initiated, and furnished with Faro, Roulette, or any other of the instruments with which the votaries of fate seek to propitiate the fickle goddess. The proprietors of the Springs stated, in extenuation of this seeming impropriety, that in so doing the unsuspicious were protected against designing knaves, and that if others chose to go there, it was with their eyes open and at their own risk.

Mr. Cauldwell, the owner of the Springs, a venerable gentleman, was surrounded by nine sons, fine looking men, who luxuriated in lives of sylvan ease, and whose vocation seemed to be to kill the enemy, lolling in the summer days under the trees, or in their white dresses and huge sombreros, cigars in mouth, galloping on their blood horses over the adjoining country. In the summer, though hot and sultry at midday, at night and morning huge fires were required in the cabins, so cold and piercing was the high mountain temperature. Words can hardly describe the delicious sensation felt as the early morning air, loaded with the aroma of the forest, the pines and hemlocks, was inhaled on the opening of the cottage door; the exhilaration of champagne without its intoxication; and from early dawn till long into the morning the whole valley was one sea of melody. It appeared as if a million of aviaries were concealed under the mist, which always hangs on the mountains till dispelled by the sun; myriads of mocking-birds and other songsters, warbling their notes as if in an ecstasy of delight.

Deer and game were plenty, and in the season the Cauldwells made the forests ring with their cheers and hunt halloos, as they followed the hounds in full chase over the mountains.

The horses went for hours at full gallop up and down precipices, which would have knocked our Northern horses up in five minutes, but they were accustomed to it —their muscles rigid as iron; they would neither snort nor blow, but appeared to enjoy the excitement equally with their riders. The Cauldwells were all keen huntsmen, and had fine blood horses in their stables, and, what is not often found in the country, a full pack of hounds. It consisted of about fifty dogs, and when they opened on the mountains (or scented "vermin" prowling around their kennels) and "gave cry," their music would make everything ring again. Man has been designated as a laughing animal, a talking animal, a dressing animal, but judging from our experience he may as well be called a *lounging* animal, for with our cigars in our mouths, we used to loll day after day under those huge trees, merely withdrawing from the sun as it circled its daily course. Sometimes, indeed, we would take our guns, and wander off to the "deer-licks," sometimes with rod to tempt the speckled lordling of the brook; but we are bound to say that much of our time was dozed away in that same lazy style. Among so many collected from all parts of the world, as were always to be found there, and which were constantly changing, there was a sufficient variety of character to afford study and amusement. Among others there was one, a Frenchman, a naturalist, whose sole passion was the collection of reptiles; a snake was a jewel; frogs, toads, and spiders invaluable treasures; and his pockets and handkerchief, indiscriminately, the place of durance for his captives. His cabin was next to mine, and one night, aroused by sundry queer thumps and jumps and bounds, I went to ascertain the cause, and there found Roussall, with tongs in hand, jumping about in his shirt in pursuit of his victims, who by accident had got loose about the floor. Occasionally snapping his tongs, he would make captive a toad or a frog, consigning him to his place, but his more frequent abortive efforts were accompanied by "*Sacres*"[3] and "*Diables*" sufficient to have scared even Uncle Toby's regiment in Flanders. But speaking of snakes, it is an old saying, and as *I found*, worthy of all credence, that if a fact isn't such, then *"there ain't no snakes in Virginy,"* for snakes were in such abundance as I never had seen till then, from the old rattler, with his sixteen rattles, surely giving his enemy warning, down to the adder blind and moccasin. I recollect we one day made up a party to go down to a "Deer Lick," four or five miles distant from the Springs, where, lying in wait, concealed under what is called a "*blind*" (a heap of logs, or pile of brush), we might get a shot at the deer as they came down to drink. They have other ways of killing them, which, though picturesque, is little better than murder for the poor deer. In their "*night-hunting*," for instance, two of the hunters go out to the "licks" (brackish, slightly saline springs, where the animals, allured by the salt, come down to drink). One carries on his head a pan or brazier, on which are one or two lighted pine-knots, throwing a circle of light upon the surrounding darkness, rendering the hunter beneath it invisible, while his companion, standing behind him, rests his rifle upon his shoulder. The deer, attracted by the light, approaches to gaze, and the hunter draws sight at his leisure, directly between the two bright eye-balls, from which in the darkness the blaze is reflected. Of course the poor animal stands no chance, and the sharp whip-like crack of the rifle, as it for an instant resounds through the forest, is followed by one or two plunges, and the victim sinks in death. On the day that I allude to, a party of five of us went out with our guns, pioneered by one of the young Caldwells (they use shot guns, and load with twelve to sixteen buck shot). It was exceedingly hot, and as we wended our way through the forest, with the exception of the hum of an insect, and the occasional rap—rap—rap of the wood-pecker, as we saw for a moment his scarlet head and blue back circling some dead tree, all was perfectly silent and still. We followed our guide in Indian file, wending our way through gullies, climbing precipices, stumbling over the huge old trunks mouldering in rottenness where they had fallen, but from whose very decay young life was springing up in conflict with its relentless enemy.

Now stopping to pluck an azalia, geranium or laurel; now to gaze on the beauty of some star-like *nameless* flower— (who shall say that it was born to blush "*unseen*," while animal life in myriads swarms around, and while other senses than those of men may appreciate the goodness of the Creator in Nature's loveliness?)—when, as we neared the place of our destination, and approached the huge trees that overhung the "Lick," we heard a woodsman's axe resounding through the forest, and soon saw a brawny negro felling timber near the very spot. Of course all chance for sport was gone, as the deer, alarmed by the noise, would not approach his favorite haunts, but dive more deeply into the recesses of the forest. As we passed a swampy bottom on our route, one of my companions, who was just behind, called to me to turn. He pointed to the ground, and there, within a foot of where I had just passed, lay an enormous black-snake, fast asleep in his coil. We, of course, all stopped and surveyed him. He was unconscious of our presence until a slight noise was made to wake him, when in an instant his coil was contracted, his head and neck elevated, his eyes glistening and tongue playing like a forked flame from his mouth, turning now this, now that way, with the quickness of electricity, on every part of the group, ready to spring on the first aggressor. He did not attempt to fly, but in defiance abode the battle. I leveled my gun, and in another instant should have sent him to the realms of his great ancestor, the devil, when my arm was arrested by one of the Cauldwells, who begged me not to fire. "He will kill," said he, "a dozen rattlesnakes before the summer is over, and therefore the hunters never destroy them." There is an abiding enmity existing between the black and rattlesnakes, and in their conflicts death is the doom of one of them. Sometimes they will be for hours, watching each other's motions, as warily as two fencers, the black always on the offensive, the rattlesnake on the defence. The latter is slow and sluggish in his movements, and his power lies in his deadly venom, but the former is as quick as light.

The black-snake watches his opportunity, when by a sudden spring he can catch his opponent behind the neck, so that he cannot use his fangs, and in an instant his body is wound round and round his enemy, and tightened till every bone in his body is broken; but woe be to the black if he misses his aim; the headsman's axe is not more fatal to its victim, than the death that follows the fangs of his enemy as they are dashed up to the quick in his lithe form. In a few moments he is writhing helplessly before his foe, who quietly and grimly watches him from his coil as he writhes in the agonies of death. On this account there is between the hunter and the black snake a sort of truce, and the law, that "the heel of man shall bruise his head," in some measure does not obtain in the mountains of Virginia. We stood for a few moments gazing at the glistening serpent, which looked as if with the plaided monarch he would say

> "Come one, come all; this rock shall fly
> From its firm base, as soon as I;"

showing neither fear nor intention of flight. After we left, we turned when at a little distance, but there was the head still elevated and the coil unmoved. We passed the same place an hour after, but he had then withdrawn, probably to his den in some more dark and secluded place in the swamp. As we returned on our way through the clearings, supposing that we should meet with more basking in the sun, I said jokingly to a little negro boy who was with us, and who rejoiced in the name of Commodore Perry:— "Com., I'll give you a sixpence if you'll kill me a rattlesnake." "Yes, sir," promptly replied the little imp, "yes, sir; shall I bring him to your room, sir?" This was being taken at my word with a vengeance, and as the idea of having a dead rattlesnake in my bed-chamber was a little too much for my nerves, I was fain to back out of my bargain.

But there is a time for all things, which reminds me that it is time to end this epistle; and so, my dear "Spirit," although you are not of the class of "black spirits and white, red spirits and gray," summoned to mingle the ingredients in the charmed caldron; nor of those called by Owen Glendower "from the vasty deep;" nor of that class of "*aerial divils* or *sprites*" which, according to old Burton, "are commanded by *Beelzebub*, and do so fill the air, that the air be not more full of flies in summer than it be of those same invisible divils;" neither the "spirit" of the grape that cost poor Cassio his lieutenancy; nor the spirit that humbugged poor old Faust; but a right-down whole-souled "Spirit;" a sort of "*Diable Boiteaux*," an "*Asmodeus*," albeit without crutches. I will now whisper farewell.

SPIRIT—Well, Hendrick, whatever demerit your sketch may have, it can't be said that you didn't take things easy.

TOM—(*waking up*).—Eh! What?

SPIRIT—Ha! ha! ha! asleep, by Juno!

TOM—Faith! I believe I must plead guilty to the charge; this cold makes me drowsy.

HENDRICK—Most likely. Come, boys, now that you are warm, let's have a glass of Burgundy or Madeira together.

SPIRIT—No, no! No wine now. It's bad to ride on in the cold.

TOM—No; that abominable punch has made my brain reel already worse than poor Cassio's.

HENDRICK—Well, then, Dinah's coffee-urn is singing in the parlor; let's have a cup of that. I confess I am no friend to Bacchus in any shape (albeit, abhorring the *cant* of temperance); his libations cloud the brain, and take away the fine tone of intellectual enjoyment. I wish in my heart that Satan had the whole vintage, from Adam down, stowed away in his infernal dominions; thereby many a fine fellow might be enjoying life as Heaven intended it should be, a boon, instead of sinking *brutalized* into an early grave.

Tom—You are right, Hendrick; I respond with all my heart to your sentiments, and feel not a little annoyed that I have accidentally given a proof to the contrary.

Spirit—Phoo! man, accidents *will* happen in the best regulated families. But, my dear boy, we can't stay a moment longer. We have got, at the end of our ride, you know, to cross that confounded ferry, and the river is full of ice. So we must be off, and that in a hurry. So good-bye to you, old boy; good-bye.

(Tom *and the* "Spirit" *jump into the sleigh; the* "Spirit," *straightning the ribbons, gives a slight circle around the ears of the leaders with his long lash, who rear bolt upright on their hind legs, with a simultaneous snort, their bells jingling a sea of melody, and in another moment, dashing forward, the sleigh, its horses and riders, are out of sight, leaving the cottage and the winter's blast far, far behind them.*)

Hendrick—(*Going into the house, stops, and turns*)—Well, Scip, what are you lingering and standing there for, scratching your head, and looking with such profound gravity into the snow bank? What wondrous crotchet is in possession of that sapient head of yours now?

Scipio—Massa, I was tinking—but p'r'aps Massa no like what old nigger was t'inking about.

Hendrick—Oh! yes—out with it.

Scip—Well, Massa, I was tinking wedder Massa "Spirit" any relation to de debil.

HENDRICK—" Relation to the d——l?" What do you mean?

SCIP—Why, my old woman—old Dinah—say as how all de spirits is relations, jis like brack folks. Now, if dis gemmen as comes here is real Spirit, den, in course, he's relation to de old Sarpent.

HENDRICK—Ha! ha! ha! that is a question too deep for me to solve, Scipio; but in with you, and tell Dinah to get my supper. (*Exit Hendrick.*)

SCIPIO—(*Slowly moving around to the kitchen door, in a reflective mood.*)—He drives like de debil, anyhow; and he right good judge of horse-flesh, too. Golly! dem brack leaders—how dey shine! dere nostrils was like burning coals, wid smoke blowing out of 'em, (*stopping and scratching his head,*) dat nigh bay on de pole, do', he was *de* beauty; he's what dis child call "zactly right." What a match he make for our Charley; dis brack man must have de felicity to curry dat horse. I tell Massa Hendrick dat de Major gitting weak in de knees, and we mus' hab him for a match. Dat's it—I—

HENDRICK—(*within.*)—Scipio—Scipio!

SCIPIO—Golly! yes, Massa—coming, sir—coming. (*Exit Scipio.*)

THE DEAD MAN'S SERMON;

OR, BILL BAXTER THE COXSWAIN'S YARN.

AN AUTHENTIC INCIDENT ON BOARD THE UNITED STATES FRIGATE PRESIDENT IN THE YEAR 1812.

"THE OLD WAGON."

IT was on a delicious afternoon in the month of July that, after making a tour of its circuit, I drew up my horse on the highest ridge of Staten Island to take a survey of the noble picture that lay on all sides extended around me. The sun had so far declined in his course as to throw the softest lights and richest shadows on the surrounding scenery; and the rolling and undulating hills, covered with a carpet of verdure of the hue of emerald, glittered with the snow-white cottages and villas scattered upon their surface. On my right the ocean stretched in majesty, his broad expanse a rising hill of waters, till reaching the blue of the horizon it mingled into one, the gallant ships swanlike floating on his bosom.

The fortifications on the Long Island shore slumbered in grim repose, the flags hanging supinely from their staffs above the ramparts, and the green fields and harvest-ripened farms smiled in beauty as they stretched onward to the city of Brooklyn, whose mansions, resting on her terraced Heights, were throwing back from all their casements the rays of the declining sun in quivering sheets of gold. New York, rising from its bed of waters, appeared a fairy city springing from the deep; while the lordly Hudson, escorted by the Palisades, coursed gallantly on his northern journey. On the left the plains of New Jersey rested in sleepy stillness, guarded by their undulating mountains; while on the west one great sea of forest verdure extended to the horizon; the Raritan, like a band of silver, glittering in its breaks and intervals as it wended its circuitous and serpentlike course.

Taking the panorama for all in all, it was the most captivating and beautiful creation that He who is the fountain of all goodness and benevolence has permitted me to gaze upon. At my feet the cheerful snow-white buildings of the Quarantine were throwing long shadows across their verdant lawns (a paradise to the poor sick mariner released from the darkness and confinement of his weary lair in the dank and dirty forecastle); and anchored on the water were vessels of all flags and burthens, from the light Bermudean shallop, with its oranges and pines, to the proud and richly laden Indiaman; but high above all, and moored at aristocratic distance from the rest, towered a dark and lofty ship, that perfection of naval architecture, a frigate of the largest class, whose stars and stripes, languidly floating at the gaff, proclaimed her nation.

I sat for some time absorbed in delight, the silence unbroken save by the occasional snort and pawing of my steed, who I doubt not likewise enjoyed the scene, till the great orb of molten gold in the western horizon, o'erhung and draped with a gorgeous canopy of clouds, slowly descending, warned me that Night's sable ministers were near, and that I must cease to linger. Putting spurs to my horse (a figurative expression, for my bonny bay required no such argument), I was soon at the landing. Dismounting, I threw the reins across the saddle and prepared with all due philosophy, as the steamer had just left, to wait her return to take me again to the city. I had the prospect of waiting for some time; so, lighting my cigar—thanks to Pandora that she left us *that* blessing!—I slowly sauntered down the pier and, leaning against a spile, puffed away in silent contemplation.

In the far distance the revolving beacons at Sandy Hook at measured intervals threw forth their warning fires like angel-guides to the home-bound mariner, and the "Yo! heave-o!" from the shipping, rendered soft and flute-like by the distance, floated gently and sweetly on the summer atmosphere.

While I thus stood absorbed, a slight jar against the pier aroused me, and looking over I saw a man-of-war's barge lying alongside, the sailors, some asleep upon the thwarts and others lolling in various attitudes, as dictated by convenience or caprice; while just beyond, partly concealed by a pile of wood, were two of her crew, seated on the pier, whom I had not before observed. Although the twilight was rapidly thickening I could see that one was old and weather-beaten, his locks grizzled by the hand of Time and his countenance channeled and scarred into the stern expression which long conflict with storm and tempest always leaves behind; while the other, with large whiskers encircling a handsome, dare-devil face, was much his junior. They were both dressed in man-of-war rig—white trousers and blue jackets, the collars, worked with a foul anchor, turned over their shoulders, exposing their bronzed chests and throats, while around the broad ribbon on their jaunty sennet hats was inscribed the name of their frigate, "The United States." Seeing the name, I involuntarily exclaimed aloud: "There, then, is the 'Old Wagon!'" the sobriquet by which the ship is known in the navy. On hearing my voice the men turned for a moment, but perceiving that I did not address them they again turned and paid no further attention to me.

After some moments the younger of the two broke the silence by saying:

"What water does they carry out over the bar of this here port, Baxter?"

Ruminating on his quid with true nautical deliberation, the elder, after a pause, slowly replied: "By the *old* channel half less four; at slack water four fathom; by this here new channel as Lieutenant Gedney has found five fathom at full tide and four fathom at low water; at the neap maybe half less six."

A pause ensued, when the younger again spoke: "I've hear'n say that they can take a line-of-battle ship, guns, water and all, out by this here new channel at any time o' tide."

"So they say," said the old man; "and it would have been well if one of the ships as has carried the stars and stripes in times gone by had known that ere channel. There is one sea-faring man not fur from here as would have been saved thereby from an English prison."

"And who is that?" asked the younger sailor.

"It is a man as hangs his hammock on board that 'ere frigate riding at anchor yonder, and is coxswain of the first cutter lying alongside this here pier; the man as is talking with you; launched into the world by the old folks with the name of William Baxter on his starn."

"Better known forward and on the gun-deck," retorted the other, "by the name of Grumbling Bill."

"Ay, ay—very like," said the other. "A gray head has no more respect shown to it nowadays, nor half as much, as an unshaved boy. Times isn't as they used to was."

Saying this, he slowly rose, and taking a short stump pipe from his pocket deliberately filled it with tobacco, and advancing toward me, touching his hat, asked whether he mought be so bold as to ask for a light.

"Certainly," said I; "but I have another cigar here; let me give you that."

"No, no, sir; many thanks, many thanks," replied the veteran. "I hopes I've been long enough in the sarvice to know my place. Pipes for the fo'castle, cigars for the cabin; pipes for the men, cigars for the officers. I likes every man to know his station; I've been aboard ship long enough to larn the valu' of disci-*pline*."

Somewhat amused at the old man's notions of propriety, I remarked: "It would be well if we had a little more of it on shore here."

"You may well say that," said he. "Things is getting to a pretty pass here; there's no respect into the times, sir. I'm hard aboard o' seventy year, and can see at the end of every cruise that the people is more snarcy and houdacious than they was before. Every man 'long shore here is master and no man mate. D'ye see, sir, I think the only place for a decent man nowadays is aboard ship, where he'll see the valu' of disci-*pline*. There every man has to toe the mark. If he does his duty he knows he desarves well of his country, and gets the good will of his officers; if he don't, he's triced up and gets the cat till he larns. I should like to know, sir, now, what would become of the sarvice without disci-*pline*. There's the 'Old Wagon' yonder. I've known the Old Man* come on deck at midnight and order the officer of the deck to beat to quarters; every man asleep in his hammock save the watch, and in *five* minutes from the first tap of the drum the crew have been at quarters, guns loose, stanchions knocked away, magazines opened; and in *eight*, hammocks stowed, decks sanded, the ship ready for action, and a gun fired from each division; every man at his post, from the powder-monkey with his leathern cartridge-bucket at the magazine hatch to the surgeon with his knife and tourniquets in the cock-pit. That's what I call disci-*pline*. What would become of that 'ere ship, I say, sir, if she was in the hands of land-lubbers? These here same shore people is mighty brave, sir, when there's no danger, and always ready to cry out for war; and d'ye see, I think there's nothing that will bring them to their senses but the d—d good licking they'll get when it comes; a parcel (*puff*) of bragging (*puff*) fools, always ready to get up a muss (*puff*), and then leave the steady men to get them out of it." (*Puff—puff—puff.*)

* The Captain is always called by the sailors " the Old Man."

"You appear very familiar with this port," said I; "you were just giving the water on the bar."

"Ay, sir," he replied; "the water on that 'ere bar I shall have cause to remember the longest day I have to live. 'Cause why?—that and another carcumstance as is not to be mentioned caused me to be made prisoner to a British fleet last war."

"Indeed!" said I. "You were, then, engaged last war?"

"You may say that, sir," said he, "and tell no lie, if some half a dozen actions and as many wounds may be called being engaged. I was in the United States frigate 'President,' Commodore Stephen Decatur, when she struck on that 'ere bar, last war, and knocked her cutwater athwartships, thereby causing one of the fastest ships in the service to sail but little better nor a Dutch Logger; and the 'Mainmast of the American Navy,'* as we called him, to strike his flag to a British fleet. Howsomever, if there had been fifty feet of water on that bar 'twould have been all the same. A carcumstance turned up in her cruise before as took the luck out of her and rendered her an onsafe craft, in my judgment, to go to sea in in time of war. When a dead man comes to life, a'ter he's been dead three hours, and preaches a sarmint and calls for a drink, 'tain't a thing as befalls a craft for nothing. No, no; a dead man don't come back into this here world for nothing, that's sartain." And he puffed away with redoubled energy.

"Did such a thing occur on board the 'President?'" said I. "I never heard of it."

"Ay, sir, very like," replied he. "You could have been

* The sobriquet given to Decatur by the seamen.

but a child then, and the thing was hushed up; but 'twan't no use. I say it caused Commodore Stephen Decatur to strike his flag to a British fleet."

"Why, Baxter," said the younger sailor, "I have hear'n say she was took by the 'Endymion.'"

"'Endymion' be d—d!" growled the old sailor. "John Bull would have to keep a double gang of ship carpenters if that 'ere was the way he conquered his inimy. The 'Endymion' got her saarce, and that hot enough, too, before the rest of the British fleet come up. Took by the 'Endymion!' D—n their impudence! They are so used to beating the French (as are not by nature a sea-faring people, but good enough for them on the land any day), and lying about it a'terwards, that I shouldn't wonder next if they said the 'President' didn't make no fight at all, and that the skipper went aboard in his gig to ask them to take possession. Took by the 'Endymion!' Why, we whipped her before the rest of the fleet came within gun-shot. Her rigging, spars and sails was cut to pieces, and she drifted a complete wrack, firing guns only at long intervals; and we could have taken possession of her, but, bating the honor of the thing, it wouldn't have been no use, for, our firing having deadened the wind, the rest of the squadron, the 'Majestic,' 'Pomone' and 'Tenedos,' came up hand over hand, choosing their positions on our quarters and pitching their old iron into us by the ton. So the commander hadn't nothing more to do, to save the spillin' of blood, but to surrender. Took by the 'Endymion!' Why, when we had to yaw, to avoid the fire of the chase, she could have raked us a dozen times; but d—n the shot did she fire! We'd 'ave whipped her with one watch and sarved out the rest if they had come on one at a time. The 'President's' men was grit;* and as for Commodore Stephen Decatur, there was no more dodge about him than there was about the mainmast. But, as I was saying, it wasn't no use; the luck was out of the ship, and she had to strike."

"But what was the circumstance you allude to?" said I. "You spoke of a dead man's coming to life."

"Well, sir," said he, slowly knocking the ashes from his pipe and carefully replacing it in his pocket, looking furtively about him at the same time and speaking low, "this here ain't the place nor the time of night I likes to speak of such things; 'cause why? Jim Austin's sperit may be haunting here away now, for aught I know, as he hailed from this here city of New York. But the carcumstance as I have mentioned occurred on board of her in her last cruise under Commodore Rodgers; it was in that very cruise. D'ye see, sir, we had been out a long time, and scoured the Atlantic and Nor' Sea from one end to the other; but somehow, and it wasn't the fault of the old commodore, neither, we hadn't the luck to fall in with the inimy, and had naither a chance for fighting nor for prize-money ; but as the cruise was nigh up we was on our way home, feeling mighty small to be sneaking into port without having fired a shot in anger nor burnt powder save in scaling the guns, when the carcumstance occurred. D'ye see, sir, there was a man on board of the ship from this same place, New York, by the name of James Austin, captain of the mizzen-top—a good seaman but a bad man, and when he had his grog aboard as profane and blasphemous a wretch as ever stepped foot on a tarred plank, but nevertheless a right bold and daring fel-

* A favorite expression of Decatur's when praising his officers.

low. Well, sir, somehow he gets this here consumption, and bleeds every day more or less from the lungs, and gets weaker and weaker, till the doctor claps him on the sick-list.

"So he gets worse and worse every day, till the doctor he condemns him as unseaworthy and turns him over to the chaplain so that he mought patch him up for his last cruise. The good man did the best he could, but d—l a bit could he make out of Jim; for while he was talking to him Jim would curse the loblolly boys about him in the sick-bay the same as if he hadn't his clearance papers all made out for the great ocean of etarnity. The chaplain told the first lieutenant (when he was in the bay one day to see that all the sick was comfortably taken care of), shaking his head and looking sorrowfully at Jim, says he, ' He fears death, sir, no more nor a drunken sleep, and is desperately mortal.' He made a kind of merit of being houdacious and hardened. As he was growing weaker and weaker, and almost suffocated by his cough, the doctor orders him, as it was hot and confined in the sick-bay, to be slung up in his hammock near the main-deck ports, so that he mought have the air; and there he was, off and on, for two or three weeks, sinking day by day; but the oath was always uppermost with him, and though his anchor was all ready to let go into the quick-sands of death he was just as wicked and profane in his whisper as he used to be when he answered the hail of the officer of the deck, in the voice of a bull, from the mizzen-top.

"Well, sir, one morning airly a sail hove in sight, and we soon made her out from the masthead to be a man-of-war, and before long from the decks, a heavy, double-banked frigate, with two reg'lar rows of teeth. I'll tell you what, sir, every man's eyes brightened up on board of that 'ere ship, from the niggers at the coppers to the commodore in his cabin. The drum beat to quarters and the ship was made ready for action; and great glee was there among the men, and congratulations—I say, Bill Blunt, ain't that 'ere the word the officers uses?—and congratulations among the officers that we shouldn't be obliged to sneak into port without having fired a shot. In course, Jim's hammock, with all the other lumber, was stowed away, and Jim placed out of harm's way with the rest of the sick. Says the surgeon to him, says he, 'My man, if we go into action, I charge you (for Jim was always ready for fight), I charge you not to leave your cot, for any exertion that you may make will start your lungs; your life will not be worth ten minutes' purchase; you'll bleed to death on the spot.' Jim said nothing, but his eyes brightened and a faint smile played across his pale lips; so the surgeon telled the lieutenant a'terwards. We clapt on all sail in chase, and so did the strange ship; but the 'President' then being in luck, the carcumstance at that time not having occurred, gradually overhauled her, and getting near enough sent a couple of shot across her forefoot to make her tell her name. Shiver my timbers if I ever seen so many long faces aboard a Yankee frigate as showed themselves of a sudden as the French flag run up and floated in the wind from her gaff. 'Stop my grog!' growled old Albro, the surly boatswain; (and Albro wasn't a man as stuck at breaking the third commandment, for every other word was with him an oath; but he never used *that* oath 'cept when he was excited) 'May my grog be etarnally stopped!' growled he between his clenched teeth, 'if it ain't a d—d Johnny Crapo after all! D—n me, if I was the skipper if I wouldn't make the Mounseer make a fight of it or co-arce him to send aboard a couple of butts of old cog-ni-ac to pay for the deception.'

"So all hopes of a fight and prize money having vanished like scud before a Nor'wester, we had nothing to do but secure the guns ag'in and make the best of a bad bargain. But as for Jim Austin, what does he do but—at the report of the first gun that was fired—what does he do but come crawling up, and, as the surgeon telled him, hardly reaches his gun before he falls, the blood gushes from his mouth and nostrils, and they takes him below, bleeding to death.

"Well, all was made snug ag'in, and the men got their breakfast, and the French ship and Jim's case was nigh on forgotten, when, as the commodore and first lieutenant was walking up and down the quarter-deck, one of the surgeon's mates comes up, touches his hat to the lieutenant and says, 'I report James Austin, sir, captain of the mizzen-top, aged forty-two years, dead of consumption at four bells.' 'Very well,' says the lieutenant; '*make it so;* let the purser square his accounts, and have him ready for burial an hour before sun-down this evening.' Now there, sir, you see the valu' of disci-*pline;* a man ain't allowed to be dead, nor the hour struck, till the officer of the watch says, '*Make it so.*' Well, sir, the day wore on; the men had got their dinners, and the officer of the watch was leaning ag'in' the capstan, with his trumpet under his arm, when the surgeon comes up and says in a low voice, 'There's something very queer going on below, sir. That man Austin, that was reported dead this morning, has come to life ag'in, and is sitting bolt upright in his hammock, addressing the men, who are crowding around him, and in language and terms so different from what was usual with him that I can hardly believe it's the same man.' 'I'll go below with you,' said the lieutenant, 'and see into the matter. He may do mischief among the crew with his nonsense.' So they went below and made their way for'ard to the sick-bay, which was surrounded by the men, crowding around and reaching over each others' shoulders; and there, as the surgeon said, sat the dead man, as white and cold and stiff as a marble statute, preaching a sarmint to the men. It warn't long before it came to the commodore's ears that there was something unusual going on below, and he was about to send to inquire into the matter, when the surgeon himself comes up and says, ' Commodore, Austin has sent for *you;* he says he has one word for *you*.'

" ' Pish !' says the commodore, as was his way when he was vexed ; ' what does the man want with *me?*' 'He says he has come from the dead, and has a message for you, commodore, and begs that you will indulge him for the moment that he has to remain.' ' Well,' said the commodore, ' I will go, lest he should work nonsense among the men, and turn my gun-deck into a Quaker meeting.'

" So he goes down to the sick-bay (and it was a great condescension for the commodore to go down at the call of a foremast man, dead or alive), and there sits Austin, bolt upright in his hammock, white as death, the surgeons each side of him, one holding his wrist and the other with his hand on his heart; and they said there was no more pulse in his wrist than there was in a marlinspike, and that his heart was as still as a pirate's conscience. ' Commodore,' says Austin, and there wasn't a muscle of his face moved save his lips; ' commodore, a few hours ago and I trembled at your frown, but *now* I do not fear you, for I'm come from the dead to warn you and this ship's company to mend your ways and take care of your immortal souls;' and he then went on for nigh on half an hour, and gin a sarmint, which the chaplain said 'in beauty of diction and elewation of sentiment was equal to that of any divine he had ever heerd, and the language that of a fine and accomplished scholard.' He told them it was their duty to stand by their flag, and fight in defence of their country (which pleased the commodore; 'cause why? he was afear'd he'd cow the men), and at the eend he warned them all to be ready to follow him; 'for,' says he, 'ship-mates, I am but a little way ahead of you, and you must all soon follow. And now,' says he, 'I'm done; my arrand is finished;' and he sunk back cold and stiff into his hammock. Well, the men disparsed and went to their duty; but there was many of them as didn't feel easy that night, and they was collected in knots, talking it over for'ard and atween the guns; and some of the hardest men aboard the ship looked sober, and allowed themselves to be disconcarted about the matter. Even old Albro clapt a belay on his tongue, and stopped swearing for hard on two hours, which is more than could be said of him before or since, 'cept once't a'terwards, in that same ship, when a musket-shot from the Tenedos went into his mouth, just as he was launching an oath at a marine as was in his way, and carried half his grinders through the opposite jaw. But, d'ye see, Austin wasn't done yet; for about half an hour after that, he rises ag'in in his hammock and says to the surgeon's mate as was looking at him, 'Give me a drink!' So the surgeon gives him a tin cup of water. Jim takes a drink, glares around him for the space of a minute, and then, staring steadily in the surgeon's eyes, slowly sinks down the third time, stock dead, into his hammock. I'll tell you, sir, there was one man aboard as would have been glad to have been out of that 'ere craft, and his name was William Baxter. I happened to be near the commodore as he and the surgeon was talking in a low tone together in the evening, while I was sweeping the weather quarter with my glass, and I listened, and I hear'n the surgeon say:

"'Yes, sir; I have seen cases, something like this, that we call in the books *catalepsy;* but I never heard of one *speaking* in that state.'

"That was enough for *me*. The smallest boy on board ship knows that a *cat* is ill luck on board any craft. Well, sir, Jim was at last dead, in airnest, and sewed up in his hammock, with a thirty-two pound shot tied to his heels; and the commodore's orders was that he should be buried next day at seven bells. Did ye ever see a burial at sea, sir? If not, to my mind you never seen the right way to return the ALMIGHTY what is left of one of His creeturs after his cruise in this world is up and his des-*tined* sarvice ended. I've seen shore folks bury their fellow-creeturs; but, like everything as landsmen does, it's onhandsome and not shipshape. It's only a few days aback that me and Bill Blunt, this man as sits here on the log, alongside o' me, was ashore on liberty, and overhauled one o' their funerals, as they call them, under way to carry some poor feller to his last mooring-ground. There was a horse towing a wagon covered with a tarpaulin, for all the world like our powder-barge, 'cept it hadn't the red flag on it; for, d'ye see, sir, when we brings powder aboard we always hoists a red flag, as a caution, on the barge, and afore we comes alongside, the boatswain pipes, 'All hands, ahoy! Put out the fires in the galleys, and all pipes, cigars and lights aboard the ship! Wake up, cooks! d'ye hear, men? d'ye hear?' And the magazine isn't opened till every particle of fire aboard ship is reported 'out' by the officer.

"But, as I was saying, this here craft was towed by a white horse, and in its wake followed a long fleet of coaches and other conweyances. In the first two or three of them, to be sure, there was passengers as had their pumps a-going, and was swabbing up the water with white handkerchers; but in all the rest the people was laughin', and talkin', and looking out of the ports, as onconcarned as if they was following a brute beast to his grave, instead of one of their kind. I say, sir, the sight was onpleasant to me; and I says to Bill Blunt, says I, 'Bill, look how little these here shore folks cares for their ship-mates;' but Bill was three sheets hauled in the wind, and he only hiccups, and, pulling off his hat, bows to the procession, and 'wishes their worships a pleasant journey.' Bill was hard up, and I seen it wasn't no use to talk to him; so I takes off my hat and stands by and looks, while he steadies himself ag'in' the lamp-post; and I'm free to say that them lamp-posts is a great convenience to sea-faring men when they has their grog aboard, as I've know'd by my own experience in a squall. But, as I was saying, we steadies ourselves by the post, with our hats in our hands, till the procession gets by; but it gin me a dislike to all shore burials; and all I ask is that when Bill Baxter's time comes he may be launched off soundings in blue water.

"Howsomdever, at seven bells the bo'swain's whistle was heerd, and old Albro and his mate's hoarse voices sounding down the hatchways, 'All hands ahoy, to bury the dead!

Below there, all hands to bury the dead!' The body of Jim was brought up out of the sick-bay, sewed up in its hammock, and laid on a grating at the gangway; the officers, with their epaulettes on their shoulders, their swords at their sides, and laced scrapers in their hands, standing on one side, and the men, in their clean jackets and trowsers, and hats off, on the other, just aft the mainmast, Jim's messmates close aboard the grating. The ship was hove to, the main-top sails aback, the flag half-mast, and nothing was heered to break the silence 'cept the slapping of the blocks and rigging occasionally ag'in the masts as she slowly rose and fell in the heavy swell. And there was the chaplain, surrounded by us sea-faring men, about to return to the ALMIGHTY the hulk of our late shipmate. A shipmate's faults, and may be vices, is forgotten at that time, when we sees him laid stiff and silent before us, and thinks that there he lies as has pulled at the same rope, laid out on the same yard, messed from the same kid, and may be fou't at the same gun, with us; I say his faults is forgotten, and the best feelings of a seaman only remain; and many an eye that has looked into the muzzle of an inimy's forty-two without winking, at such times runs down with tears like a child; but somehow that 'ere wasn't the case with the body of Jim Austin as he lay there on the grating. The men was afeard; and when the chaplain comes to the part in the sarvice, ' we consign him to the deep,' and the body plunged overboard, every man aboard of that craft, officers and all, breathed freer, as if they'd got rid of a sort of Jonah as boded ill to the ship. The men rushed to the ports, expecting to see the body rise ag'in and float, and sure enough it did. It shot half out of the water, and then sunk again—rose and sunk—and then slowly rising, floated half its length above the swell, in which it surged and rolled from side to side, as if it were trying to regain the ship; and there it remained, floating in our wake, until, as the ship got way, it gradually grew less and less, and finally disappeared. Now, sir, it's my belief, and the belief of some of the oldest sea-faring men I have met, that Jim Austin's sperit always haunted about that 'ere ship arter that, and in spite lent a hand to knock her cut-water athwart ship when she thumped on the bar, and that thereby, as I said, she had to strike her flag to a———"

"First cutter, ahoy!" hailed a fine deep voice.

"Ay, ay, sir!" answered the veteran, abruptly breaking off his narration; and by the light of the wharf-lantern and the glitter of the uniforms I perceived a couple of officers approaching along the pier. In a moment or two more they were seated in the stern-sheets of the barge, the old seaman at the tiller.

"Oars!" said the officer, and each man's oar elevated, stood upright before him. "Shove off!" and the bowman gave the bow a sheer with his boat-hook. "Let fall!" The oars fell simultaneously into the water, dashing around them phosphorescent fire as they fell. "Give way, men!" The boat shot away, and soon the measured roll of the oars in the row-locks became fainter and fainter, and the boat was lost in the darkness.

A few moments more and my horse was pawing impatiently the deck of the steamer as we dashed up the bay on our way to the good and ancient city of Gotham.

A TRIP THROUGH LONG ISLAND SOUND.—

No. 1.

HELL GATE.

SO at five o' the clock in the afternoon of the — of August, Anno Domini————wind S.S.W, and the sky as clear as a bell, I stood in *propria persona*, my stick in my hand, and cape on my shoulders, on the deck of the steamer at the Battery, surrounded by all the noise, hubbub and confusion attending the departure of that Leviathan on its nocturnal journey. The Pilot's signal was given, the voice of the Captain, "All ashore that's going" was heard, the plank hauled in, the fasts cast off, the huge paddles revolved, the wharf slid by us, we passed the pier head, and with gathering speed shot out on to the bosom of the calm and beautiful bay.

We swept around the Battery, and dashed like a race horse, with momentarily increasing velocity, on our course, through the various craft crowding the east river. Gliding past the borders of the great city, the busy industry of man every where evident to eye and ear, soon we were hurrying through the beautiful scenery of Hell Gate, the gay and cheerful villas shining among the green trees on the island of Manhattan, while Blackwell's reared her castellated and looped prisons at our sides.

With steadiness our huge line steamer with undiminished

speed, rushed upon her course, reckless alike of boiling eddies, and rocks, and tides and whirlpools. A wide and beautiful bay opened on our left. Here in our youthful days did we watch with awe the diving bell at work, suspended above the submerged wreck of the British man-of-war, "Hussar," and here in our boyish fancy did we see "wedges of gold, great anchors, heaps of pearl, inestimable jewels, all scattered in the bottom of the sea." The Hussar struck upon a rock in passing through the Gate in the Revolution, and was with difficulty kept afloat, till running her into this bay she sunk in deep water near the shore, her crew escaping with their lives. She was supposed to have had the military chest of the troops on board, containing a hundred thousand pounds in silver.

Whether true or not, the probability was sufficient to induce the formation of companies at different times to explore her slimy and kelp-covered timbers in its pursuit, and much real treasure was sunk in the vain effort to obtain that which in all probability never has been. The tradition handed down, that she was a *frigate*, is incorrect; she was a *sloop of war*, with a single gun deck and consequently but one battery.

An old man (a stout lad at the time), relates that passing one morning down by the Flymarket, he was accosted by "a soldier officer" (her Lieutenant of Marines) who requested him to carry on board a pair of shoes that he had just purchased.

He went down to the end of the wharf, and finding one of her barges putting off, jumped in, and was soon set on board of her, as she lay moored in the middle of the stream. Enquiring for the Purser, he delivered the shoes and his message, and receiving the pistareen, his promised reward, ascended the deck again to return, but to use his own expression, "found that getting *into* a King's ship and getting *out* were two very different things." While he was below, the crew, it appears, had been mustered to receive certain prize money, and all his inquiries and solicitations as to how

DUTCH MANSION.

he was to get ashore, were answered by such jeers and jibes, such pushing and hustling, that his soul fairly sunk within him, and to avoid the boatswain's cats, which began to fly around among the rioters with the most impartial plenty, and in the distribution of which he came in for his share, he was forced to creep in between two of the guns opposite the main hatch, waiting a favorable opportunity for escape. He eventually succeeded in getting again below, and representing his case to the Purser. That officer commiserating his situation, came on deck, and directed him to be put on shore by a boat, much to the dissatisfaction of the rough men-of-war's men, who by no means restrained their mutterings, as they "gave way," to stem the tide which ran almost as swiftly then as now.

In those days the carters loaded their wood from *alongside* the vessels in Coenties Slip, and the salutes were fired from old Fort George, just below the Bowling Green. The Powder Magazine was placed well without the city limits on the "Common," the spot where now stands the City Hall. The Hessians quartered on the Bowery Road, well nigh as far out as Grand street, and the English Red Coats barracked at a distance, on a line now known as Chambers street. Wall street was the " West end," where were to be found the Howes and Clintons, the Knyphausens and De Heysers, with their liveried servants, and powdered and laced footmen. The *Theatre*, "that wicked school of Satan," where the English Officers, many of them, themselves performed, was in John street, the present site of Thorburn's Seed Store. "I was never into it but once't," said the old man ; " I was never into it but once't, and then it cost me a gold half Jo, for I stood treat for the whole company. Talk about dress! Why, the people don't know how to dress now-a-days. You ought to a-seen the gentle folks then— why, there was the fine cloth coat with its broad flaps, and buttons the size of a dollar ; the shirt of Holland, seventeen hunder' fine, and the cambric cravat with its lace ends, tied in a handsome knot in front; the brocade vest, covering the hips, and the velvet breeches, with the paste, or it mought be, diamond buckles at the knees; silk stockings, with their embroidered clocks half up the legs, and the polished Spanish leather shoes; the queue, tied with its black ribbon, hanging down the back, playing forward and backward in the powder on the shoulders; the long gold-headed cane, and the cocked hat under the arm." However, to return to the wreck. Nothing was ever recovered from her, save some trifles: rusty cannon and small arms were got up, and a bottle of "Old Jamacia," crusted over with oysters and barnacles, which, they say, was delicious. Large sums of money were expended at different times, but no return ever realized.

Sir Peter Parker afterwards passed through the gate in his frigate, holding a pistol to the ear of the pilot, with the comfortable assurance that if the ship touched, his brains should be the forfeit. Fortunately skill and good luck saved the pilot from this naval Judge Lynch. As we passed on, the beautiful shores, with their gay villas, glided by us like a moving diorama. Trim yachts with gaudy streamers, sloops careering in the breeze till their green bottoms were thrown almost entirely out of the water, and square rigged vessels bellying out their white canvas in lordly dignity, were all left behind us, as we rounded "Throg's," opposite to which lies the fortress, erected by the general Government, to cover the city upon its Eastern side, which with a work of corresponding magnitude upon the Long Island shore, will protect it from any attack in that direction. As we sped out upon the bosom of the broad blue Sound, our gallant boat rushed forward with increased vehemence, and "in going we did devour the way." As we plowed its surface, the day was closing and the last rays of the setting sun seemed to linger, to gild the white sails here and there resting upon it, before gathering himself into a huge globe of fire, he should reluctantly sink beneath the horizon, leaving the Christain here, to warn the Hindoo and the Mussulman, that Brahma and Alla, in the other Hemisphere, were there awaiting prayer.

The gray twilight, like mist, gradually gained upon us, and ere long the constellations were quivering in the heavens, while the kindly lights and beacons erected by the hand of man, shone steadily and hospitably along the shores.

A S I pursued my solitary walk up and down the promenade deck, my mind was aroused from its train of reflections by the Light shining in the distance on the Connecticut shore, and with little effort I recognized it as marking the spot where were passed my school-boy days. There thou liest, thought I; thy fields are just as green and verdant, the meadow-lark raising his wild notes as sweetly from their midst, thy shady woods as still, the squirrel and partridge in their depths; thy swamps as thick, entangled with undergrowth, brilliant with wild flowers, the muskrat and graceful teal sailing as safely in their waters; thy creeks as fresh and clear, the oysters clinging to the rocks waiting to be taken, the fish sweeping around the rustic skiff all ready to be speared; and thy orchards! with just such tempting fruit waiting *other* schoolboys' appetites. The scene of my boyish frolics and truant days—days when there was no "satis to the jam," there thou liest, still—still enough—yet it was not always so of yore. Thou hast known the pomp, the pride—ay, *felt* the circumstance of war.

The town was burnt by the British during the Revolution, and acts of great atrocity and cruelty committed by the licentious soldiery. I well recollect how I used to listen with all my ears to the narrations of "Old Kit," one of Africa's blackest sons, who, torn in his childhood from his native sands in Guinea, had been passed, for nearly three generations, from master to master, outliving them all into freedom and four-score. After firing most of the houses the enemy's column moved toward Ridgefield, with the intention of destroying the neighboring town of Danbury, about ten miles farther on. As they moved along the main road they were fired upon by the enraged inhabitants from every spot that would afford a cover. As they passed the cornfields, which were then in full height, they were particularly exposed, their officers picked off and numbers thinned, by an unseen foe, whose whereabouts was only marked by the smoke of his musket rising above the tall green stalks, and who was out of reach long before the fire could be returned. "De Red Coats fire whole platoons in dem dar fields ob corn," said Kit, "but dar no use—our people was off as soon as dey fire; sarve 'em right, burnin' people's housen." In one place, a company of militia that had ensconced themselves behind a stone fence until they came within musket range, poured in a fire that made a complete chasm in the column, retreating and escaping under the smoke of their own guns. Among other deeds of brutality that are related of them, the troop seized upon a poor old man, who had remained behind in the town in the hope that his age and infirmities might protect him, and having enveloped him in a blanket soaked in rum, they set fire to it, bidding him, with savage laughter, run for his life. The poor man hurried, with all the strength he had, to throw himself into an adjacent pond, but before he could reach it was bayonetted to death amid the jeers and execrations of the demons in human shape. Some few of the houses escaped the conflagration, as being residences of tories, or adjoining them. One of the latter stands to this day, with the hole made by a cannon-shot in its side. The last forty years, swarms of bees have ensconced themselves annually within the walls, and collected large stores of honey within the ceilings, which the owner will not allow to be disturbed.

"Young Massa," said Kit, "you see dat little rise by de Meetin' House, dar, jis by dat trees? well, arter de British was gone, dar I see little red rag stick up out of de ground—old nigger's eyes was better den dan day is now—dat was next day. Well, me and Hi. Lewis—not dat little noisy debbil dar, dat young Hi, as is making him mischief—but old Hi' him's grandfather as is dead and gone—me and old Hi' dig and find—what you tink we find dar, eh?—we find body of young soldier officer in him regimentals, him red coat and epcrletts and sword and all, buried two feet under ground jis where he fell. Old Kit seen handsome men in him day, but dat young soldier officer was de handsomest man dat he ever did see. Him had light hair and blue eyes and little picter in his bosom, him sweetheart I reckon, hung round him neck by blue ribbon, but muskit-ball dat kill him jag in one corner of it, as it went right tro' his heart. Oh! but dat dar war beautiful man—old nigger say him war beautiful young man. Massa Dr. Clark say, 'Pity, pity; him fine young man, but neber know what hurt him'—but we lay him down decent in de burying-ground after dat." Numberless were the traditions treasured up by the old people, and little, less than little, was the love they bore the British. But for thee, old Kit—dark, charcoal, jetty Kit, I ne'er shall see thee more—ne'er shall my truant steps again linger at thy cabin door in the little dell in the woods. Ne'er again shall I drink thy spruce beer whizzing from its black bottle, nor see the yellow of thine eyes beaming with satisfaction as thou dost watch its transfer to my youthful lips; no more shall I hear thy legends of witches and hobgoblins; alas! no more e'en believe in ghosts and spirits; no more in early morning see the blue smoke rising in its spiral columns above thy rustic home; thou hast gone, long, and long ago; gone to that bourne where old Dinah's voice shall not follow thee, nor e'en the bark of "Spot," thy little trundle tail, fall sweetly on thine ear.

No more on thy block in the corner shall I see thee puffing from thy smoke-enameled pipe, while thou dost turn the fish caught in the neighboring creek upon the coals; thy hearthstone and thy hut are gone—a pile of clay and stones, relics of the old chimney, are all that remain to tell that there was human habitation. Peace to thy ashes, Kit, they rest in the black people's "section" in the graveyard, not even in death mingling with the white race.

The old giant elms tower above thee, but no carved monument, with boasting epitaph, marks thy whereabouts ; two gray stones, the one at thy head and the other at thy heels, show where were consigned thy ashes. Farewell, honest, simple-hearted Kit; should I reach thy years, I still should carry in remembrance the happy hours I passed with thee, the squeaking of thy violin, the shrill notes of thy "wry-necked fife ;" even the toll of thy funeral bell, honest old negro, shall rouse in my memory my happy hours with thee.

The British proceeded to Danbury, and destroyed a large quantity of stores and provisions which had been deposited there for the American forces. The streets literally ran ankle deep in fat from the burning beef and pork. In the height of the conflagration a somewhat ludicrous exhibition was made by a squad of troopers chasing an old man, endeavoring to escape on horseback with a roll of cloth, his property, under his arm. The cloth, unfolding and flying behind him, so frightened the horses of the dragoons, that, although they were more fleet, they could not reach the old man with their sabers in their attempts to cut him down. "Give in, old daddy," they at length shouted ; "give in, and take quarter." But the old daddy, tenacious of his property, would not give in, and won the race, saving his cloth and skin.

The surrounding country was soon in arms, and the enemy, having effected their object, commenced their retreat. At one time, when the column was in full march, it was brought to a halt, and the artillery hurried up to the front, by the appearance of a mounted man on a ridge just above them, who appeared to be giving commands to a force behind in tones of decision and authority. As soon as his words could be distinguished, they heard the imposing orders: " Halt—the whole universe! Break off by kingdoms! Empires to the front!" They of course discovered that it was a madman. Wooster and Arnold hung upon their rear as they retreated, and they were glad to effect a hurried embarkation in their boats, which were awaiting them off Compo. Wooster was killed, shot through the body, as he turned in his saddle to cheer on his men. Arnold came near sharing the same fate, but exhibited his usual cool daring and intrepidity. His horse was shot by an English grenadier, and fell upon him in such a manner that he was entangled, and could not immediately arise. The soldier hurried up to bayonet the disabled officer; but Arnold, disengaging himself, drew his pistol from the holsters, and shot the man dead as he approached.

A TRIP THROUGH LONG ISLAND SOUND.

No. III.

NIGHT ALARM.

BUT to return to our journey. As the evening wore on group after group disappeared from the deck, and by and by I myself descended to the cabin, prepared to try to rest. I threw myself into my berth, and soon all was still, save here and there a sleepy waiter might be seen gathering the boots together, or obeying the instructions given him by some passenger in undertones. But the quiet of the cabin was before long broken by the entry of several noisy young men, who had, by drinking at the bar, deprived themselves of the slight modicum of sense with which nature had endowed them. The noise and profanity were borne by the passengers for a time in silence; but finally, by absence from restraint, became so insufferable that we were induced to call a waiter and send him with a message to the captain, complaining of the unreasonable disturbance. The captain was soon on the spot, and by his remonstrances the disturbance quelled; but he had no sooner left the cabin than it was resumed, and became worse than before. I had heard for some time ominous sounds of dissatisfaction proceeding from the berth above me; and sundry creaks and broken exclamations of wrath warned me that its occupant was about bestirring himself. At length a night-capped head protruded itself over its side, and a solemn voice, in tones and gravity becoming a country deacon proceeded from it. "I think that it is a great and manifest wrong," said the speaker, "that all the passengers in the cabin of this public conveyance are to be disturbed in this manner by a parcel of noisy, riotous young men, who——" "Bah! Uncle, pull in your night-cap," was the insulting interruption called forth by this reasonable remonstrance; but, instead of silencing, my neighbor's pluck was thoroughly up, and raising his voice so that it could be heard to the very extremities of the cabin, completely drowning the vociferations of the rioters, he continued: "I think it a shame—I see no reason why we should be deprived of our rest, more than our money; and of the two I had rather be robbed of the last." The yells of the rioters now became perfectly outrageous. "I move that if these fellows are not instantly quiet, that they be put out of the cabin in their shirts"—and suiting the action to the word, throwing his legs over the side of the berth—" and I will be the first to do it." "I second that motion," cried one passenger; "and I," "and I," "and I," resounded from every part of the cabin. "D—n their eyes," growled a deep bass voice, from the berth just beyond me, in tones that had evidently been modulated by a speaking trumpet, "d—n their eyes, if they give us any more of their noise, I'll thrash the whole raft of them myself. Shut up, you infernal whelps!"

The spirit of wrath was up among the passengers, and the rioters were effectually subdued. They slunk away, and quiet was restored. I supposed all this time that my friend of the night-cap was simmering in wrath and indignation in his berth above me, but was equally surprised and amused when, after a lapse of some ten minutes, the head again bent over the side towards me, and a good-natured voice issued from its mouth: "I say, we put them fellows down nice, didn't we?" as calm and good-naturedly as if its owner had had no hand in the belligerent manifestations so lately made.

The regular jar and clank of the machinery was soon all that disturbed the restored quiet of the cabin, and the moan or sigh of some uneasy sleeper all that gave evidence that a hundred souls were resting within its confines. I gradually lost my recollection, and fell asleep, but could not have been long in that state when I was aroused by a cry so shrill and agonizing—" Stop her, stop her, for God's sake stop her!"– that, in common with twenty others, I was out of my berth, hurrying upon deck, before I was well aware of what I was about. Supposing that we were running on the rocks, or about to be run into by some other vessel, the passengers, some dressed, others not, as they had sprung from their berths, rushed up the companion-way. There we found the captain standing in his shirt and pantaloons, apparently as much in amazement as ourselves. The engineer, hearing the cry, had stopped the engine without waiting for orders from the pilot; and there we all stood, staring at each other like the drunkards in Auerbach's cellar in Leipsic.

The upshot of the affair turned out to be that one of the deck passengers had dreamed that he was overboard, and the screams which he had sent forth in his sleep had thus alarmed the whole boat. Order was of course again restored, and we returned to our berths. As I went to mine, I was amused by the nonchalance exhibited by an English half-pay officer whose berth was near mine. He was very coolly finishing his elaborate toilette previous to going upon deck to ascertain the cause of the alarm. "You take matters coolly, sir," said I. "Oh, yes," he replied; "I thought that if I had got to drown, I might as well drown with my clothes on, like a gentleman.

A TRIP THROUGH LONG ISLAND SOUND.

No. IV.

"THE BOYS."

NEVER a good sleeper on board of a steamboat, and my nerves somewhat jarred by the alarm, I remained for a long time awake after the sounds from the various berths showed me that at least it was forgotten by their occupants.

While cogitating upon the events of the night, my mind in connection with the uproar of the noisy youths in the earlier part of it, recurred to some humorous scenes and adventures to which I had been witness years by gone at N——. It so happened that I was there at a time, and thrown into company and companionship with a laughter-loving, fun-seeking, mirth-requiring set, whose nocturnal quarters were at "the Colony," the Bachelor's row, at ——— Hall, and ill betide any unfortunate wight who sought his slumbers there until long after the witching time of night. "By'r Ladie!" it was a place profane, that entry. Little was heard of grace, but shouts of uproarious laughter, loud and long-continued, bass voices in merry chorus, the ringing of bells, and cries for "waiter," "sherry cobblers," "mint juleps," "punches strong and sweet," "cigars and pipes," for its noisy denizens. But with all their youthful jollity and excess, the gentleman still predominated, and there were right witty, generous and noble spirits among them.

A few short years have glided by, and where are they? Some are dead; one fine fellow has killed his man, and wanders a homicide, with the mark of Cain upon his brow, too late awakened to the pangs of conscience; another—but why moralize? They are dispersed on their life journey, some on the blue ocean, some on the green prairie, some on mountain top, some in the toiling city, each in his vocation, but not likely to meet again. One evening " L.," of our number, the most popular and amusing, was missing from his seat upon the back piazza, where our body politic with their cigars used to congregate in the earlier part of the night, and his absence soon became object of remark and speculation. Various were the surmises—some thought he had dined out, others that he'd been shot dead with the bright " glances of some white wench's merry black eye," that— but surmise was soon silenced by the fact that he had gone— to bed. " To be up betimes was to be up after midnight," but to be abed before was strange—" 'twas passing strange " —unnatural, not to be allowed. To be in bed by nine!— 'twas monstrous; such innovation on time and place was not to be permitted—not even thought of; and it was determined that "come what, come may, sleep to his eyelids should be a thing forbid." To second so laudable a determination, a waiter was summoned, and being duly advised of his duty, soon reached the door of " No. 6," where the unfortunate " L." was paying his devotions to the sleep god. A gentle, modest, then louder knock was heard, and again repeated; finally followed the drowsy reply of the inmate, " Who's there? What do you want?" " Here it is, sir," was the obsequious answer; "here it is." "Here's what?" "The warm water, sir." "Warm water?" "Yes, sir, the warm water for the sick gentleman." "Warm water—why, I'm not sick, it must be for some other room." "Beg pardon, sir." And the waiter returned to inform his employers on the piazza that it was a mistake, and that the gentleman in "Six" was "not in the laste unwell."

A suitable time being allowed to elapse for "L." to forget the disturbance, and be again upon the shores of Lethe, another waiter was summoned, and soon standing with thundering knock at his chamber door. "Hallo! What do you want? Who's there?" replied the startled voice within. "Here's the medicine, sir." "Medicine! what medicine?" "Why, sir, the rhubarb and magnesia for the sick gentleman." "Confound your stupidity; the sick man is in some other room—clear out!" and the astonished waiter, like his predecessor, returned to tell his story to those that sent him. A longer interval of quiet was now allowed, and the occupant of "No. 6" was far gone into forgetfulness, when thump, thump, thump, again at his door, started him wide awake. "What in the foul fiend's name do you want?" "The Docthur is below, sir; *will* I tell him to come up?" "Will you put your head inside the door, you stupid scoundrel, that I may throw my boot at it; this is the third time I have been disturbed to-night; off with you, and find your sick man somewhere else!" and the frightened waiter retured to the gentlemen with, "Sure, there's nothing the matter with the gentleman, save wrath." A sufficiently long time elapsed, and the waiters, to speak in a military sense, having, like tirailleurs, done the skirmishing, it was determined that the main body, the party on the piazza, should charge in solid column, and make a final, determined and desperate attack.

Preceded by a servant with a large supply of lights, cigars, cobblers, slings and juleps, and of drinks "*id genus omne*," their measured tramp was heard along the entry leading to its fated portal. "Halt!" from the van. The column faced to the right, and the long still entry returned the echo; knock, knock, knock, thundering at the door of devoted "No. 6." Suspecting what was in the wind, "L." remained perfectly still, and returned no answer; "thump, thump, thump." and the clatter of the opposite windows returned the jarring sound—thump, thump, thump, each blow given with more urgent emphasis, and the reluctant "What's wanting?" at length heard in reply. R——'s deep voice, deepened into sepulchral tones, slowly answered, "Here's the undertaker to measure the dead gentleman for a coffin in "No. 6." This lugubrious information elicited from the occupant no reply. There ensued a pause. "He's jumped out of the window," said the van, "committed suicide," growled the center, "*crumpit, crupit, cvasit!*" shouted the rear. A suitable and befitting time having elapsed for the opening of the door, snuffled R. in the tones of a Methodist preacher, "I move that we now enter the room of our deceased friend and make suitable provision for his obsequies. Open sesame!" and suiting the action to the word, followed by a press of the shoulder, the door flew open, and there sat L. bolt upright, his hands folded before him in his bed, resignedly awaiting coming events, and that that the gods had for him in store. He was too good a fellow to be sulky, however much he was annoyed by this unwelcome intrusion upon his quiet; besides "it would have been no use," and with his glass in his hand, surrounded by jolly companions, some seated on the bed, some on the tables and on each other's laps, the atmosphere of the room opaque with smoke, his voice was heard ere long in the Bacchanalian chorus with which the wise pates saw fit to surround him. There were among them some exceedingly "hard youths," to whom mischief and fun were synonymous.

One night they changed all the boots that the porter had cleaned and left at the doors of the rooms for their respective occupants, and the next morning a little before the second bell, such ringing and shouting for "waiter" had rarely been heard e'en in that noisy quarter; such objurgations, such imprecations, not deep only, but loud, as were hurled at the head of the unfortunate "boots." There was "No. 2" with feet the size of Goliah, tugging at a pair of delicate patent leathers, into the leg of which he could scarcely squeeze his toes, while the unfortunate dandy in "No. 9" stood staring in speechless astonishment at the huge clumsy thick soled "country makes" which had taken their place.

"Washington ties," the comfort of gouty old gentlemen, were awaiting feet that cared not a stiver for a twenty mile tramp, while morocco pumps were provided for feet acquainted only with twinges and bandages of flannel. "No. 13's" straps were cut off, and "22" had his filled with whiskey punch, whilst "17" found two tumblers and a wine glass in his; "27" and "28's" door handles, the rooms being opposite, were made fast by a rope across the entry, and "32's" bed, bedding and carpet were formed into a pyramid in the center of the room, with the wash bowl and pitcher as its apex, while "No. 7" was horrified by having all the furniture of the adjoining unoccupied room piled against his door, tumbling in upon him as he opened it in the morning. A few years only have passed by, and as men sadder and wiser, how do many of the actors look back in wonder at *such* pleasure?

A TRIP THROUGH LONG ISLAND SOUND—

No. V.

THE UNFORTUNATE LOVER.

BUT while upon practical jokes, I recollect one that occurred at Yale, that venerable academic matron, in years gone by. B., a somewhat sentimental youth, roomed with two brother soph's who had about as much romance in their composition as could be analyzed from a blacksmith's anvil. Now the suites of rooms in that ancient institution are composed of three, two bed, and one sitting-room, to say nothing of the luxury of a wood closet. B., besides writing poetry and playing on the flute, was also desperately in love, and used to go and see his inamorata every night, where his stay in " lengthened sweetness, long drawn out," usually terminated at about the witching hour.

One very cold night, his chums, being instigated by the father of evil, determined as an offset to his enjoyment that they would have some fun at his expense. So, getting a large cat, which was in the habit of prowling about the mess hall, they by coaxing and a little gentle force succeeded in placing her snugly in the centre of B.'s bed, where, the quarters being warm and comfortable, puss was contented to remain. Raking up the fire and putting out the lights, these two wicked youths then retired to their beds, and there, chuckling in anticipated delight, awaited the *cat*-astrophe. By and by up came B., fumbled at the door, and opening it walked in. Finding all cold, dark and comfortless, he grumbled at the want of consideration that had thus left him so inhospitable a reception, but, summoning his philosophy, made the best of a bad bargain, and proceeded with what alacrity he might to divest himself of his garments in the dark, his movements not the less expeditious from the cold.

Having proved Plato's definition of humanity, he gave one spring, and in an instant was beneath the bed clothes; but in another Grimalkin's claws, suddenly disturbed from her slumbers, were planted in his unfortunate legs. With a scream of terror B. bounced out of bed on one side, while the cat, in equal alarm, darted out on the other. Dashing around the room, frantic with alarm, springing at the windows and rushing through the fire-place, scattering the sparks and live embers about the room, the cat screamed and yelled, while B., in amazement, his hair standing on end, and the drops of perspiration rolling off his forehead with terror, danced first on one leg and then on the other, shouting for assistance at the top of his lungs in the center.

The mirth soon "became so fast and furious" that to save poor B. from more dire consequences, the mischief-makers, pretending to awake from slumber, were fain to interpose, and by opening the door allow the cat to escape into the entry, from whence she soon again ensconced herself in her favorite haunts under the roof in the garret of the "old South Middle."

A TRIP THROUGH LONG ISLAND SOUND.

No. VI.

ADVENTURE ON THE MISSISSIPPI.

MARQUETTE DESCENDING THE MISSISSIPPI.

THE alarm that had so seriously aroused us from our berths soon, as I have said, subsided, and all was again silent, except the measured jar and clank of the machinery. For my own part, although I could not hear a voice crying "Macbeth hath murdered sleep," I found that I could "sleep no more," pitching and tumbling, rolling first on one side and then on the other in my berth in vain attempts to enjoy its balmy influence, my imagination running wild in all sorts of freaks and fantasies. Now, my imagination is of such a perfect devil-me-care character that it will, under such circumstances, jump on and ride, without bridle or halter, whatever subject first presents itself, and, ere I was aware, it was galloping back to a ludicrous scene I once witnessed in the cabin of a steamer ascending the Mississippi.

It so happened that I left New Orleans, in the season when duels and yellow fever were becoming rife, in one of the fastest steamers out of that port. The usually monotonous voyage up was enlivened with an occasional race with some boat ahead, in which all the spare bacon and hams among the freight were thrown into the furnaces to feed the boilers, while to save unnecessary trouble the firemen lashed down the safety valves. Indeed, in our case we might be said to be especially favored, for even in the absence of the excitement of the race we could always recur to the fact that we had four hundred kegs of gunpowder, marked "buckwheat," stowed in interesting proximity to the furnace, which at any instant might, by sending us among the stars, leave it a matter of doubt in our minds whether the boilers did or did not give way at exactly four hundred atmospheres. When arrived at Natchez, from that interesting suburb yclept "Natchez under the hill," to which district the "Five Points" is a church swept out and garnished—where the bowie-knife and pistol are the arbiters in all disputes, where a pack of cards is the only Bible, and the demand, "Stranger, will you drink or fight?" the first salutation— there came on board "an individual" extremely "wolfy about the head and shoulders," "a yellow flower of the forest,"—in short, a regular " hoosier," his long elf-locks streaming around his shoulders, and his deep-sunken black eyes cast furtively about him with a sinister expression, indicating that " he was considerably troubled with the rascal."

He was surly in his appearance, and dirty, but, as he paid his fare for the cabin, cabin accommodations of course he was entitled to, and had. The fellow's whereabouts was undesirable in the morning, when he was sober, but when drunk, in the afternoon, extremely annoying to us of the more cleanly sort that used our own tooth-brushes; so much so that we endeavored to have him sent forward, but the captain said that he could not turn the man out of the cabin without some specific charge of offense; and that, although he would not go out of the way of his duty to shun consequences, he would rather avoid the chance of having a rifle-ball put through him, perhaps some years afterwards, from behind a tree or wood-pile along shore, when he might least expect it.

To an argument so forcible, we could not of course make reply. But when we came to retire at night, and the *mauvais sujet* was ensconced in his berth, o'ercome, if not with " wine and wassail," with potations of whisky " pottle deep," the rest of us sinking into calm repose, there began to rise from his berth such snores and groans and grunts that it appeared as if all the hogs of the last litter were there huddled together. By and by, an individual, getting entirely out of patience, sprung from his berth, and rushing up and shaking him with all his might, consigning him at the same time to all the d——ls in the infernal regions, insisted that he should stop his noise. The man sat upright in his berth, with drunken gravity, looking at the speaker with lack-lustre eyes, essaying a reply, but stopped by a hiccough, sunk slowly down, and was asleep again before he was well on his side. But no sooner had the excited passenger got back to his berth, and the rest of us begun to think that the disturbance was over, than at it again he went, as if in very defiance; so that it was soon determined, *nem. con.*, that he must go, willingly if he would—" we would not stand upon the order of his going"—but go he must.

The captain was again apealed to, and by his directions the sot was carried out, and placed in one of the berths forward, where he remained most of the time drunk during the rest of the passage. It was not until the last day of our voyage that we found we were indebted to a very clever fellow, a ventriloquist, who slept in the next berth, for the relief. From him came the sounds which appeared to emanate from the form of the unfortunate "hoosier." There were several professed gamblers on board, who were incessantly engaged in their vocation during the day, snatching time only for their meals, and many an unfortunate wight was relieved of his superfluous cash on the passage. One game in particular appeared to be a favorite one. It was called "Poker," and not only the gentlemen gamblers, in the cabin, but the more common sort, forward, were equally absorbed in it.

There was a fascination about the game which took with all. The lower classes and the boatmen, I understood, frequently staked the coats off their backs upon the game, and it is said that there have been instances when the negro firemen, after losing everything, have staked and lost their freedom. Speaking of this game reminds me of an incident that occurred on the passage, which at the time strongly touched my feelings.

I was one morning measuring the hurricane deck with my usual walk, our boat breasting the turbid expanse of waters, her high-pressure engines panting as if with the effort;—now viewing, as we were gliding almost beneath them, the huge forest trees trembling on the brink, which, ere long, undermined by the current, would fall, and be swept onwards to form the dreaded snags and sawyers; and now, aroused by the sudden change in our course, as we ran across the stream to double a bend or bar; now watching the phalanxes of wild fowl winging their way to the limpid pools and splashy lakes of the north, now some gaunt heron or gigantic crane slowly and heavily winging his awkward flight, while from the lofty tree in the adjoining forest, sitting motionless as death upon a withered branch, the lordly eagle, with cruel eye fixed upon his victim, was "biding his time," when, throwing himself upon the blue ether, he should commence the death-chase, circling higher and higher, till, descending upon him like a meteor, he would bear him, screaming and struggling, to feed his eaglets in their mountain eyrie; now, in imagination, tracing the thousand tributary streams, from the frozen regions of the north, from mountain grim and prairie green, from the silver lake, where the bronzed trapper watched the busy beaver, and the turbid river where floated the free Indian in his bark canoe, tracing the thousand streams which, by this "father of waters," send their offering to the ocean through the great Gulf of Mexico;—when my attention was diverted by a stout negro man leaning over the side of the railing, in true negro abandon, watching the ceaseless revolution of paddles. As I passed him, I stopped. "Boy," said I (for all negroes at the South, old or young, great or small, are called boys); "boy, to whom do you belong?" He turned his round, fat face, shining with content, and his row of ivory, the color of snow, contrasted with his jetty skin, and replied, with the utmost simplicity and "sang-froid," "Well, sir, I doesn't rightly know. I did belong to Massa John, but he and de captain been playin' poker for de last two hours, and I can't rightly say who I does belong to now." And yet he appeared as happy and contented as any man, white or black, on board. The simplicity and *naiveté* with which he spoke of his transfer affected me for the moment much.

A TRIP THROUGH LONG ISLAND SOUND.

No. VII.

NEW LONDON AND STONINGTON.

BUT to return from our long digression. Our steamer plowed her course along the Sound with unremitting speed and steadiness.

> "The air was cut away before,
> And clos-ed from behind."

Finding that, so far as sleep was concerned, I was "a man forbid," I folded my cloak about me, and ascended the deck. The night-mist hung damp and heavy on plank and railing, and far ahead New London light was shining in the distance. This was the port, it will be recollected, where Commodore Decatur was blockaded with two American frigates during the war by the British squadron. He was in some measure reconciled to the spirit of inaction, so galling to his feelings, by the reflection that he was chaining down a large force of the enemy from doing further mischief. It is said that, as in a similar case on the coast of South America, the captain of one of the American frigates sent a challenge to the commander of one of the English squadron, to run out a few miles from the port, and meet with equal force in regular naval duel, Commodore Decatur endorsing on the back of the challenge, that it was with his sanction, pledging his honor that no assistance should be afforded the American frigate, but that she should abide the result of the conflict, provided Commodore Hardy would guarantee the same on his part. The British Commodore sent in, in reply, that he forbade the acceptance of the challenge, for, although he felt perfect confidence in the bravery and skill of his officers and men, he could not justify himself to his country in allowing a mere spirit of chivalry to prevent his annoying his enemy by every means in his power. Hardy was a fine, hearty old gentleman, and, Saxon-like, went into his work, because it *was* work, and had got to be done. He was quite popular with the people along the shores of New England, from the fact that he never wantonly injured individuals. He had, withal, a large share of humor. At the bombardment of Stonington, where, with a couple of old iron eighteens, whose cartridges, in default of other flannel, were made from the petticoats presented by the women, he saw through his glass the boys scampering after the bombs as they fell, frequently pulling out the fuses before they could explode, while a raw countryman in his tow frock was whoaing and geeing his oxen among the shot and shells, picking them up and throwing them into the cart as a good speculation, with as much coolness as if they had been pumpkins in his own cornfield. This tickled the old gentleman's fancy immensely, and the next day an officer coming in with a flag was directed to ask the authorities whether they would sell some shot. The "Selectmen," with equal humor and shrewdness, replied that, "if the Commodore would send them in some powder, they would return him his shot gratis on its receipt."

Long before day, our steamer had performed her devoir, and was lying still at the side of the Stonington pier, her Eastern passengers transferred to the cars, hurrying with even greater velocity over terra-firma than they had been on the aqueous element. As the day dawned, we that were destined for Newport, were transferred with our luggage to the Mohican, a large and powerful boat, and were soon again reaching out toward the ocean, rising and falling gracefully on its long; swell, as we approached that terror to all sea-sick passengers, "Point Judith." The white lighthouse shone bright and lonely in the morning sun; and as we emerged from breakfast, the beautiful and peculiar shores of Rhode Island opened to our view. The rounded gray rocks, presenting an impenetrable barrier to the ocean waves, were covered to the very edge with a carpet of verdure green as emerald and velvet-like in texture, while flocks of sheep and cattle, grouped here and there upon its surface, afforded lovely pictures of still life. The entire absence of trees, save some of recent growth, those that had previously wooded its surface having been cut down by the armies of the Revolution, left the view unobstructed as far as the eye could roam, and the exquisite clearness of the atmosphere gave the vault above the hue of the sapphire. As we ran up through the outer roads, the surf was breaking high upon that most dangerous ridge of rocks, known by many a tale of disaster as "Brenton's Reef," on our right; while the shores of Connecticut, with the "Dumplings," masses of rude rock seamed and gashed by the wear of the elements for ages, were on our left—the summit of one of the latter surmounted with the already crumbling ruins of a circular fortress from which it was intended in the last war to furnish John Bull with a supply hot enough of that proverbially indigestible food.

As we passed along up the channel, the fishermen in their fishing-boats lazily looked over their shoulders at us, as they pulled in their tautog and bass (their light shallops rising and falling gently in the long swell), enjoying a freedom from care and a pleasure in existence to which the lordly nabob is a stranger. The magnificent fortification which, when completed, will mount five hundred cannon, was soon before us, and, shooting into the inner harbor, we were ere long ensconced with bag and baggage, rolling in a comfortable coach up the long wharf, into the ancient and unique town of Newport.

THE BLIND OFFICER.

["The hand of the reaper
Takes the ears that are hoary,
But the voice of the weeper
Wails manhood in glory."]

A FEW years since might occasionally be met, promenading Broadway, in the city of New York, a man of fine appearance, in the prime of life, of remarkably erect and soldierlike carriage (usually clad in military undress, his eyes covered with large green glasses), led by a young lad, or supported on the arm of a friend, whose military port and handsome person, aside from the peculiar bearing of a blind man, almost necessarily attracted the attention of the passer-by. We allude to the late Captain Henry W. Kennedy, and in so doing know that we shall revive his memory in the recollection of many warm friends, who, while they recall his generous and noble qualities, will sigh at his premature withdrawal from the stage of life. To those friends, the following brief sketch of his career may not be uninteresting.

He was born in Pennsylvania, and with his parents removed during his infancy to the West Indies, where his earlier days were passed. Returning to his country while yet in his boyhood, he was deprived by death of their protection, and left alone in the world without a single blood relation. At the age of nineteen he determined to adopt the military profession, and having received a commission as lieutenant in the United States marine corps, soon after sailed in a frigate for the Mediterranean, where he expected to take part in the war with the Barbary powers ; but before he arrived on the field of contest, the pride of the Ottomite had been humbled, and the stars and stripes floated over the crimson flag of the corsair states, Tripoli, Tunis, Algiers and Morocco having all been forced to unconditional submission. Returning to the United States, he found the enthusiasm of the country awakened by the Patriot revolution in South America, and, impatient of the dullness and inactivity of peace, with a number of other adventurous spirits resigned his commission, embraced their cause, and, accepting highly flattering propositions from one of the distinguished leaders, sailed, with the rank of captain, for that country. His cool judgment and intrepidity soon made him conspicuous, and it was not long before he received, from his desperate and adventurous courage, the sobriquet of the *"Gallo Ingles,"* or *"English Game-cock,"* the people of that country not making any distinction between the North Americans and the English, deeming all who spoke the language Britons. He received accession of rank, and was engaged in a number of actions, and his adventures and hair-breadth escapes, in the battles with the Spaniards and Royalist party, would almost afford material for a volume of romance.

The appearance of the wild native cavalry which he commanded was picturesque in the extreme. His particular corps was clad in a costume made of tiger-skins, their helmets representing the head of the ferocious animal—a silk handkerchief, twisted so tightly as to turn the edge of a saber, knotted round their necks. Dashing in at the head of these wild warriors, he would lead them into the thickest of the fight, cheering them on by his voice, " but rarely," to use his own words, " taking any part in the butchery, other than to ward off the attacks made personally upon himself." The character of the warfare partook of that ferocity which appears to have pertained always to the Spanish arms, forming such an anomaly to their lofty, high-minded, and generous qualities; and the heart sickens at the savage fury that, under the sanction of the sacred garb of contest for liberty, prevailed in their conflicts.

Neither party, as a general rule, gave or received quarter, and it was at the risk of his own life that he, in several instances, succeeded in saving the lives of the vanquished. In one case, a Spanish cadet, of noble family, besought his protection on the battle-field, and, reckless of the danger of being shot down by his own excited soldiery, he mounted the young officer behind him, and, galloping out of the action, conveyed him to a place of security. But perhaps the following incident, one of many related by him, may give a more distinct idea of the character of the warfare waged upon that unhappy soil. In an action where, after very severe fighting, the Patriot party had been successful, and the Spanish defeated, his attention was attracted by an isolated group, where a very powerful negro soldier was defending himself with his musket against the attack of a half-dozen Patriot dragoons, who were dashing like hawks around him, endeavoring to cut him down with their sabers. The black knew that his case was hopeless, and was apparently determined to sell his life at as dear a rate as possible. The swords of the troopers occasionally took effect, causing deep gashes and flesh-wounds, from which the blood streamed profusely; but the thick wool of his head had the same effect as the hair-crests on the helmets of our cavalry, turning the edge of their sabers, which glanced off, inflicting comparatively slight wounds. The contest continued for some time, the negro bleeding from twenty gashes, while Captain K. was obliged to remain a mute spectator of the scene, any attempt at his rescue being almost equivalent to his own destruction. At length a Patriot officer, deeming it a mercy to put him out of pain, put spurs to his horse, and, galloping in, gave him the *coup de grace*, ending the barbarous and unequal combat.

After four years of hardship, adventure, and battle, now victor and now vanquished, now stimulated by the cause of freedom and now disgusted by the atrocities of savage warfare, the recital of which would fill a volume (which might perhaps be useful to those who, ignorant of its horrors, are so ready to throw down the gauntlet and rush into the fell arena), he was severely wounded and his military career terminated on the plains of Cordova. The party of which he was the leader had been victorious, and the enemy were in full retreat. Halting his horse for a moment, he had loosened the rein, and was bending forward for some purpose on his neck, when he found himself enveloped in utter darkness. He clapped his hand to his head, supposing that he had been struck by a ball across the forehead, and that the blood flowing from the wound had thus deprived him of sight.

> "His clotted locks he backward threw,
> Across his brow his hand he drew,
> From blood and mist to clear his sight."

But the next instant betrayed to him too well his dreadful loss. The blessed light of the sun was thenceforth to be to him a stranger; the green fields, the blue skies, "the plumed troop" with "all the pride, the pomp and circumstance of war," were to be forever shut out from him; the smile of friendship, the scowl of enmity, to be alike unheeded; youth's glowing hopes were quenched — "Othello's occupation gone!"

A spent ball, entering his left eye, had torn it from its socket, passed through the bones of his nose, and buried itself in the right orbit, distorting the eye and destroying its vision forever. A soldier who was near him at the time said that he saw him eject the ball from his mouth with the blood, and although Drs. Hosack, Rogers, and Mott gave it as their opinions, after his return to this country, that the ball was still in the right orbit, behind the eye, he was incredulous as to the fact. (The risk of inflammation attending the operation, with the exceeding uncertainty and improbability of any benefit being derived, prevented the trial suggested by those gentlemen to ascertain it.) With his usual self-collectedness, he sent for the officer next in command, and gave him the conduct of his party and his instructions; but, in a few days after, they were in their turn defeated, and most of the officers made prisoners by the Spaniards, Captain Kennedy among the number, helpless from his wounds. They were subsequently conveyed to Callao, and imprisoned in one of the castles, from which every few days some were marched out and shot.

While imprisoned, among others who took an interest in him was the officer in command of the castle. His fate hung some time in suspense, and his request of the officer was not a little characteristic of the man. "I beg," said he, "that when my time comes I may not be shot like a dog in the castle ditch, but that I may be allowed to march out and meet my fate like a soldier and a man." This the officer promised, and not long after his prison doors were opened, and, preceded by a band of music and a military guard, he was conducted out into the public *plaza* for execution. A regiment, forming three sides of a hollow square, was drawn up, and, standing in the center with a bandage tied around his eyes (to him useless precaution), he awaited his fate. He heard the voice of the officer, and step of the firing party as they marched out from the ranks; he heard their approach and halt within a few paces, the orders distinctly given, the jar of the muskets as they came to an aim, and the next moment expected to be in eternity, when the officer read from a paper in his hand that, in consideration of the blindness of the prisoner, and his inability to do any further injury to the Royal cause, the Governor had been pleased to pardon him. He had so made up his mind to his fate, and his situation was so utterly desolate, that, to use his own words, he "received the information without emotion, and without the quickening of a pulse."

Turned thus adrift, without friends, or money, or shelter, his situation was truly deplorable; and if it had not been for the assistance afforded by a young Spanish girl, whose compassion was aroused for him, and other casual charities, he must have perished of want. One morning, standing in the street, his ear was struck by a voice which appeared familiar, and at a venture he called to the passer, "*Ramsay*, is that you?" "My heavens! *Kennedy*, is that *you?*" after a moment's surprise, replied the person addressed; and in another moment he was in the embrace of his friend, Lieutenant Ramsay, of the U. S. Ship Constellation. The frigate had arrived in the bay; and in a few hours, clothed, and fully provided for, he was welcomed by his brother officers, and received into the ward-room mess. He remained some time on board the frigate, and in her returned to the United States. Arriving here, the marine corps took their old comrade under their protection, until government provided for his wants, by appointing him sutler at the Brooklyn Navy Yard, an office which he could perform by deputy.

His firm and patient deportment, his cheerful and uncomplaining disposition, and his high-minded and generous sentiments, attracted around him a crowd of admiring friends, among whom were many of the more gentle sex, whose sympathies were strongly excited by his situation. As was said in the earlier part of this sketch, he was without a relative on the earth, but his general information, and powers of entertainment, drew around him many to supply their place, and his rooms were the regular lounge of his brother officers and other friends (among whom were many men of talent and standing), who always found him in uniform good humor and cheerfulness. He never alluded to the calamity which had befallen him, unless questioned upon the subject, and then spoke of it with as much coolness and equanimity as if he had no particular interest in the affair. The ball, a heavy ounce musket ball, was taken, after his death, from the socket of the eye, in whose orbit it had been so long buried, confirming the opinion of the surgeons. Singular as it may seem, it gave him no uneasiness, but if it had gone the sixteenth part of an inch further, he must have been instantly killed, when he received the wound on the plains of Cordova.

But his term of life was measured, and he was not destined to reach the three score years and ten of man's alloted pilgrimage. After having been stationed about two years at the navy yard, a complaint of the heart, an enlargement and ossification set in, and after six or eight months of most intense and agonizing suffering, which he bore with his characteristic fortitude, and in the intervals of the paroxysms of which his voice was heard, with the same kindness and concern, in inquiries for the interests of his friends, he gradually sank and expired, aged thirty-two years. Though his pillow was smoothed by no wife, nor mother, nor sister, there were not wanting warm friends to bend over his bedside and soothe him in the hour of his last sad journey; and as they stood around him, and beheld the manly form, from which the spirit defeated had fled, lying cold and still, released from its conflict with pain and agony, the countenance tranquil as was its wont, and calm, they could not but feel that, "after life's fitful fever, he slept *well*."

It was on the afternoon of Sunday, the day following his death, that a coffin, shrouded in the American flag, borne upon the shoulders of soldiers, preceded by the guard of marines, with arms reversed, and followed by a long procession of sailors and citizens, passed from the marine barracks, the instruments of music wailing a mournful dirge, amid the continuous and melancholy roll of the muffled drums, as it slowly and solemnly moved upon its journey along the avenue to the Episcopal cemetery. As it proceeded, numbers of sympathizing spectators joined and followed in the procession, and the soft yellow rays of a declining autumnal sun appeared to throw, as if in unison, a sad and congenial light upon the scene. Arrived at the gate of the cemetery, the guard halted and opened to the right and left, their hands clasped on the reversed butts of their muskets, the muzzles of which rested at their feet, their bronzed and weather-beaten countenances bent sorrowfully upon the ground, and preceded by the chaplain, wrapped in its country's flag, all that remained of the gallant soldier passed forward to its final resting-place. The group collected around the grave, and the coffin was lowered and rested upon the bottom of the sepulchre. The beautiful and consoling service of the church was said, and many a heart among the mourners responded to the hollow jar of the sods as they fell upon the coffin lid. "Ashes to ashes"—and the religious services were ended. The crowd, with uncovered heads, still stood looking wistfully and mournfully into the narrow pit, when the silence was broken by the stern "*Forward!*" of the officer, and the measured heavy tramp of the soldiers of the guard was heard rustling and pressing down the long grass as they approached. The crowd opened, and the swarthy veterans halted and stood statue-like in double ranks beside the grave. A momentary clang of arms, the same voice was heard, and a sheet of flame, followed by the sudden peal of musketry, glanced over the soldier's sepulchre. Another volley, and another, echoed among the silent chambers of the dead, and their stern farewell was said. The white smoke wreathed mournfully, and hung above the monuments as if reluctant to take its departure, when the column wheeled, and again was heard their heavy tramp retreating through the hollow graves to the outlet of the cemetery. A few moments more, and we saw the beams of the setting sun dancing around their bayonets, as with quick step they were returning to their quarters. The crowd and mourners slowly retired, and on the narrow mound then left alone, now lies a marble tablet inscribed, "*Here rest the remains of Henry W. Kennedy.*"

GREENWOOD CEMETERY.

WHERE, THEN, IS DEATH?—and my own voice startled me from my reverie, as, leaning on my saddle-bow on the summit of an elevation in the Greenwood Cemetery, I asked: *Where, then, is death?* The golden sun of a summer's afternoon was streaming o'er the undulating hills of Staten Island, lighting more brilliantly the snow-white villas and emerald lawns; the Lazaretto, its fleet gay with the flags of all the nations, was nestling like a fairy city at its feet; the noble bay before me was one great, polished mirror, motionless vessels, with white sails and drooping pennants, resting on its surface like souls upon the ocean of eternity, and everything around was bright, and still, and beautiful, as I asked myself the question: *Where, then, is death?*

The islands with their military works lay calm and motionless upon the waters; the grim artillery, like sleeping tigers, crouched upon the ramparts and the castle's walls, but the glistening of the sentry's polished musket, and the sudden, clamorous roll of drums, showed me that—*not there was death.*

I turned. The great, fierce city, extending as far as eye could reach, the sky fretted with her turrets and her spires, her thousand smokes rising and mingling with the o'erhanging clouds, as she rose above her bed of waters, with hoarse, continuous roar, cried to me: "*Look not here, not here, for death!*" Her sister city, with her towers and cupolas—her grassy esplanades surmounted with verdant trees and far-extending colonnades embowered in shrubbery—from her high terraced walls, re-echoed the hollow roar: "*Not here for death!*"

The island lay extended far before me, its farms and towns, its modest spires, its granaries, its verdant meadows, its rich cultivated fields, its woods, its lawns, all wrapped in silence; but still its whisper softly reached me: "*Not here; not here, is death!*" E'en the great, distant ocean, closed only from my view by the far-reaching horizon, in sullen, continuous murmurs moaned: "*Not here is death!*"

Where, then, I cried—*where, then, is death?* I looked above me, and the blue vault hung pure and motionless: light, fleecy clouds, like angels on their journeys, alone resting on its cerulean tint; around, the evening breeze played calm and gently, and beneath, the flowers and leaves were quivering with delight, while the incessant hum of insect life arising from the earth with ceaseless voice still cried: "*No, no; not here is death!*"

Ah! said I; this beautiful world shall be forever, and there is—there is no death; but, even as I spoke a warning voice struck with deep solemnity upon my startled ear: "Man that is born of woman hath but a short time to live, and is full of misery. He cometh up and is cut down like a flower; he fleeth as it were a shadow, and never continueth in one stay." And as I turned, the funeral procession, its minister and its mourners, passed onward in their journey with the silent dead.

I looked after the retiring group, and again from beyond the coppice which intervened, heard rising in the same deep, solemn tones: "Write, from henceforth, blessed are the dead who die in the Lord; even so saith the Spirit, for they rest from their labors." And my soul cowered within itself like a guilty thing, as it said, Amen!

I looked again upon the scene before me and sighed; e'en such is human reason. That gorgeous sun shall set, the gay villas and verdant lawns, the crowded shipping, the beautiful bay with all that rest upon its bosom, shall soon be wrapped in darkness, the gleaming watch-light disappear from yon tall battlement, as the bugle sounds its warning note, the great fierce city be stilled in silence, while the beating hearts within her midnight shroud, like seconds, answer her tolling bells upon the dial of eternity, and the insect myriads, the flowers and leaves, ay! the great heavens themselves, shall from the darkness cry, "*This is the portraiture of death!*"—for the darkness and the silence are all that man can realize of death.

The hardy Northman with trembling finger points to the mouldering framework of humanity, and shudders as he cries, "*Lo! there is death!*" and the polished Greek smiles delightedly on the faultless statue of the lovely woman with the infant sleeping on her breast, as he also cries, "*Lo! there is death!*" yet both alike, with reverence, do lay their final offering before his gloomy shrine. The squalid Esquimaux scoops out the cavern in the never-melting snows, for the frozen form whose conflicts with the grizzly bear and shuddering cold are done; and the mild Hindoo, with affection, feeds the funeral pyre, and as the fragrant column does arise, cries, "Soul of my brother—immortal soul, ascend!" The red man, in the far distant prairie's lonely wilds, pillows the head of the warrior-chief upon his slain desert steed within its mound, while the bronzed pioneer, throwing aside his axe and rifle, hastily dashes away the tear as he inhumes beneath its flowery bed his scar-marked comrade's form.

The secluded village hamlet, with pious care, within the quiet grove, encloses a resting-place for its silent few, disappearing at long intervals; and here those great living cities have chosen this silent city for their dead; falling like the forest leaves in autumn.

For the great army, who must, ere long, march forth to ground their arms before the grim and ghastly Conqueror, 'twere difficult to find more beautiful and lovely resting-place. E'en the sad mourner lingers as he beholds its broad and lovely lawns, stretched out in calm serenity before him; its sylvan waters in their glassy stillness; its antique elms, arching with extended branches the long, secluded lanes; its deep, romantic glens; its rolling mounds, and all its varied scenery, ere with a softened sadness he turns him to his desolate and melancholy home. Spirits of our departed ones! we know that you have gone forth from your human habitations, and that we shall behold your loved forms no more forever; therefore will we lay your deserted temples within this consecrated ground, and, in imagination, fondly see you sleeping still in tranquility beneath its green and silent sward!

But lo! where upon the broad and verdant lawn, the loose clods and dark black mould heaped carelessly aside, the narrow pit awaits, ere it close again from light, its tenant in his dark and narrow house. The sorrowing group collect around, and the pall slowly drawn aside, one moment more exhibits to the loved ones the pallid countenance of him about to be hidden from their sight forever. The weeping widow, in her dark habiliments, leans upon the arm of the stern, sad brother, her little ones clinging to her raiment in mingled awe and admiration of the scene before them. "Ashes to ashes," she writhes in anguish, as the heavy clods fall with hollow, unpitying jar upon the coffin lid—how like a lifeless thing she hangs upon the supporting arm in which her countenance is buried in agony unutterable; and see the little ones, their faces streaming with wondering tears, clasping her hands; how in happy ignorance, they innocently, with fond endearing names, still call upon him to arise.

But the narrow grave is filled, the mourning group has gone, the evening shadows fall, the declining sun sinks beneath his gorgeous bed in the horizon, and in the thickening twilight the dead lies in his mound—alone. The night advances, the stars arise, and the joyous constellations roll high onward in their majestic journeys in the o'erhanging heavens, but beneath, the tenant of the fresh-filled grave lies motionless and still. The morning sun appears, the dew, like diamonds, glitters on every leaf and blade of grass, the birds joyously carol, and the merry lark, upon the very mound itself, sends forth his cheerful note; but all is hushed, in silence, to the tenant who in his unbroken slumber sleeps within. The Autumn comes, and the falling leaves whirl withered from the tree-tops, and rustle in the wind; the Winter, and the smooth broad plain lies covered with its pure and spotless cloak of driven snow, and the lowly mound is hid from sight, and shows not in the broad midday sun, nor e'en at midnight, when the silver moon sailing onward in her chaste journey turns the icicles into glittering gems on the o'erhanging branches as they bend protectingly towards it. The Spring breathes warmly, and the little mound lies green again ; and now the mother, bending o'er it, lifts the rose and twines the myrtle, while the little ones in joyous glee from the surrounding meadows bring wild flowers and scatter them in unison upon its borders. Then, were consciousness within, would the glad tenant smile.

But let him, whose tears as yet fall not for any dear one beneath its sod, ascend again with me the Mount, and with retrospective gaze behold the living drama which has passed before it. The great world around, the stage, lies still the same; but the actors all have passed onward to their final rest. Into the still gleaming past bend your attentive gaze. Lo! the features of the scenery are still the same; the bay's unruffled bosom, and the islands; but no sail now floats upon its surface; no gilded spires in the distance loom, nor does the busy hum of man reach us, as listening we stand; nought we see but the far forest, covering the main and islands, even to the waters. The coward wolf howls in yon distant glen; the partridge drums upon the tree-top; and the graceful deer, e'en at our sides, browse in conscious safety. Yon light dot moving upon the water?—'tis the painted Indian paddling his canoe. Yon smoke curling on the shore beneath us?—it is the Indian's wigwam. The joyous laugh arising among the trees?—it is his squaw and black-eyed children; the Indian reigns the lord, reigns free and uncontrolled.

But look again: upon the water floats a huge and clumsy galliot, its gay and gaudy streamers flaunting in the breeze; how the poor savages congregated on yonder point gaze in wonder as it passes, sure 'tis the Great Spirit; and the quaint figure with the plumed hat, and scarlet hose glistening with countless buttons, on its poop; some demi-god! and as she onward moves, behold the weather-worn seamen's faces in her rigging, how anxiously they return the gaze. The forest children muster courage; they follow in their light canoes. The galliot nears the Manahattoes; they ascend her sides: hawks-bills, and rings, and beads, and the hot strong drink are theirs; their land—it is the white man's. See with what

confidence he ensconces himself upon the island's borders. In his grasp he has the fish, the furs, the game—the poor confiding Indian gives him all. Lo! the embryo city's fixed!

But see! Is that the Dutch boor's cabin at our feet? Is that the Indian seated on the threshold, while the Dutchman lolls lazily within? Where, where then is the Indian's wigwam? Gone!

Look up again: a stately fleet moves o'er the bay, in line of battle drawn; the military music loudly sounds, dark cannon frown from within the gaping ports, and crews with lighted matches stand prepared; they near the Manahattoes, and—and—the Orange flag descends; the Dragon and St. George floats from the flag-staff o'er the little town. Who is the fair-haired man that drinks with the Dutchman at his cottage door, while the poor Indian stands submissively aside? "It is the Briton." I hear the laugh of youth; sure 'tis the Indian's black-eyed brood? "'tis the Englishman's yellow-haired, blue-eyed children." Alas! alas! poor forest wanderer; nor squaw, nor child, nor wigwam, shall here be more for thee. Farewell, farewell.

The little town swells to a goodly city; the forests fall around; the farms stretch out their borders; wains creek and groan with harvest wealth; lordly shipping floats on the rivers; the fair haired race increase; roads mark the country, and the deer and game, scared, fly the haunts of men. Hah! the same flag floats not at the Manahattoes! now, 'tis Stars and Stripes. See! crowding across the river, men in dark masses, cannon, muniments of war, in boats, on rafts, in desperate haste. Trenches and ramparts creep like serpents on the earth; horsemen scour the country, divisions, regiments, take position, and stalwart yeomen hurrying forward, join in the ranks of Liberty! Hear! hear the wild confusion, the jar of wheels, the harsh shrill shriek of trumpets and the incessant roll of drums, the rattling musketry, the sudden blaze and boom of cannon; it is the roar of battle—it is the battle field. Hear! hear the distant cry, "St. George and merry England." "Our Country and Liberty." Ah! o'er this very ground the conflict passes. See! the vengeful Briton prostrate falls beneath the deadly rifle, while the yeoman masses fade beneath the howling cannon shot; and hark! how from amid the sulphurous cloud the wild "hurrah" drowns e'en the dread artillery.

The smoke clouds lazily creep from off the surface, the battle's o'er, and the red-cross banner floats again upon the island of Manahattoes, and now again the Stars and Stripes stream gently in the breeze.

The past is gone, the future stands before us. Here on this spot, once rife with death, yonder cities shall lay their slain for centuries to come—their slain, falling in the awful contest with the stern warrior, against whom human strength is nought, and human conflict vain. Years shall sweep on in steady tide, and these broad fields be whitened with countless sepulchres; the mounds, covered with graves where affection still shall plant the flower and trail the vine. In the deep valleys, and romantic glens, to receive their ne'er returning tenants, the sculptured vaults still shall roll ope their marble fronts, and on this spot, the stately column shooting high in air; to future generations tell, the bloody story of the battle field.

All here shall rest; the old man, his silver hairs in quiet, and the wailing babe in sweet repose; the strong from fierce conflict with fiery disease, and bowing submissively, the poor pallid invalid, the old, the young, the strong, the beautiful, all here shall rest in deep and motionless repose.

May that Being, Infinite and Glorious—UNSEEN—shrouded from our vision in the vast and awful mists of immeasurable Eternity! CREATOR! throned in splendor inconceivable, mid millions and countless myriads of worlds, which still rushing into being at his thought, course their majestic circles, chiming in obedient grandeur glorious hymns of praise; God of Wisdom, that hast caused the ethereal spark to momentarily light frail tenements of clay; grant, that in the terrors of final dissolution, we may meet the splendor of the opening Heavens with steadfast gaze, and relying on his love, in ecstasy, still cry—WHERE—WHERE, THEN IS DEATH?

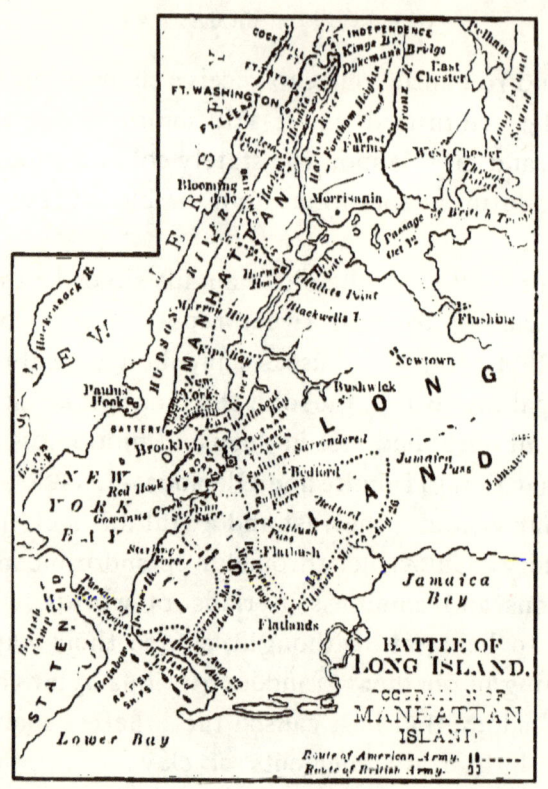

APPENDIX.

CONTENTS.

Note to the RESURRECTIONISTS.—Ghost in the Grave Yard.
" " OLD KENNEDY, No. I.—Lieutenant Somers.
" " OLD KENNEDY, No. III.—"The Parting Blessing."
' " OLD KENNEDY, No. IV.—Explosion at Craney Island.
" " GREENWOOD CEMETERY.
" " NIGHT ATTACK ON FORT ERIE—The Officer's Saber.
" " LUNDY'S LANE—Rainbow of the Cataract.
                The Day after the Battle.
                The two Sergeants.
                Death of Captain Hull.
                Scott's Brigade.
                Death of Captain Spencer.
" " LAKE GEORGE.—Attack on Fort Ticonderoga.
" " BASS FISHING.—Crew of the Essex frigate.
                Mutiny on board the Essex.
" " LONG ISLAND SOUND.—New England Traditions.

APPENDIX.

Note to the Resurrectionists.—GHOST IN THE GRAVE YARD.—In New-England most of the burying-grounds, as they are called, are at some distance from the villages, and generally neglected and rude in their appearance, frequently overgrown with wild, dank weeds, and surrounded by rough stone walls. Dr. W., a physician, whose extensive practice gave him a large circuit of country to ride over, relates that returning late one night from visiting a patient who was dangerously ill, his attention was attracted by a human figure clad in white, perched upon the top of the stone wall of one of these rustic cemeteries. The moon was shining cold and clear, and he drew up his horse for a moment and gazed steadily at the object, supposing that he was laboring under an optical illusion, but it remained immoveable and he was convinced, however singular the position and the hour, that his eyesight had not deceived him. Being a man of strong nerves, he determined to examine it, whether human or supernatural, more closely, and leaping his horse up the bank of the road he proceeded along the side of the fence toward the object. It remained perfectly motionless until he came opposite and within a few feet, when it vanished from the fence, and in another instant, with a piercing shriek, was clinging round his neck upon the horse. This was too much, for even the Doctor's philosophy, and relieving himself with a violent exertion from the grasp, he flung the figure from him, and putting spurs to his horse galloped into the village at full speed a torrent of ghostly lore and diablerie pouring through his mind as he dashed along. Arousing the occupants of the nearest house, they returned to the scene of the adventure, where they found the object of his terror—a poor female maniac, who had escaped from confinement in a neighboring alms-house, wandering among the tombs.

Note to Old Kennedy, No. I.—CAPT. SOMERS.*—The name of Somers, the twin brother in arms of Decatur, shines brightly on the History of American Naval Warfare; and the last desperate action which terminated his short and brilliant career with his life, is stamped in colors so indelible, that nothing but the destroying finger of Time can efface it from its pages. After severe and continued fighting before Tripoli, the Turkish flotilla withdrew from the mole, and could not be induced to venture themselves beyond the guns of the Tripolitan Battery. The ketch Intrepid was fitted out as a fire-ship, filled to the decks with barrels of gunpowder, shells, pitch, and other combustible materials; and Capt. Somers, with a volunteer crew, undertook the hazardous, almost desperate, task, of navigating her, in the darkness of night into the middle of the Turkish flotilla, when the train was to be fired, and they were to make their escape as they best could in her boats.

Lieutenants Wadsworth and Israel were the only officers

* The U. S. Brig Somers, in which a daring mutiny was suppressed by the prompt and decided measures of Lt. Alexander Slidell McKenzie, was named after this hero of the Tripolitan war.

allowed to join the expedition, which was comprised of a small crew of picked men. The Intrepid was escorted as far as was prudent by three vessels of the squadron, who hove to, to avoid suspicion, and to be ready to pick up the boats upon their return: the Constitution, under easy sail in the offing.

Many a brave heart could almost hear its own pulsations in those vessels, as she became more and more indistinct, and gradually disappeared in the distance. They watched for some time with intense anxiety, when a heavy cannonade was opened from the Turkish batteries, which, by its flashes, discovered the ketch determinedly progressing on her deadly errand. She was slowly and surely making for the entrance of the mole, when the whole atmosphere suddenly blazed as if into open day; the mast with all its sails shot high up in the air; shells whizzed, rocket like, exploding in every direction; a deafening roar followed and all sunk again into the deepest pitchy darkness. The Americans waited, and waited, in anxious, at last sickening, suspense. Their companions came not, the hours rolled on; no boat hailed, no oar splashed in the surrounding darkness. The East grew grey with the dawn, the sun shone brightly above the horizon, nought but a few shattered vessels lying near the shore, the flotilla, the batteries, and the minarets of Tripoli, gilded by the morning sunbeams, met their gaze. Those noble spirits had written their history. Whether consigned to eternity by a shot of the enemy, prematurely exploding the magazine, or from the firing of the train by their own hands, must always remain untold and unknown.

Note to Old Kennedy, No. III.—"THE PARTING BLESSING."—An officer of the Lawrence engaged in this desperate action informed the writer that he observed, in the latter part of the battle, the captain of one of the guns, who was a perfect sailor, and remarkable for his neatness and fine personal appearance, ineffectually endeavoring to work his gun himself, after all its crew had fallen. He was badly wounded by a grape shot in the leg; and although in that situation, he was supporting himself on the other, while he struggled at the tackle to bring the piece to bear. The officer told him that he had better leave the gun, and join one of the others, or, as he was badly wounded, go below. "No, no, sir," said the brave tar; "I've loaded her, and if I've got to go below, it sha'n't be before *I give 'em a parting blessing!*" The officer then himself assisted him in running the gun out of the port. The sailor, taking a good and deliberate aim, discharged her into the British ship, and then dragged himself down to the cockpit, fully satisfied with the parting compliment that he had paid the enemy. General Jackson, during his administration, granted the man a pension.

Note to Old Kennedy, No. IV.—EXPLOSION AT CRANEY ISLAND.—One of the oldest of the surgeons now in the navy, who was present when the British were defeated in their attempt to cut out the Constellation at Craney Island, in Hampton Roads, in the last war, relates the following anecdote.

The fire of the Americans was so heavy that the British flotilla was soon obliged to retire, a number of their boats having been disabled by the cannon shot—one, in particular, having been cut in two, sunk, leaving the men struggling in the water for their lives. It was thought that it contained an officer of rank, as the other boats hurried to her assistance, and evinced much agitation until the individual alluded to was saved. But to let the doctor tell his own story:—

"Well, they retreated, and we made prisoners of those whose boats having been cut up, were struggling in the water. Among others, there was a fine looking fellow, a petty officer, who had been wounded by the same shot that had sunk the boat; so I got him up to the hospital-tent, and cut off his leg above the knee, and having made him comfortable, (!) walked out upon the beach, with my assistant, for a stroll. We had not gone far, when we were both thrown upon our backs by a violent shock, which momentarily stunned us. On recovering ourselves, we observed the air filled with cotton, descending like feathers. We did not know how to account for the phenomenon, till, advancing some distance farther, we found a soldier lying apparently dead, with his musket by his side. I stooped down, and found that the man was wounded in the head, a splinter having lodged just over the temple. As I drew out the splinter, he raised himself, and stared stupidly about him. I asked him what he was doing there? 'I'm standing ground over the tent, sir,' he replied. What tent? 'Why, sir, the tent that had the gunpowder in it.' How came it to blow up?—what set it on fire? 'I don't know, sir.' Did nobody come along this way? 'Yes, sir; a man came along with a cigar in his mouth, and asked if he might go in out of the sun; I told him, yes!—and he went in and sat himself down—and that is the last I recollect, until I found you standing over me here.' Upon going a few hundred feet farther, we found a part, and still further on, the remainder of the body of the unfortunate man, who ignorantly had been the cause of the explosion, as well as his own death. He was so completely blackened and burnt that it would have been impossible, from his color, to have distinguished him from a negro."

Note to Greenwood Cemetery.—To the untiring exertions of Major D. B. Douglass, Messrs. Joseph A. Perry, Henry E. Pierrepont, Gerrit G. Van Wagenen, and a few other liberal minded gentlemen, the public are indebted for the design and completion of this beautiful place of repose for the dead.

Night Attack on Fort Erie.—THE OFFICER'S SABER.—The writer saw in the possession of Major ———, a beautiful scimitar-shaped saber, with polished steel scabbard; the number of the regiment, (119th, he thinks,) embossed on its blade, which one of the soldiers picked up and brought in from among the scattered arms and dead bodies in front of the works on the following morning. The white leathern belt was cut in two, probably by a grape-shot or musket ball, and saturated with blood. Whether its unfortunate owner was killed, or wounded only, of course could not be known. It was a mute and interesting witness of that night's carnage and had undoubtedly belonged to some officer who had been in Egypt, and had relinquished the straight European saber, for this favorite weapon of the Mameluke.

Night Attack on Fort Erie, and Battle of Lundy's Lane.— These two articles elicited the following reply from the pen of an officer of the U. S. army, since dead. The authenticity of the statement can be relied upon, as the documents from whence it was derived were the papers of Major-General Brown, and other high officers engaged in the campaign. It is proper to observe, that in the rambling sketch of a tourist, where a mere cursory description was all that was aimed at, the apparent injustice done to that gallant officer and eminently skillful soldier, Major-General Brown (who certainly ought to have been placed more prominently in the foreground), was entirely unintentional.

* * * * "Deeming that a 'local habitation and a name' may be affixed to my friend the 'Major,' and that he may be considered responsible for inaccuracies, if any, for which others alone are accountable, I hasten to say, that in the description of the battle of Lundy's Lane (with the exception of some of the personal anecdotes), the title is retained merely as a *nom de guerre* to carry the reader through the different phases of the action. The description of the night attack on Fort Erie, as well as that of the character and personal appearance of Lieutenant-Colonel Wood, is, however, almost literally that given at the fireside of my friend. The information received at the British camp on the following morning, through a flag, was, as near as could be ascertained, that Colonel Wood had been bayoneted to death on the ground. The account of the battle at Lundy's Lane was compiled from one of the earlier editions of Breckenridge's History of the Late War (I think the third), the only written authority that I had upon the subject, and from conclusions drawn from rambles and casual conversations on the battle-ground. In how far a rough sketch, which was all that was aimed at, has been conveyed from that authority, the reader, as well as your correspondent, can best determine by referring to the history alluded to." P. 269-70.

* * * * "The enemy's artillery occupied a hill which was the key to the whole position, and it would be in vain to hope for victory while they were permitted to retain it,

Addressing himself to Colonel Miller, he inquired whether he could storm the batteries at the head of the Twenty-first, while he would himself support him with the younger regiment, the Twenty-third. To this the wary, but intrepid, veteran replied in an unaffected phrase, 'I'll try, sir;'* words which were afterwards given as the motto of his regiment.

* * * * "The Twenty-third was formed in close column under its commander, Major McFarland, and the First regiment under Colonel Nicholas, was left to keep the infantry in check. The two regiments moved on to one of the most perilous charges ever attempted; the whole of the artillery opened upon them as they advanced, supported by a powerful line of infantry. The Twenty-first advanced steadily to its purpose; the Twenty-third faltered on receiving the deadly fire of the enemy, but was soon rallied by the personal exertions of General Ripley. When within a hundred yards of the summit, they received another dreadful discharge, by which Major McFarland was killed, and the command devolved on Major Brooks. To the amazement of the British, the intrepid Miller firmly advanced, until within a few paces of their line, when he impetuously charged upon the artillery, which, after a short but desperate resistance, yielded their whole battery, and the American line was in a moment formed in the rear upon the ground previously occupied by the British infantry, In carrying the larger pieces, the Twenty-first suffered severely; Lieutenant Cilley, after an unexampled effort, fell wounded by the side of the piece which he took; there were but few of

---

* The Twenty-first carried the celebrated '*I'll try, Sir,*' inscribed upon their buttons during the remainder of the war.

the officers of this regiment who were not either killed or wounded.

"So far as I can recollect, the personal narrative of my friend was as follows: Miller, quietly surveying the battery, coolly replied, 'I'll try, sir;' then, turning to his regiment, drilled to beautiful precision, said, 'Attention, Twenty-first.' He directed them as they rushed up the hill, to deliver their fire at the port-lights of the artillerymen, and to immediately carry the guns at the point of the bayonet. In a very short time they moved on to the charge, delivered their fire as directed, and after a furious struggle of a few muments over the cannon, the battery was in their possession.

* * * * "To show with what secresy the arrangements were made for the sortie of Fort Erie, it is believed that the enemy was in utter ignorance of the movement. To confirm him in error, a succession of trusty spies were sent to him in the character of deserters, up to the close of the day of the 16th; and so little did the army know of what were General Brown's plans for that day, that even if an officer had gone over to the enemy, the information he could have given must have been favorable to the meditated enterprise, as no one had been consulted but General Porter, and the engineers, Colonels McRae and Wood.

"At nine o'clock on the evening of the 16th, the general-in-chief called his assistant adjutant-general, Major Jones, and after explaining concisely his object, ordered him to see the officers whom the General named, and direct them to his tent. The officers General Brown had selected to have the honor of leading commands on the 17th, came; he explained to them his views and determinations, and enjoyed much satisfaction at seeing that his confidence had not been misplaced. They left him to prepare for the duty assigned to them on the succeeding day. At twelve o'clock the last agent was sent to the enemy in the character of a deserter, and aided, by disclosing all he knew, to confirm him in security.

"The letter, of which the following is an extract, was written by General Brown to the Department of War early in the morning of the 25th July, 1814:

"'As General Gaines informed me that the Commodore was in port, and as he did not know when the fleet would sail, or when the guns and troops that I had been expecting would even leave Sackett's Harbor, I have thought it proper to change my position with a view to other objects.'

"General Scott, with the first brigade, Towson's artillery, all the dragoons and mounted men, was accordingly put in march towards Queenston. He was particularly instructed to report if the enemy appeared, and to call for assistance if that was necessary. Having command of the dragoons, he would have, it was supposed, the means of intelligence. On General Scott's arrival near the Falls, he learned that the enemy was in force directly in his front, a narrow piece of woods alone intercepting his view of them. Waiting only to despach this information, but not to receive any in return, the General advanced upon him.

"Hearing the report of cannon and small arms, General Brown at once concluded that a battle had commenced between the advance of his army and the enemy, and without waiting for information from General Scott, ordered the second brigade and all the artillery to march as rapidly as possible to his support, and directed Colonel Gardner to remain and see this order executed. He then rode with his aids-de-camp, and Major McRee, with all speed towards the scene of action. As he approached the Falls, ;about a mile from Chippeway, he met Major Jones, who had accompanied General Scott, bearing a message from him, advising General Brown that he had met the enemy. From the information given by Major Jones, it was concluded to order up General Porter's command, and Major Jones was sent with this order. Advancing a little further General Brown met Major Wood, of the engineers, who also had accompanied General Scott. He reported that the conflict between General Scott and the enemy was close and desperate, and urged that reinforcements should be hurried forward. The reinforcements were now marching with all possible rapidity. The Major-General was accompanied by Major Wood to the field of battle. Upon his arrival, he found that General Scott had passed the wood, and engaged the enemy upon the Queenston road and the ground to the left of it, with the 9th, 11th and 22d regiments, and Towson's artillery. The 25th had been detached to the right, to be governed by circumstances. Apprehending these troops to be much exhausted, notwithstanding the good front they showed, and knowing that they had suffered severely in the contest, General Brown determined to form and interpose a new line with the advancing troops, and thus disengage General Scott, and hold his brigade in reserve. By this time Captains Biddle and Ritchie's companies of artillery had come into action. The head of General Ripley's column was nearly up with the right of General Scott's line. At this moment the enemy fell back, in consequence, it was believed, of the arrival of fresh troops, which they could see and begin to feel. At the moment the enemy broke, General Scott's brigade gave a general huzza, that cheered the whole line. General Ripley was ordered to pass his line and display his column in front. The movement was commenced in obedience to the order. Majors McRee and Wood had rapidly reconnoitered the enemy and his position. McRee reported that he appeared to have taken up a new position with his line, and with his artillery, to have occupied a height which gave him great advantages, it being the key of the whole position. To secure the victory, it was necessary to carry this height, and seize his artillery. McRee was ordered by the Major-General to conduct Ripley's command on the Queenston road, with a view to that object, and prepare the 21st regiment, under Colonel Miller, for the duty.

"The second brigade immediately advanced on the Queenston road. General Brown, with his aids-de-camp and Major Wood, passing to the left of the second brigade in front of the first, approached the enemy's artillery, and observed an extended line of infantry formed for its support. A detachment of the first regiment of infantry, under command of Colonel Nicolas, which arrived that day, and was attached to neither of the brigades, but had marched to the field of battle in the rear of the second, was ordered promptly to break off to the left, and form a line facing the enemy on the height, with a view of drawing his fire and attracting his attention, while Colonel Miller advanced with the bayonet upon his left flank to carry his artillery. As the first regiment, led by Major Wood, and commanded by Colonel Nicolas, approached its position, the commanding General rode to Colonel Miller, and ordered him to charge and carry the enemy's artillery with the bayonet. He replied in a tone of great promptness and good humor, It shall be done, sir.'

" At that moment the first regiment gave way under the fire of the enemy; but Colonel Miller, without regard to this circumstance, advanced steadily to his object, and carried the height and the cannon in a style rarely equaled—never excelled. At this point of time, when Colonel Miller moved, the 23d regiment was on his right, a little in the rear. General Ripley led this regiment; it had some severe fighting, and in a degree gave way, but was promptly reformed, and brought upon the right of the 21st, with which were connected a detachment of the 17th and 19th.

" General Ripley being now with his brigade, formed a line (the enemy having been driven from his commanding ground), with the captured cannon, nine pieces, in the rear. The first regiment having been rallied, was brought into line by Lieutenant-Colonel Nicolas, on the left of the second brigade, and General Porter coming up at this time, occupied with his command the extreme left. Our artillery formed the right between the 21st and 23d regiments. Having given to Colonel Miller orders to storm the heights and carry the cannon as he advanced, General Brown moved from his right flank to the rear of his left. Major Wood and Captain Spencer met him on the Queenston road; turning down that road, he passed directly in the rear of the 23d, as they advanced to the support of Col. Miller. The shouts of the American soldiers on the heights, at this moment, assured him of Col. Miller's success, and he hastened towards the place, designing to turn from the Queenston road towards the heights up Lundy's Lane. In the act of doing so, Maj. Wood and Capt. Spencer, who were about a horse's length before him, were near riding upon a body of the enemy; and nothing prevented them from doing it but an officer exclaiming before them, 'They are the Yankees.' The exclamation halted the three American officers, and upon looking down the road they saw a line of British infantry drawn up in front of the western fence of the road, with its right resting upon Lundy's Lane.

"The British officer had, at the moment he gave this alarm, discovered Maj. Jesup. The Major had, as before observed, at the commencement of the action, been ordered by Gen. Scott to take ground to his right.

"He had succeeded in turning the enemy's left, had captured Gen. Riall and several other officers, and sent them to camp, and then, feeling and searching his way silently towards where the battle was raging, had brought his regiment, the 25th, after a little comparative loss, up to the eastern fence at the Queenston road, a little to the north of Lundy's Lane. The moment the British gave Jesup notice of having discovered him, Jesup ordered his command to fire upon the enemy's line. The lines could not have been more than four rods apart—Jesup behind the south fence, the British in front of the north. The slaughter was dreadful; the enemy fled down the Queenston road at the third or fourth fire. As the firing ceased, the Major-General approached Major Jesup, advised him that Col. Miller had carried the enemy's artillery, and received information of the capture of Gen. Riall.

"The enemy having rallied his broken forces and received reinforcements, was now discovered in good order and in great force. The commanding General, doubting the correctness of the information, and to ascertain the truth, passed in person with his suite in front of our line. He could no longer doubt, as a more extended line than he had yet seen during the engagement was near, and advancing upon us. Capt. Spencer, without saying a word, put spurs to his horse, and rode directly up to the advancing line, then, turning towards the enemy's right, inquired in a strong and firm voice, ' What regiment is that?' and was as promptly answered, 'The Royal Scots, Sir.'

"General Brown and suite then threw themselves behind our troops without loss of time, and waited the attack. The enemy advanced slowly and firmly upon us: perfect silence was observed throughout both armies until the lines approached to within four to six rods. Our troops had leveled their pieces and the artillery was prepared: the order to fire was given. Most awful was its effect. The lines closed in part before the enemy was broken. He then retired precipitately, the American army following him. The field was covered with the slain, but not an enemy capable of marching was to be seen. We dressed our men upon the ground we occupied. Gen. Brown was not disposed to leave it in the dark, knowing it was the best in the neighborhood. His intention, then, was to maintain it until day should dawn, and to be governed by circumstances.

"Our gallant and accomplished foe did not give us much time for deliberation. He showed himself within twenty minutes, apparently undismayed and in good order."

Extract of a private letter from the writer of the above article, dated January 15, 1841. * * * *

"As to the fate of the gallant and accomplished Wood.— You supposed a flag from the enemy reported he had been bayoneted to death on the ground; like enough, but how did the enemy recognize his body? Gen. Porter thinks he fell at the close of the action at Battery No. 1, but I never heard that any one saw him fall. His body never was recovered. Those of Gibson and Davis, the leaders of the two other columns in Gen. Porter's command, were.

"Soon after the war, McRee, one of the best military engineers this country ever produced, threw up his commission in disgust and died of the cholera at St. Louis.

"From the time I lost sight of Gen. Scott in my narrative until after the change referred to at the end of the narrative, Gen. Scott with three of his battalions had been held in reserve. The commander-in-chief now rode in person to Gen. Scott, and ordered him to advance. That officer was prepared and expected the call. As Scott advanced toward Ripley's left, Gen. Brown passed to the left to speak with Gen. Porter and see the condition and countenance of his militia, who, at that moment, were thrown into some confusion under a most galling and deadly fire from the enemy: they were, however, kept to their duty by the exertions of their gallant chiefs, and most nobly sustained the conflict. The enemy was repulsed and again driven out of sight. But a short time, however, had elapsed, when he was once more distinctly seen, in great force, advancing upon our main line under the command of Ripley and Porter. The direction that Scott had given his column would have enabled him in five minutes to have formed a line in the rear of the enemy's right, and thus have brought him between two fires. But in a moment most unexpected, a flank fire from a party of the enemy, concealed upon our left, falling upon the centre of Scott's command, when in open column, blasted our proud expectations. His column was severed in two; one part passing to the rear, the other by the right flank of platoons toward the main line. About this period

Gen. Brown received his first wound, a musket-ball passing through his right thigh and *carrying away his watch seal*, a few minutes after Capt. Spencer received his mortal wound. * * * *

"This was the last desperate effort made by the enemy to regain his position and artillery. * * * *

"Porter's volunteers were not excelled by the regulars during this charge. They were soon precipitated by their heroic commander upon the enemy's line, which they broke and dispersed, making many prisoners. The enemy now seemed to be effectually routed; they disappeared. * * * *

"At the commencement of the action, Col. Jesup was detached to the left of the enemy, with the discretionary order, to be governed by circumstances. The commander of the British forces had committed a fault by leaving a road unguarded on his left. Col. Jesup, taking advantage of this, threw himself promptly into the rear of the enemy, where he was enabled to operate with brilliant enterprise, and the happiest effect. The capture of Gen. Riall, with a large escort of officers of rank, was part of the trophies of his intrepidity and skill. It is not, we venture to assert, bestowing on him too much praise to say, that to his achievements, more than to those of any other individual, is to be attributed the preservation of the first brigade from utter annihilation.

"Among the officers captured by Col. Jesup, was Capt. Loring, one of General Drummond's aids-de-camp, who had been despached from the front line to order up the reserve, with a view to fall on Scott with the concentrated force of the whole army and overwhelm him at a single effort. Nor would it have been possible to prevent this catastrophe, had the reserve arrived in time; the force with which General

Scott would have been obliged to contend being nearly quadruple that of his own. By the fortunate capture, however, of the British aid-de-camp, before the completion of the service on which he had been ordered, the enemy's reserve was not brought into action until the arrival of Gen. Ripley's brigade, which prevented the disaster that must otherwise have ensued, and achieved, in the end, one of the most honorable victories that ever shed lustre upon the arms of a nation. * * * *"

Note to Lundy's Lane.—RAINBOW OF THE CATARACT.—The afternoon of the action presented one of those delicious summer scenes in which all nature appears to be breathing in harmony and beauty. As General Scott's brigade came in view, and halted in the vicinity of the cataracts, the mist rising from the falls was thrown in upon the land, arching the American force with a vivid and gorgeous rainbow, the left resting on the cataract, and the right lost in the forest. Its brilliance and beauty was such, that it excited not only the enthusiasm of the officers, but even the camp followers were filled with admiration.

Note to Lundy's Lane.—THE DAY AFTER THE BATTLE.—" I rode to the battle-ground about day-light on the following morning without witnessing the presence of a single British officer or soldier. The dead had not been removed through the night, and such a scene of carnage I never before beheld. Red coats, blue and gray, promiscuously intermingled, *in many places three deep,* and around the hill, where the enemy's artillery was carried by Colonel Miller, the carcasses

of sixty or seventy horses added to the horror of the scene."
—*Private letter of an Officer.*

The dead were collected and burnt in funeral piles made of rails, on the field where they had fallen.

Note to Lundy's Lane—THE TWO SERGEANTS.—For several days after the action, the country people found the bodies of soldiers who had straggled off into the woods, and died of their wounds. At some distance from the field of battle, and entirely alone, were found the bodies of two sergeants, American and English, transfixed by each other's bayonets, lying across each other, where they had fallen in deadly duel. It is rare that individual combat takes place under such circumstances in the absence of spectators to cheer on the combatants by their approval, and this incident conveys some idea of the desperation which characterized the general contest on that night. Yet in this lonely and brief tragedy, these two men were enacting parts, which to them were as momentous as the furious conflict of the masses in the distance.

Note to Lundy's Lane.—DEATH OF CAPTAIN HULL.—Captain Hull, son of General Hull, whose unfortunate surrender at Detroit created so much odium, fell in this battle. He led his men into the midst of the heaviest fire of the enemy, and after they were almost, if not all, destroyed, plunged sword in hand into the center of the British column, fighting with the utmost desperation, until he was literally impaled upon their bayonets.

In the pocket of this gallant and generous young officer,

was found a letter, avowing his determination to signalize the name or to fall in the attempt.

Note to Lundy's Lane.—SCOTT'S BRIGADE.—Part of Gen. Scott's command were dressed in gray (probably the fatigue dress), at the battle of Chippewa. An English company officer relates that: "Advancing at the head of my men, I saw a body of Americans drawn up, dressed in gray uniform. Supposing them to be militia, I directed my men to fire, and immediately charge bayonet. What was my surprise to find, as the smoke of our fire lifted from the ground, that, instead of flying in consternation from our destructive discharge, the supposed militia were coming down upon *us* at 'double quick'—at the charge. In two minutes I stood alone, my men having given way without waiting to meet the shock."

Note to Lundy's Lane.—DEATH OF CAPT. SPENCER.—Capt. Spencer, aid-de-camp to Maj. Gen. Brown, a son of the Hon. Ambrose Spencer, was only eighteen years of age at the time he closed his brief career. He was directed by Gen. Brown to carry an order to another part of the field, and, to avoid a more circuitous route, he chivalrously galloped down, exposed to the heavy fire in the front of the line, eliciting the admiration of both armies, but, before he reached the point of his destination, two balls passed through his body and he rolled from his saddle.

The following letter to Gen. Armstrong, Secretary of War, will show in what estimation he was held by Gen. Brown:—

Copy of a letter from Major Gen. Brown, to Gen. Armstrong, Secretary of War.

"HEADQUARTERS, FORT ERIE,
20th September, 1814.

"SIR:—Among the officers lost to this army in the battle of Niagara Falls, was my aid-de-camp, Captain Ambrose Spencer, who, being mortally wounded, was obliged to be left in the hands of the enemy. By flags from the British army, I was shortly afterwards assured of his convalescence, and an offer was made me by Lieutenant General Drummond, to exchange him for his own aid, Captain Loring, then a prisoner of war with us. However singular this proposition appeared, as Captain Loring was not wounded, nor had received the slightest injury, I was willing to comply with it on Captain Spencer's account. But as I knew his wounds were severe, I first sent to ascertain the fact of his being then living. My messenger, with a flag, was detained, nor even once permitted to see Captain Spencer, though in his immediate vicinity.

"The evidence I wished to acquire failed; but my regard for Captain Spencer would not permit me longer to delay, and I informed General Drummond that his aid should be exchanged even for the *body* of mine. This offer was, no doubt, gladly accepted, and the *corpse* of Captain Spencer sent to the American shore."

Note to LAKE GEORGE AND TICONDEROGA.—This important position, situated on Lake Champlain near the foot of the Horicon (called by the English Lake George, and by the French St. Sacrament), was first fortified by the French, and was the point from which they made so many incursions, in conjunction with the Indians, upon the English settlements. Lord Abercrombie led an army of nearly 16,000 men against it in the year 1658, but was defeated with a loss of 2,000 men, and one of his most distinguished officers, Lord Howe, who fell at the head of one of the advance columns. In the following year it surrendered to General Amherst, who led a force of nearly equal number against it. Its surprise and capture by Ethan Allen, at the commencement of our revolution, is, we presume, familiar to every American, as also the fact of Burgoyne's getting heavy cannon upon the neighboring mountain, which had heretofore been considered impracticable, and from which the works were entirely commanded. The necessary withdrawal of the army by St. Clair, after blowing up the works, is as related in the text.

Note to Bass Fishing.—CREW OF THE ESSEX FRIGATE.— In the bloody and heroic defence of the Essex, in which, out of a crew of two hundred and fifty-five men, one hundred and fifty-three were killed and wounded! a number of instances of individual daring and devotion are recorded of the common sailors. Besides the act of Ripley, which is mentioned in the text, one man received a cannon ball through his body, and exclaimed, in the agonies of death, "Never mind, shipmates, I die for free trade and sailors' rights." Another expired inciting his shipmates to "fight for liberty!" and another, Benjamin Hazen, having dressed himself in a clean shirt and jacket, threw himself overboard, declaring that "he would never be incarcerated in an English prison." An old man-of-war's-man, who was in her, informed the writer that her sides were so decayed by exposure to the climate in which she had been cruising, that the dust flew like smoke from every shot that came through the bulwarks, and that at the close of the action, when the Essex was lying perfectly helpless, a target for the two heavy British ships, riddled by every ball from their long guns, without the ability to return a single shot, he was near the quarter-deck and heard Commodore Porter, walking up and down with hurried steps, repeatedly strike his breast and exclaim, in great apparent agony, "My Heaven! is there no shot for me?"

Note to Bass Fishing.—MUTINY ON BOARD THE ESSEX FRIGATE.—While the Essex was lying at the Marquesas Islands, recruiting and refreshing her crew from one of the long and arduous cruises in the Pacific, Commodore Porter was informed, through a servant of one of the officers, that a mutiny had been planned and was on the eve of consummation. That it was the intention of the mutineers to rise upon the officers, take possession of the ship, and, after having remained as long as they found agreeable at the island, to hoist the black flag and "cruise on their own account." Having satisfied himself of the truth of the information, Commodore Porter ascended to the quarter-deck, and ordered all the crew to be summoned aft. Waiting till the last man had come from below, he informed them that he understood that a mutiny was on foot, and that he had summoned them for the purpose of inquiring into its truth. "Those men who are in favor of standing by the ship and her officers," said the commodore, "will go over to the starboard side; those who are against them will remain where they are." The crew, to a man, moved over to the starboard side. The ship was still as the grave. Fixing his eyes on them steadily and sternly for a few moments, the commodore said, "Robert White, step out." The man obeyed, standing pale and agitated, guilt stamped on every lineament of his countenance, in front of his comrades. The commodore looked at him a moment, then seizing a cutlass from the nearest rack, said, in a suppressed voice, but in tones so deep that they rung like a knell upon the ears of the guilty among the crew, "Villain! you are the ringleader of this mutiny—jump overboard!" The man dropped on his keees, imploring for mercy, saying that he could not swim. "Then drown, you scoundrel!" said the commodore, springing towards him to cut him down—"overboard instantly!" and the man jumped over the side of the ship. He then turned to the trembling crew, and addressed them with much feeling, the tears standing upon his bronzed cheek as he spoke. He asked them what he had done, that his ship should be disgraced by a mutiny. He asked whether he had ever dishonored the flag, whether he had ever treated them with other than kindness, whether they had ever been wanting for anything to their comfort, that discipline and rules of the service would allow, and which it was in his power to give. At the close of his address he said: "Men! before I came on deck, I laid a train to the magazine, and I would have blown all on board into eternity, before my ship should have been disgraced by a successful mutiny; I never would have survived the dishonor of my ship; go to your duty.' The men were much affected by the commodore's address, and immediately returned to their duty, showing every sign of contrition. They were a good crew, but had been seduced by the allurements of the islands, and the plausible representations of a villain. That they did their duty to the flag, it is only necessary to say, the same crew fought the ship afterwards against the Phebe and Cherub, in the harbor of Valparaiso, where, though the American flag descended, it descended in a blaze of glory which will long shine on the pages of history. But mark the sequel of this mutiny, and let those who, *in the calm security of their fire-sides*, are so severe upon the course of conduct pursued by officers in such critical situations, see how much innocent blood would have been saved, if White had been cut down instantly, or hung at the yard-arm. As he went overboard he succeeded in reaching a canoe floating at a little distance and paddled ashore. Some few months afterwards, when Lieutenant Gamble of the Marines was at the islands, in charge of one of the large prizes, short-handed, in distress, this same White, at the head of a party of natives, attacked the ship, killed two of the officers and a number of the men, and it was with great difficulty that she was prevented from falling into their hands. The blood of those innocent men, and the lives of two meritorious officers, would have been spared, if the wretch had been put to instant death, as was the commodore's intention. It will be recollected that the Essex, in getting under way, out of the harbor of Valparaiso, carried away her foretopmast in a squall, and being thus unmanageable, came to anchor in the supposed protection of a neutral port; nevertheless the Phebe, frigate, and Cherub, sloop-of-war, attacked her in this position, the former with her long guns selecting her distance, cutting her up at her leisure, while the Essex, armed only with carronades, lay perfectly helpless, her shot falling short of the Phebe, although they reached the Cherub, which was forced to get out of their range. "I was standing," said my informant, then a midshipman only fourteen years old, "I was standing at the side of one of our bow-chasers (the only long guns we had), which we had run aft out of the stern-port, when the Phebe bore up, and ran under our stern to rake us. As she came within half-pistol shot (!) she gave us her whole broadside at the same instant. I recollect it well," said the officer, "for as I saw the flash, I involuntarily closed my eyes, expecting that she would have blown us out of the water, and she certainly would have sunk us on the spot, but, firing too high, her shot cut our masts and rigging all to pieces, doing little injury to the hull. Singular as it may seem, the discharge of our one gun caused more slaughter than the whole of their broadside, for while we had but one man wounded, the shot from our gun killed two of the men at the wheel of the Phebe, and glancing with a deep gouge on the main-mast, mortally wounded her first Lieutenant, who died on the following day.

Long Island Sound.—NEW ENGLAND TRADITIONS.—There are few countries where traditions and legends are handed down from generation to generation with more fidelity than in New England, more particularly along the sea-coast and the shores of the Sound. The "fire ship" was supposed by the old fishermen to be seen cruising occasionally in the vicinity of Block Island in the furious storms of thunder and lightning. The tradition was that she was taken by pirates, all hands murdered, and abandoned after being set on fire by the buccaneers. Some accounts stated that a large white horse, which was on board, was left near the foremast to perish in the flames, and in storms of peculiarly terrific violence that she was seen rushing along enveloped in fire, the horse stamping and pawing at the heel of the foremast, her phantom crew assembled at quarters. In the early part of the last century, a ship came ashore a few miles beyond Newport, on one of the beaches, all sails set, the table prepared for dinner, but the food untouched, and no living thing on board of her. It was never ascertained what had become of her crew, but it was supposed that she had been abandoned in some moment of alarm, and that they all perished, although the vessel arrived in safety.

The phantom horse will recall to mind a real incident, which occurred not long since in the conflagration of one of the large steamboats on Lake Erie. A fine race-horse was on board, and secured, as is usual, forward. Of course his safety was not looked to, while all were making vain efforts to save themselves from their horrible fate. As the flames came near him he succeeded in tearing himself loose from his fastenings, rushing frantically through the fire and smoke fore and aft, trampling down the unfortunate victims that were in his way, adding still more horror to a scene which imagination can hardly realize, until, frenzied with the pain and agony of the fire, he plunged overboard and perished.

But the favorite and most cherished traditions are those relating to hidden treasure. The writer well recollects one to which his attention was attracted in his childhood. Mr. ———, inhabiting one of those fine old mansions in Newport, which had been built fifty years before, by an English gentleman of fortune, where taste and caprice had been indulged to the extreme, and where closets, and beaufets, and cellars, and pantries, appeared to meet one at every turn, was engaged late one winter's night writing in his study, when he found it necessary to replenish his fire with fuel. The servants having retired, he took a candle and went himself to the cellar to procure it, and as he passed the vault known as the "wine cellar," his attention was attracted by a light streaming through the key-hole of the door. He stopped a moment and called out, supposing that some of the family were in the apartment—but instantly the light vanished. He stepped up to the door and endeavored to open it, but found to his surprise that it was fastened,—a thing that was unusual, as the door constantly stood ajar. Calling out again, "Who's there?" without receiving any answer, he placed his foot against the door, and forced it open, when a sight met his eyes, which for a moment chained him to the spot. In the center of the cellar, in a deep grave, which had been already dug, and leaning upon his spade, was a brawny negro, his shirt-sleeves rolled up to his shoulders, and the sweat trickling down his glistening black visage, while on the pile of earth made from the excavation stood another negro, a drawn sword in one hand, a lantern with the light just extinguished in the other, and an open bible, with two hazel rods across it, lying at his feet—these swarthy laborers, the moment that the door was thrown open, making the most earnest signs for silence. As soon as Mr. ——— could command his voice, he demanded the meaning of what he saw, and what they were about. They both simultaneously then declared that the charm was broken by his voice. One of the worthies, who was the groom of the family, had dreamed five nights in succession that old Mr. E——, the builder of the house, had buried a boot'ul (!) of gold in that cellar, and, on comparing notes with his brother dreamer, he found that his visions also pointed to treasure in the old house, and they had proceeded *secundem artem* to its attainment, both vehemently declaring that they intended to give part of the treasure to Mr. ———. Of course, the door being opened, the strange negro was required to add the darkness of his visage to that of night, while the groom was, on pain of instant dismissal, together with the threat of the ridicule of the whole town, directed to fill up the grave, and thereafter to let the buried treasure sleep where its owner had seen fit to deposit it.

A Gallop among American Scenery:

OR,

Sketches of American Scenes and Military Adventure.

BY

A. E. SILLIMAN.

* * * "Mr. Silliman's 'Gallop among American Scenery' is an eminently readable book, consisting of sketches, historical and descriptive, everything dashed off with a champagne sparkle, and withal, scholarlike and finished. The talent for this kind of writing is as rare as the tenor among singers, and we are glad to hear of the existence of such a writer, though his light shine from the 'Vale of Mammon.' * * *N. P. Willis.*" *Bro. Jo., April* 1, 1843.

* * "It is a most agreeable volume, and we commend it to the lovers of the *champagne* style in literature." * * *N. Y. Com. Adv.*, 1843 (4).

* * "With an eye to observe the beauties of nature, and a heart to appreciate them; with a pen to "gallop" as fast as the thoughts of the writer; and language fluent enough to depict the quick ideas of the mind, Mr. Silliman has brought together a work of the most captivating character." * * *Boston Transcript*, 1843 (4).

* * "C'est une véritable course au galop que le volume de Silliman, etdans cette société qui va si vite les meilleurs livres et les plus agréables styles sont ceux qui s'élancent à toute bride, ne s'embarrassant ni de philosophie, ni de beau langage. Il y a dans les Esquisses de Silliman une peinture magnifique de la Cataracte du Niagara, pendant l'hiver; cet immense palais de glace, suspendu et étincelant, ce mouvement gigantesque arrêté dans l'air par une force magique, composent un des plus étourdissans spectacles dont on puisse s'aviser. La touche de l'auteur américain est facile, rapide, hazardeuse, un peu incorrecte, mais chaud n'en vaut que mieux." * * *La Revue des Deux Mondes*, Tome Septième (15 Août 1844), Paris.

"A GALLOP AMONG AMERICAN SCENERY. By A. E. SILLIMAN. This volume seems to have been rapidly written, but it displays uncommon qualities of style and powers of observation. * * * His sketches are brilliantly drawn and his stories and anecdotes well told. Unlike most books so miscellaneous in character, this has a spirit and life which keep up the reader's interest to the end; it is drawn from fresh nature and is therefore free from vague or unmeaning epithets. It is written in a hearty and honest tone, and we strike up a pleasant acquaintance with the author at once. We are amused, excited, and frequently instructed by our agreeable companion, and part from him with regret. * * We are particularly pleased with the dazzling picture of Niagara in the winter, though it is not done at sufficient length. * * * We take leave of our author with a lively sense of his descriptive powers, his gaiety and good humor, and with many thanks for reviving so agreeably the recollection of places made classical by striking events in American history, or that have grown dear to the heart by the gratification they have afforded to the love of the beautiful." *North American Review*, 1843 (4), Vol. LXII, pp. 252-3.

A. S. BARNES & CO., - NEW YORK.

www.ingramcontent.com/pod-product-compliance
Lightning Source LLC
Chambersburg PA
CBHW030312240426
43673CB00040B/1142